VIVIAN BIRD

STAFFORDSHIRE

B. T. Batsford Ltd
London

I dedicate this book to
my second grandson
DOMINIC HARVEY LANGRIDGE,
but warn my children that at my age
I cannot promise a new book for each
new grandchild

First published 1974

© Vivian Bird 1974

Printed and bound in Great Britain by Cox and Wyman
Ltd, London, Fakenham and Reading for the publishers
B. T. Batsford Ltd, 4 Fitzhardinge Street, London W1H 0AH

ISBN 0 7134 2863 5

CONTENTS

List of *Illustrations*   viii
Map of Staffordshire   x
Author's Foreword   xi

One   Lichfield and Tamworth   13
Two   Lost Territory – The Black Country   38
Three   The Green Borderland   64
Four   Penkridge and the River Penk   73
Five   Burton-on-Trent and the Needwood Forest   85
Six   Abbots Bromley and the River Blithe   103
Seven   Rugeley and Cannock Chase   113
Eight   Stafford and Stone   128
Nine   Eccleshall and the Woodland Quarter   143
Ten   Cheadle and the Churnet Valley   163
Eleven   The Potteries   181
Twelve   Leek and the Moors   192

Index   216

LIST OF ILLUSTRATIONS

1	Lichfield Cathedral	*frontispiece*
2	Lichfield Cathedral, the nave	17
3	Market Square, Lichfield	18
4	Penkridge Parish Church	21
5	Chillington Hall – the Tudor Hall	22
6	Speedwell Castle, Brewood	39
7	Himley Hall	39
8	Hoar Cross	40
9	Barton under Needwood	57
10	Halfhead Cottage, Shallowford	57
11	Tutbury parish church	58
12	Queen Mary's Tower, Tutbury Castle	58
13	Trent & Mersey Canal – the Horninglow Basin	75
14	Rugeley Power Station	75
15	Abbots Bromley, the Horn Dance	76
16	Abbots Bromley, the old Butter Cross	76
17	Cannock Chase	93
18	Shugborough Hall – Hadrian's Arch	94
19	Ingestre	111
20	Tixall Gate House	112
21	Ingestre Hall	112
22	Broughton Hall	129
23	Aqualate Hall	129
24	Alton Towers	130
25	St Giles, Cheadle	147
26	Kilns of the Five Towns	148
27	Alstonfield looking towards Steep Low	165
28	Longnor	166
29	Leek	183
30	Mill Dale	184
31	Rudyard Lake	184

ACKNOWLEDGEMENTS

The author and publishers would like to thank the following for permission to use photographs in this book :

Hallam Ashley F.R.P.S. (Pl. 30)
Barnaby's Picture Library (Pl. 12)
J. Allan Cash (Pls 13, 29, 31)
Herbert Felton, F.R.P.S. (Pl. 2)
Fox Photos (Pl. 7)
A. F. Kersting, F.R.P.S. (Pl. 15)
Eric de Maré (Pl. 26)
National Monuments Record (Pls 5, 18, 21, 23)
Kenneth Scowen, F.I.I.P., F.R.P.S. (Pls 1, 3, 16, 27, 28)
The late Edwin Smith (Pls 8, 9, 19, 24, 25)
Leslie Stonehouse (Pls 4, 6, 10, 14, 20)
Spectrum Colour Library (Pl. 17)
Map by Patrick Leeson

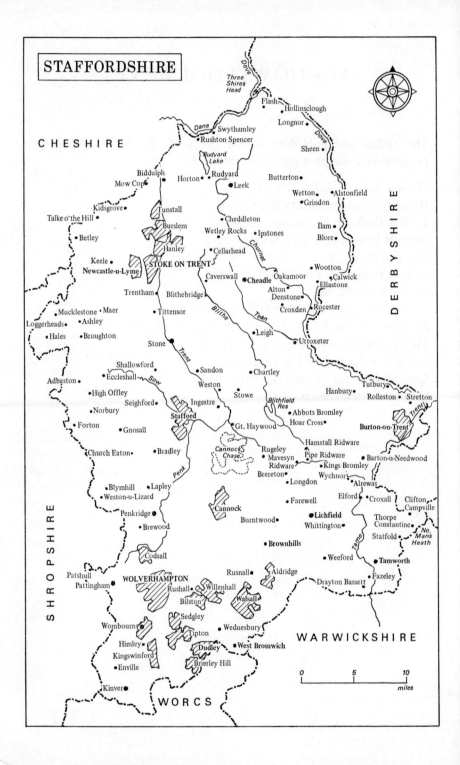

STAFFORDSHIRE

CHESHIRE

DERBYSHIRE

SHROPSHIRE

WARWICKSHIRE

WORCS

Three Shires Head
Flash
Hollinsclough
Longnor
Dove
Sheen
Swythamley
Dane
Rushton Spencer
Rudyard Lake
Butterton
Wetton
Grindon
Alstonfield
Biddulph
Horton
Rudyard
Mow Cop
Leek
Kidsgrove
Talke o' the Hill
Tunstall
Cheddleton
Ilam
Blore
Burslem
Wetley Rocks
Ipstones
Betley
Hanley
Cellarhead
Wootton
Keele
STOKE ON TRENT
Caverswall
Cheadle
Oakamoor
Calwick
Newcastle-u-Lyme
Alton
Denstone
Ellastone
Trentham
Blithebridge
Croxden
Rocester
Mucklestone
Maer
Tittensor
Tean
Loggerheads
Ashley
Leigh
Hales
Broughton
Utoxeter
Stone
Shallowford
Sandon
Chartley
Adbaston
Eccleshall
Sow
Weston
Stowe
Hanbury
Tutbury
Rolleston
Stretton
High Offley
Ingestre
Blithfield Res
Seighford
Abbots Bromley
Burton-on-Trent
Norbury
Stafford
Gt. Haywood
Hoar Cross
Forton
Gnosall
Hamstall Ridware
Barton-u-Needwood
Church Eaton
Bradley
Cannock Chase
Rugeley
Pipe Ridware
Mavesyn
Kings Bromley
Wychnor
Brereton
Longdon
Alrewas
Blymhill
Lapley
Penk
Cannock
Farewell
Elford
Croxall
Clifton Campville
Weston-u-Lizard
Burntwood
Lichfield
Thorpe Constantine
Penkridge
Whittington
Statfold
No Mans Heath
Brewood
Brownhills
Weeford
Codsall
Tamworth
Patshull
Rusnall
Aldridge
Fazeley
Pattingham
WOLVERHAMPTON
Rushall
Willenhall
Drayton Bassett
Bilston
Walsall
Wombourn
Sedgley
Himley
Tipton
Wednesbury
Kingswinford
Dudley
West Bromwich
Enville
Brierley Hill
Kinver
Trent
Churnet
Blithe
Penk
Tame

0   5   10
miles

Author's Foreword

In the belief that people do not read county books in order to learn about cities I omitted Birmingham and Coventry from my *Warwickshire* (B. T. Batsford, 1973) without apparently causing any offence. The two great Staffordshire conurbations, the Black Country and the Potteries, are much more closely associated with their county and cannot equally legitimately be disregarded – even though the Black Country has been transferred to the West Midlands Metropolitan County under the new local government reorganisation, at which I am pleased to cock a snook by including it in Staffordshire.

With these built-up industrial areas at its north and south extremities, Staffordshire is scorned by a multitude of country-lovers. Yet it has much exhilarating walking country as I can testify, not only from countless walks within the county, but from a walk round its entire boundary, such as I have done serially for my newspapers with several Midland counties.

If any theme emerges from this book I hope it will be 'Staffordshire the Surprising'.

Yet again I thank the editor of the *Sunday Mercury* for allowing me to call upon experiences and material collected while writing for that newspaper. Once more I thank my diligent friend Norman Williams, who must by now have read as many miles of typescript for my books as we have walked together, and I am happy to acknowledge some help from another old friend, Tom Coxon of Tutbury.

Hall Green, Birmingham
December 1973

CHAPTER ONE

Lichfield and Tamworth

In the eighth century, Midland Mercia was for a while the most powerful kingdom in the Saxon Heptarchy. Offa, no petty princeling but a great king who negotiated with continental rulers of the calibre of Charlemagne, selected Tamworth as his capital, and built a palace where Market Street runs today. He reigned from 757 to 796, and in 787 he saw neighbouring Lichfield elevated to an archbishopric, and it is there, in the ecclesiastical capital of the county, that we begin our wanderings in Staffordshire.

The traveller from Birmingham, entering Staffordshire by the Ryknield Street at Watford Gap, soon comes under the seductive influence of the county as he finds himself beckoned on by the 'Ladies of the Vale'. The Vale is that of the River Trent which, flowing in a south-easterly direction from its Staffordshire source on Biddulph Moor, reaches its southernmost point near Alrewas and turns north-eastward to provide the boundary with Derbyshire for six miles on its course towards Burton. The Ladies are the three spires of Lichfield Cathedral, but however inviting the welcome thrust into the wide Midland skies, we must turn aside for a mile where the Watling Street traffic enters an enormous merry-go-round, and pay reverence to the Romans at Wall, which they called Letocetum. On that mile of Roman road we might well reflect that, where thunderous lorries impose a well-nigh impenetrable wall today, Alfred the Great once fixed the northern boundary of his Saxon kingdom with that of the Danelaw.

The roar of traffic pervades the small community at Wall – the Trooper Inn, the Old School House, the old school, a small museum, and the path to the Roman baths alongside the so-English Rose Cottage. A furnace with cold, tepid, and hot baths is displayed by the National Trust, and beyond this, above the upward slope of a field, a trim church spire rises among some trees, the kind of pastoral vignette which will become familiar in Staffordshire, a county never cluttered with trees, but offering rather the felicitous group or hilltop eye-catcher.

Lichfield is held by some to be the 'lych' field – the field of the corpses of Christians believed to have suffered martyrdom at the decree of the Roman emperor Diocletian. The seal of Lichfield, which can be seen with eight various coats-of-arms on the railway bridge across St John Street, shows the three British kings who defied the Romans lying dead with their swords beside them as they are said to do beneath a tumulus on Borrowcop Hill, south of the city. An alternative interpretation of the name is the grey, or lichenous trees (lich) in open country (feld). This lilliputian city describes itself on its welcoming sign as 'Mother of the Midlands', and it carries its welcome so far as to provide excellent free parking facilities, one of the car parks being alongside the Ebor Café, the original owner of which came from York, the Roman Eboricum. If this sets visitors thinking of horse-racing, of the Ebor Handicap, a pub in Lichfield Market Street keeps up the association, the 'Scales' – a name unique in Britain in my experience – with a sign showing a jockey in blue and yellow seated on the scales in the weighing-in room.

Up to 1701 Lichfield had a race meeting on Fradley Heath, but in 1702 this was transferred to Whittington Heath. Fifty years later the races were held under exceptional circumstances, as is shown by a handbill in the William Salt Library, Stafford, advertising the meeting to take place on 'Tuesday, Wednesday, and Thursday, the 1st, 2nd, and 14th of September MDCCLII'. These three days were consecutive, for September 1752 saw a calendar change in which the 11 days from 3 to 13 September, inclusive, were 'lost' – to the consternation of the masses who demanded that the Government give them back their 11 days. Prior to the change the calendar year, which began on 1 January, differed from the legal year commencing on Lady Day, 25 March, and events between the dates were recorded as being in two years, such as 'died 3 February 1749–50.'

From the racehorse owners' names, including Earl Gower and Mr Warren, the September 1752 races seem to have been the Whig race meeting, for Lichfield's politics overflowed on to the race course. This stemmed from the 1747 election when two Whigs unseated Lichfield's sitting Tory M.P.s and chose to celebrate at the race meeting, to which the Whig leader, the Duke of Bedford, was invited. A riot ensued, the duke was assaulted, and the Tory gentlemen met to consider the race situation – a meeting which became a Jacobite demonstration, with Burton and Birmingham mobs drinking the health of Bonnie Prince Charlie and singing treasonable songs. The Tories staged their first races in August 1748, but the Whigs, loyal to the Hanoverians, took the shine out of them by putting up at their race meeting a week later a Royal Plate of 100 guineas with the consent of George II.

These rival events continued until 1753 when they were amalgamated, and in 1769 the famous horse Eclipse won the King's Plate. In the 1830s Wolverhampton took over from Lichfield as the premier meeting, and, with Whittington Barracks built on the heath, 1895 saw Lichfield's last race meeting. One of the great supporters of Lichfield Races was General William Dyott of the Manor of Freeford, who recalled Eclipse's victory as 'the great event of an old man's memory.' He died in 1847, aged 86, and his memorial can be seen in the Dyott Chapel of St Mary's Church, which rises beside the Market Place. He was carried from his home at Freeford Hall by torchlight for midnight burial, the outcome of a strange boon granted to his ancester 'Dumb' Dyott by Charles I in recognition of his having shot and killed Lord Brooke, the Commonwealth commander during the siege of Lichfield Cathedral in 1643 – a boon observed until the end of the nineteenth century that all Dyotts be thus buried.

St Mary's tall spire tapers heavenward opposite the birthplace of Dr Samuel Johnson, who sits ponderously in an armchair above the Market Place cobbles and the canvas stalls, while Boswell, who did so much to ensure Johnson's fame, trips lightly on a neighbouring plinth with tricorn hat and his sword beside him. These Market Place cobbles glowed in the flames that consumed three Protestant martyrs during the Marian persecution, and flames sprang up again on 14 January 1873 when a house fire in the Market Place wiped out the Corfield family of seven. They were buried in St Michael's Churchyard though they were Roman Catholics, and something on the three large head-stones offended Church of England susceptibilities, so they were not placed above the graves. They were placed instead alongside the wall of Holy Cross Roman Catholic Church, and there they remain to this day. Then, none can say when or how, a stone commemorating all seven Corfields appeared on the graves in St Michael's Churchyard. So this Lichfield jeweller, William Corfield, and his family, have a foot in both camps, and they share the churchyard, among countless others, with Dr Johnson's father, mother, and brother.

Samuel Johnson was born in September 1709 at his father's book-shop on the corner of Breadmarket Street and Market Street. Today it is a museum, and the various rooms with their high narrow windows enshrine collections of his works and many of the domestic trifles connected with this ungainly man of letters who occupies, to my mind, a place in English literature disproportionate to his attainments, for which he has largely to thank his devoted biographer. Here displayed are such items as Johnson's walking stick, his teapot, his wife's wedding ring, and his shoe buckles. Round the corner of the Market Place in Dam Street an inscription commemorates Dame Oliver's School, where the infant Samuel learned his first lessons in the English language which he collected eventually into his Dictionary.

Little Lichfield can lay claim to more than a fair share of famous figures either from birth or residence. On the far side of what was the Three Crowns Inn next door to Johnson's birthplace, Elias Ashmole was born in 1617. His title to fame is that as 'the greatest virtuoso and curioso' that England had ever known he gave his great collection of rarities to Oxford, thus originating the Ashmolean Museum. David Garrick, the actor, born in 1717 at Hereford, lived his first 20 years in this smaller cathedral city on the site now the city museum. Near the entrance to the cathedral close Dr Erasmus Darwin, grandfather of Charles Darwin, lived from 1756 to 1781, studiously avoiding Dr Johnson, in whose company he could not get in a word edgeways.

Erasmus Darwin's biographer, Anna Seward, the eighteenth-century poetess known as the 'Swan of Lichfield' lived with her father, Canon Seward, in the bishop's palace, built in 1687. The famous Lunar Society, that gathering of philosophers, scientists, and eccentrics, meeting for a monthly luncheon on the Monday nearest the full moon

2   *The soaring majesty of the nave at Lichfield Cathedral*

– which provided light on their homeward way after protracted discussions – could have begun around 1766 in Erasmus Darwin's Lichfield home, though it is more frequently associated with Soho House, the Handsworth home in Birmingham of Matthew Boulton. The society certainly met occasionally at Lichfield, a note having been preserved in which Boulton offers one Dr William Small a lift to Lichfield to enjoy 'a philosophical feast'. Dr Darwin himself wrote of the Lunar Society : 'Lord, what invention, what wit, what rhetoric, metaphysical and mechanical, and pyrotechnical, will be on the wing, bandied like a shuttlecock from one to another of your troop of philosophers'. He travelled to Lunar Society meetings in a carriage provided with food, books, and writing material. With others of the members he was an inventor, his productions including a rotary pump, a manifold writer, and a speaking machine with the somewhat limited vocabulary of 'Mama' and 'Papa'.

Richard Lovell Edgeworth, the literary father of novelist Maria Edgeworth, and inventor of a pedometer and a velocipede; and Thomas Day, an eccentric minor author, barrister, educationalist, and social scientist, were two other Lichfield 'Lunatics' whose antics must have caused their fellow members much mirth. Each lived in turn at Stowe House, gracious against its lawns at the far end of Stowe Pool. Of Day, Edgeworth once wrote that he was 'the most virtuous human being I have ever known'. This paragon had one obsession, a search for the perfect woman as his wife. One turned down his suggestion that she 'live unnoticed with him sequestered in some secluded grove'. Another took unkindly to his habit of never combing his hair – though he enjoyed washing. Eventually, taking with him his friend, James Bicknell, he visited Shrewsbury Foundling Hospital, and selected for adoption a blonde child whom he named Sabrina after the River Severn. Then, from a London foundlings' home he chose a brunette, Lucretia, intending training the girls to play the perfect wife to him, the one not chosen being given a gratuity of £500. This was Lucretia. Sabrina he sent to a boarding school at Sutton Coldfield nearby when she became too old decently to live in his home.

In her absence he fell in love successively with two sisters, Honora and Elizabeth Sneyd, of a prominent Lichfield family. Both ladies rejected him for his lack of refinement and, rubbing salt in the wound,

3 *Dr. Samuel Johnson presides over the Market Square at Lichfield and memories of him still pervade his native city*

became in time the second and third wives of his friend Edgeworth. So Day had to fall back on Sabrina despite some imperfections he had failed to eradicate. But she, grown into a considerable beauty, married the friend with whom he had picked her out at Shrewsbury, James Bicknell. Eventually Day found a suitable mate, and in 1778 married a wealthy heiress, Esther Milnes, first requesting that her fortune be placed beyond his reach should she regret the marriage and leave him. He allowed her no servants, saying: 'We have no right to luxuries while the poor want bread.' Nevertheless the marriage succeeded until, on 28 September 1789, trying out his theory that kindness would control any animal, Day was thrown by an unbroken colt and killed.

Among past occupants of Lichfield Deanery was the father of the essayist Joseph Addison, creator of Sir Roger de Coverley. Young Addison attended King Edward vi Grammar School, Lichfield, which despite only Eton and Winchester of famous schools being older, and three of its old boys, Addison, Johnson, and Garrick having come to rest in Westminster Abbey, now has to share its fame with the former Kinghill Secondary Modern in an enlarged comprehensive school of 1,200 pupils known as the King Edward vi School. By long tradition the school captain always replies to the toast to 'Dr Johnson's old school' at the Johnson Supper in the Guildhall each September.

Most of the aforementioned Lichfield alumni, along with Lady Mary Wortley Montague, who anticipated both Benjamin Jesty of Dorset and Edward Jenner of Gloucestershire in applying inoculation as a preventive against smallpox, have memorials in Lichfield Cathedral. Standing at the west end of this glorious building, breathless with wonder at the soaring majesty of the thirteenth century nave, the visitor becomes aware of a peculiarity – the weeping chancel. Far away at the east end the Lady Chapel inclines to the north. Some church builders who fail to stay on a straight line explain their error by claiming that the angle represents the inclination of Christ's head on the Cross. Lichfield proffers no such excuse. The axis is out of true because the south wall of the Lady Chapel follows a convenient bed of sandstone taking it ten degrees out of straight.

Lichfield's greatest treasure adorns the Lady Chapel, the sixteenth-century Herckenrode windows from a dismantled Cistercian convent

4 *Penkridge Church, with its Littleton memorials, is one of the most interesting churches in the county*

near Liège. Early last century Sir Basil Brooke of Ashbourne, Derbyshire, bought the glass in Belgium for £200 and made it over to Lichfield Cathedral at that price. To the seven Herckenrode windows are added two others in the Lady Chapel with a story, the two westernmost. These, too, are Flemish, bought in Belgium for a destination in Ireland, but the purchaser died when they had reached no farther than Crewe. There the glass lay for many months before it was offered for sale at Christie's, where a friend of the cathedral purchased it and had it installed in the Lady Chapel in 1895.

Age in glass appeals less to me than a pictorial story, and a window in the south choir aisle, dedicated only in 1901 to the memory of John Hacket, Bishop of Lichfield in the mid-seventeenth century, tells of his restoration of the cathedral after the Cromwellian depredations. He is depicted seated outdoors as he discusses plans with the architects while work proceeds on the cathedral behind them, a cathedral with the central tower reduced to the stump of its spire by Commonwealth artillery. A story is told that the new Bishop Hacket began removing the debris from the siege in his own carriage on the morning of his arrival, and the window shows a horse drawing away a cartload of fractured masonry.

During the siege in February and March 1643 Lichfield Cathedral was defended by the Royalists under Lord Chesterfield and Sir Richard Dyott. It was St Chad's Day, 2 March, when Sir Walter Scott's 'fanatic Brooke', leader of the Cromwellian besiegers, raised his helmet to observe the bombardment of the Royalist three-pounder gun positions on the central spire, and was shot through the eye and killed by Sir Richard's son, 'Dumb' Dyott. On 5 March the Royalists surrendered and the despoilers stormed in, destroying what they were able and introducing a pack of hounds into the building with which, day after day, they hunted cats.

St Chad was, it seems, watching over his own on his festival day in 1643, for he was the inspiration for the birth of Lichfield Cathedral. A pupil of St Aidan at Lindisfarne, his great mission was the fostering of friendship between the Britons and the Angles of Mercia. Created Bishop of Mercia, he moved his seat from Repton to Lichfield, where he built a church at Stowe, a pleasant short walk beside Stowe Pool from the Cathedral. The present Stowe church is mainly fourteenth

5   An interior at Chillington Hall, home of the Giffards who came to England with William the Conqueror and stayed to help another king – Charles II

century, and in its chancel are memorials to Lucy Porter, Dr Johnson's step-daughter, and Catherine Chambers, a Johnson family servant for many years, whose stone bears the doctor's own poignant words: 'My dear old friend Catherine Chambers. She buried my father, my brother, and my mother . . . I humbly hope to meet again and part no more.'

In a garden adjacent to the church is St Chad's Well, where probably the saint baptised his converts. At Stowe on 2 March 672, Chad died, seven days after angelic songs had announced his forthcoming end. He was buried at Stowe, but his successor, Bishop Hedda, built a new church where the cathedral now stands, and 28 years after Chad's death his body was re-interred there, and the cathedral constructed around it until the completion in 1420.

At the Reformation, although Henry VIII was more considerate of Lichfield Cathedral than Cromwell later was to prove, Prebendary Arthur Dudley thought it expedient to remove Chad's relics for safe keeping, and on his death passed them to his nieces Bridget and Kathleen Dudley of Russell Hall, near Dudley. Fearful of the Penal Laws these ladies passed them to Henry Hodshead of Woodsetton, Sedgley. On his deathbed Hodshead called repeatedly on St Chad, which intrigued Father Peter Turner who was ministering to him, and to whom, when pressed, he revealed some of the saint's bones wrapped in buckram on a bedpost. Turner then took the relics into his keeping, passing them at his death in 1655 to a Jesuit, John Leveson, who sent some to Flanders for veneration. The remainder were placed in the charge of Father Collingwood at Boscobel House – where Charles II had hidden some years earlier during the royal oak episode. From this home of the Fitzherberts the relics were moved to another Fitzherbert residence at Swynnerton Hall, Stone, but on the family moving to a nearby Aston Hall the bones went missing. Not until 1837, when the missioner at Aston Hall was clearing out the chapel, did they reappear – four large bones along with a casket containing relics of four other saints. These bones were accepted by Pope Gregory XVI as St Chad's relics as they came to their present resting place in the new Roman Catholic cathedral of Birmingham which was about to be dedicated – to St Chad.

The archbishopric of Lichfield which commenced in 787 and

covered seven dioceses lasted only 16 years, and Lichfield's status was further depressed in 1075 when the bishop's seat was transferred to the much more important town of Chester, from where, 20 years afterwards, Bishop Robert de Lymsey moved to Coventry and took the title Bishop of Coventry. Lichfield was later added to this, but took precedence in 1660 when the names were transposed, the diocese becoming Lichfield and Coventry. The existing title, Bishop of Lichfield, was established in 1836 with the transfer of the Archdeaconry of Coventry to the Diocese of Worcester.

One of the great glories of Lichfield Cathedral is the west front with its array of kings and saints, the Queen Victoria among them being designed by her daughter Louise, Duchess of Argyll. Three only of the figures are originals – on the north-west tower. With them is Charles II, moved there in a Victorian restoration from the position in the central gable now filled by Christ in Majesty. During this restoration Henry Williams fell from the tower to his death on 11 July 1878, and was buried on the spot, his fellow workmen providing a memorial stone which can be seen on the lawn near the north-west angle of the cathedral.

To condense the items of interest in Lichfield Cathedral into a reasonable space is a thankless task. You will not miss Chantrey's exquisite 'Sleeping Children', an early work of the sculptor, who came once a year to sit before it hoping for similar inspiration in his current work. The children were daughters of Canon William Robinson, one of whom died when her frock caught fire at a party, the other dying shortly afterwards. In the choir stalls and the bishop's throne is some century-old woodwork by George Evans – uncle of George Eliot (Mary Ann Evans) – who was the prototype of Seth Bede in her novel *Adam Bede*. The chapter house shows in its windows St Aidan teaching the infant Chad at Lindisfarne, and the grown-up Chad baptising the sons of King Wulfhere. Here, too, Lichfield's earlier relationship with Chester is portrayed in stone on a capital where a Cheshire cat toys with a mouse. My own favourite Lichfield window is that in the south transept full of saints who are particularly associated with the early churches throughout Europe and the Near East such as Polycarp with Antioch, Patrick with Ireland, and Boniface with Germany.

Perhaps the most surprising thing about Lichfield Cathedral was told me in 1962 by the head verger.

'When I was in France during the First World War', he said, 'I met a New Zealand unit. Somehow it was mentioned that I came from Lichfield, and at once the Maoris and the white New Zealanders remembered that Bishop Selwyn, the first Bishop of New Zealand, had left there to become Bishop of Lichfield.'

This is a remarkable tribute to Bishop Selwyn. None of those soldiers in Flanders could have known him, for he was Bishop of New Zealand 110 years ago, and Bishop of Lichfield from 1868 to 1878. His memorial chapel is decorated with tiles bearing the arms of various New Zealand cities. Here, too, the visitor can see the bishop's Maori friends in their villages and paddling their canoes about the lovely lakes of their homeland – strange exotic items in the cathedral at the heart of the Midlands. Decorative wall tiles commemorate George Augustus Selwyn in many churches of Lichfield diocese; Selwyn College, Cambridge, was built by public subscription as his memorial in England; and his portrait appears on the New Zealand £1 note.

Lichfield is famous for two annual customs, the Greenhill Bower on Whit Monday, and the Sheriff's Ride in September. The Court of Arraye and Greenhill Bower date from the twelfth century when citizens had to provide armour for the defence of the cathedral walls. This was inspected by the Court of Arraye of Men and Arms, and trading concessions were granted to those making a contribution, with fines for absentees. Men still dress in armour of sorts for the Arraye, and then take part in the procession of flowers known as Greenhill Bower, which commemorates a mediaeval fair.

It was Edward VI in 1549 who first commanded the bailiff and citizens of Lichfield to perambulate the bounds every year on 1 May. In 1553, Edward's half-sister, Queen Mary Tudor, designated Lichfield a county separate from Staffordshire with its own Sheriff. She changed the date of the perambulation to her own saint's day, 8 September, the nativity of the Virgin Mary, and by custom the Sheriff's Ride now takes place on the Saturday nearest that date. This is to accommodate the schoolchildren who now join the procession from their riding schools instead of the one member of each city household decreed by

Lichfield Court Leet in 1645 on pain of a fine. Boys were always taken on the ride and beaten or bumped on the boundary stones to impress these places in their memory, rough treatment which paid off in 1656 when, the relevant documents having been destroyed in the Civil War, Lichfield won a boundary dispute with Lord Paget of Longdon on the testimony of an old man who remembered the boundary line from his boyhood bumpings.

The Sheriff's Ride is said variously to cover from 19 to 24 miles. One year I walked the course a week before the ride – a kind of pedestrian muck-cart preceding the Lord Mayor's Show – across farmland, arable, and pasture, through parkland at Freeford, along the dry bed of the Wyrley and Essington Canal, by woodland glades through Leamonsley, and I estimated the distance at 20 miles.

The best time to browse about Lichfield is when, in Alfred Noyes' words 'all the chestnut spires are out' for the city is liberally hung with white and pink candelabra of many chestnut trees particularly around the Minster Pool and the Museum Gardens. Here two of the most tragic events this century, separated in 1912 by two short weeks, come together. These were the loss of Captain Robert Falcon Scott and his four companions as March moved into April on their return journey from the South Pole, and, on 14–15 April, the sinking of the 'unsinkable' White Star liner *Titanic* in the Atlantic on her maiden voyage. Little more than two years later came the unveiling in the peace of the Museum Gardens on 29 July 1914, of the bronze statue of Commander Edward John Smith, the 62-year-old master of the *Titanic* who was lost with his ship. The statue was the work of Scott's widow, Lady Kathleen Scott.

There seems some mystery why Commander Smith's statue was placed in Lichfield rather than his native Hanley in the Staffordshire Potteries. I was told in 1967 by Mrs Helen Russell Cooke, Commander Smith's only daughter, who, as a girl of 12, unveiled the Lichfield statue: 'I seem to remember something about a town rejecting the statue.' Yet on 16 April 1913, a year after the disaster, a brass memorial tablet to Commander Smith was unveiled at a civic ceremony in the apse facing the entrance to Hanley Town Hall. Many tributes were then paid him, including one that 'he did all that was humanly possible to save his passengers and his ship, and died the death of a true

27

Englishman.' A portrait was also dedicated in his old school at Etruria, where he was remembered as 'a senior boy who never put himself to the front very much, but was always ready to defend the weaker lads'.

It has been reported that as Hanley Town Hall had the plaque, a memorial statue was placed at Lichfield as the ecclesiastical centre of Staffordshire, easily accessible to travellers between London and Liverpool. There was opposition to the statue at Lichfield in a petition to the city council on 17 June 1914, signed by 73 citizens. Admitting that Commander Smith was 'a brave sailor' they nevertheless objected (a) that he had no claim on the city; (b) that such memorials should be erected only to distinguished and eminent men; and (c) that very great care must be taken in who they would commemorate in such close proximity to the statue of Edward VII, already in Museum Gardens.

The petition was rejected, and on 29 July 1914 a distinguished company gathered for the unveiling, including the Bishop of Willesden; Millicent, Duchess of Sutherland; Admiral Lord Charles Beresford; Lady Kathleen Scott; Lady Diana Manners, and the Marchioness of Anglesey.

Mrs Cooke remembers her father only as 'the man who came home on Wednesday – every fourth Wednesday – a gay man, a funny man, always laughing.' Through his statue at Lichfield posterity is reminded of Commander Smith's sterner qualities: 'A great heart, a brave life, and a heroic death.'

At every turn Lichfield has something to show of interest, and St John's Hospital has the striking sight of eight lofty chimneys raised in the fifteenth century when chimneys first became a feature of domestic architecture. With my surname I have always been somewhat concerned at the conjunction of two of Lichfield's main thoroughfares, Bird Street and Bore Street. Bird, I find, is a corruption of Brigge or Bridge Street – the bridge running across by the Minster Pool. Bore Street has also been Boar Street, and, anciently, Borde Street or Draper Street, and here is the Guildhall on the site of the Guild House which stood in the reign of Richard II. Lichfield has made practice of completely changing its street names; thus Market Street was Sadler Street, and before that Rope, and Robe Street after Hugh

Robe, a fourteenth-century property owner. Breadmarket Street was Whoman's Cheppynge – the latter word meaning market.

The traveller choosing to make his landfall of Staffordshire at the secular capital of Mercia rather than the ecclesiastical, will enter the county four miles south of Tamworth, where the A4091 holds two points of interest. His right hand neighbour alongside the road is the Fazeley Canal coming up from Birmingham to meet the Coventry Canal at Fazeley – a circular route through Birmingham known as the 'Bottom Road' to the old boatmen who brought their cargoes of metal ingots or tomato puree from Brentford to Birmingham, and continued via Fazeley to load up at the Warwickshire coalfield with fuel for Hertfordshire mills around Watford, rejoining the main Grand Union Canal at Braunston. This necessitated a right turn into the canal at Fazeley. A left turn, and in 11 sylvan miles one came to Fradley Junction on the Trent and Mersey Canal.

Barely has it entered Staffordshire than the Fazeley Canal is crossed by an ornamental bridge with miniature turrets at either side. This is at Drayton Bassett, near Drayton Manor, now a pleasure park but once the home of Sir Robert Peel, the Prime Minister who gave his name to the 'peelers' of the Police Force which he founded. Secretary for Ireland at the tender age of 24, Peel became, in the words of Disraeli 'the greatest Member of Parliament'.

Fazeley, once noted for its ribbon making, stands on the Watling Street, and once this is safely crossed Tamworth Castle looms above the water meadows ahead. The riverside clearing in the woodlands at the confluence of the Tame and the Anker was an ideal spot for the Saxons who built the first settlement at Tamworth. Barely a mile north of the Watling Street, it gave easy access to the road network left by the Romans. No wonder Offa selected Tamworth as his capital and built a palace where Market Street runs today.

A well in the castle gardens links Tamworth with the growth of Christianity in the Mercian kingdom. It is called Ruffin's Well after one of the two sons of King Wulfhere, and it is known to have existed in 1276 when a man was fined for obstructing the pathway to it. In all probability Wulfhere dedicated the well to the son he slew in the seventh century. Ruffin's brother, Wulfhade, was converted by St Chad whom he met at Stowe while out hunting, and Ruffin's conversion soon followed. Their pagan father was enraged and murdered them both, to repent later and become a Christian so that his statue is now among those on the west front of Lichfield Cathedral.

The bridge across the Tame beneath Tamworth Castle is known as Lady Bridge, the lady being the Virgin Mary, not, as many think, Ethelfleda, Lady of the Mercians, who raised the mound and crowned it with a wooden stockade, the forerunner of the castle we know. Ethelfleda's statue, which represents her with her favourite nephew Athelstan, greets visitors just inside the castle grounds. The daughter of Alfred the Great, Ethelfleda was responsible for the rebirth of Tamworth in 913 after the Danes had destroyed Offa's settlement. She built her own residence at the foot of the fortified mound, protecting it by a ditch sometimes attributed to her predecessor, Offa – well known as a builder of dykes – and she may also have built the splendid herringbone curtain wall, ten feet thick, still to be seen between the Market Street lodge and the castle keep. Ethelfleda died in 918 and, with Athelstan on the throne of England, Tamworth remained a royal residence and a meeting place of the Witenagemote, the parliament of Saxon days.

At the time of a treaty of peace between the Saxons and the Danes, Athelstan gave his sister, Editha, in marriage to the Danish king of Northumbria, Sihtric, on the understanding that he renounced his paganism and became a Christian. But the Dane proved a backslider, jettisoning both his new faith and his wife. Editha then devoted her life to the Church and established a convent in the royal palace at Tamworth. This presumably survived another Danish attack which destroyed Tamworth in 943, for the nuns were still there in 1066, only to be expelled by Robert de Marmion, who came from Normandy with the Conqueror, and who was granted Tamworth Castle for his services in the Battle of Hastings. The evicted nuns moved no farther than Polesworth Abbey across the county boundary in Warwickshire, founded by Edith a daughter of King Egbert. Marmion was, however, also granted the lordship of Polesworth, and was able to turn the nuns out of their refuge.

From his ruthlessness springs the ghost story of Tamworth Castle, which the custodian once told me on the haunted staircase.

'One night', he said, 'Marmion had gone to bed after an entertainment when, in a dream, Edith appeared to him dressed as an abbess. She criticised his harsh treatment of her nuns and struck him on the side with her crozier, prophesying that he would meet with a horrible death if he did not let them take up residence again at Polesworth. Marmion awoke sweating with fear, a fear that was intensified when he found himself bleeding from a wound in the side, so he promptly gave orders that the nuns be allowed to return to Polesworth. A Black Lady is said to have haunted these stairs to his room ever since, and someone claimed to have photographed her around 1950.'

With the end of the male line the Marmion tenure of Tamworth Castle ended in 1294, so obviously the hero who gave his name to Sir Walter Scott's epic *Marmion* was a fiction, dying as he did at Flodden in 1513 when 'Charge, Chester, charge; on, Stanley, on' were the last words of Marmion. Somewhere at Tamworth Castle Sir Walter Scott's signature is kept, scratched on a piece of glass which was removed from its window for safety.

Shortly after the Marmions gave place to the deFrevilles the castle lost its association with the office of Royal Champion. The original Robert had been Champion to William the Conqueror back in Normandy, and the gift of Tamworth Castle and the Manor of Scrivelsby in Lincolnshire carried the obligation to become Royal Champion of England. After the first deFreville at Tamworth, Sir Alexander, had appeared as Royal Champion at the Coronation of Edward III in 1327, the successors of the Marmions on the female side who had inherited Scrivelsby Manor claimed, successfully, that the role of Champion went with it. But Tamworth retains a memory of the Royal Champion in Fontenaye Road, for Scott had written of his Marmion

> They hailed him Lord of Fontenaye,
> Of Lutterward and Scrivelsbaye,
> Of Tamworth tower and town.

Following the deFrevilles in 1423 the Ferrers have left their mark on Tamworth Castle after a 260-years stay with such permanent reminders as their coat-of-arms in most of the 52 panels of the state drawing-room, and again in the oak room. Among the exciting collection of weapons and armour in the Henry VIII banqueting hall is the sword used by Lord Thomas Ferrers at Bosworth, which is inscribed 'He who loses me loses honour'. From 1790 to 1792 this hall was rented by a Mr Peel as a forge in connection with a cotton industry which he had brought into the area from Lancashire. He became Sir Robert Peel, Bart, and his son, another Sir Robert, that 'model of all Prime Ministers'. During the time of the Ferrers, Tamworth Castle had one of its royal visitors, James I, whose bedchamber is still shown. Accompanying him was his son, later Charles I, who thus became familiar with a castle which supported him during the Civil War. A thorn in the side of the Roundheads in their attempts to capture Lichfield, the castle fell to them in 1643.

The Shirleys of Chartley and the Comptons, Earls of Northampton, both obtained Tamworth Castle by marriage before it passed, again by marriage, in 1751 to the Townshends, and it was from Marquis Townshend that the Corporation of Tamworth bought the castle to commemorate Queen Victoria's diamond jubilee. Tamworth had a mint in the reign of Athelstan, and a collection at the castle includes several Saxon coins minted in the town. Brass-rubbers, too, will find the Allsopp collection of great interest, with examples from as far apart as Lincolnshire and Sussex.

Tamworth's splendid collegiate church, dedicated to St. Editha, has one unique feature – the double staircase entered either from the churchyard or the church, and so constructed that the roof of one spiral of steps is the floor of the other, the staircase comprising 101 and 106 steps. The windows suffer where they depict dreary Old Testament characters or William Morris consumptives, but come to life with an excellent land girl and miner in the War Memorial. Among the churchyard monuments are an obelisk commemorating 'the melancholy and awful deaths of six female servants, who were hurried from time into eternity' by a fire at the Castle Inn on 2 November 1838; and a stone to Edward Farmer, 'Author of Little Jim', born in Derby but long resident in Tamworth, who died on 10 July 1876. Farmer was a railway detective, best known for the heart-rending ballad on the death of Little Jim – a miner's only child – but author, too, of other works, including pantomime scripts.

The Sir Robert Peel, whose bronze statue stands beside the Town Hall, is the father of the statesman who represented Tamworth in

Commons from 1837 to 1850. One of his predecessors was Thomas Guy, founder of Guy's Hospital, London, remembered in Guy's Close among Tamworth street names as Peel is commemorated in Peel Rise. Guy built the almshouses in Lower Gungate, Tamworth, but, annoyed at losing his parliamentary seat in 1707, he refused any place in them to his ungrateful constituents. 1200 years are spanned by the street names of Tamworth, from Offa Street, to names of astronauts and lunarnauts on the Lichfield Road Industrial Estate – Gagarin, first man in space; Armstrong, first man on the Moon; Borman, Lovell, and Anders, with Apollo thrown in for good measure.

A charming tract of sylvan country follows the valley of the Black Brook between Lichfield and Tamworth, from Shenstone where one of Nelson's captains, Admiral Sir William Parker, lies; through Weeford, birthplace in 1700 of James Wyatt, who beat Richard Arkwright to the invention of the spinning machine; to sequestered Hints. Between Hints and Hopwas, with an astonishing church, tall ash trees have clothed the quarry from which was hewn the stone to build Tamworth Church, turning it into a delightfully spooky spot known as the Devil's Dressing Room.

Eastward from Tamworth, Staffordshire pushes a salient towards the Four Counties Inn at No Man's Heath, bounded on the south by the A.453, and on the north by the River Mease. Statfold and Thorpe Constantine are redolent of the country-house society of Jane Austen, the latter in particular, one of those charming Georgian villages where the old rectory is three times the size of the church, and the church is in the grounds of the hall. Lordly pheasants honk, and partridges whirr in a parkland alive with sheep and cattle, while the rambling red brick estate buildings resound with busy noises. Haunton is a village of saints and mice where St Charles Cottages, St Edward's Cottage, two houses – St Bernard's and St Michael's; St Joseph's Convent School for Girls; and St James Major's church all speak of a Roman Catholic atmosphere. St James's Church has a window depicting St Gertrude of Nivelles with field mice on her staff. The patroness of cats, she is invoked by people who are afraid of mice; but this does not include the girls at the convent, who eat their meals with legs nestling against the 'church mice' with which Robert Thompson of Kilburn, Yorkshire, signs his wood-carving, in this case the refectory table.

In the convent chapel the front of the organ loft was carved by Agnes de Trafford of near-by Haselour Hall, while other carving on the altar is the work of a past mother superior, Mother Scholastica.

Rising above this pleasant countryside is the magnificent 189-foot spire of Clifton Campville, the resident cloud of jackdaws always playing about it, but the church flatters to deceive, with spacious but colourless expanses of plain glass, its walls cluttered with fulsome but uninteresting nineteenth-century epitaphs. The screen is its best feature, beautifully carved, and inscribed 'Master Gilbert – Parson of Clifton – 1684'.

The little River Mease, rich in dace, chub, pike, perch and roach, flows beside many-gabled Croxall Hall which has an association with one of the most exquisite poems in the language. Lady Anne Wilmot-Horton was the wife of Sir Robert of the hall, a cousin of Lord Byron, who first saw her dressed in a black spangled gown at a ball. He was so captivated by her beauty that he at once wrote the poem beginning

> She walks in beauty, like the night
> Of cloudless climes and starry skies . . .

Sir Robert was largely responsible for the suppression of the memoirs Byron left with Thomas Moore to be published after his death, but which were deemed too unseemly for publication and so were solemnly burned.

Away across the River Mease from Croxall stands a farmhouse named 'Oakley', the seat of Sir John Stanley, ancestor of the Earls of Derby, who died in 1474 and lies to the south-westward at Elford Church in the chantry he built. The people of Elford were for some time concerned about the bearded mystery man, a bachelor, Stanley Whitehead, who gave his black and white home a foreign name, 'Framheim', and with the comings and goings of Land-Rovers with Irish voices in the night. Far from being sinister those voices denoted a healthy movement away from the Irish troubles. They came from groups of young Irishmen travelling to and from the Continent on one of the seven adventure Land-Rovers run by Mr Whitehead on a non-profit-making basis, the cost merely replacing the vehicles as they wear out. The 'Fram' project is as remarkable a venture as I have known.

In 1953 Stanley Whitehead acquired his first Land-Rover to take boys' clubs, scouts, and other groups on adventure week-ends in the mountainy parts of England and Wales. His brother, killed in the Harrow rail disaster, was a youth club leader, and, dedicating the 'Fram' idea to him, Stanley hoped it would do some of the good for boys that his brother might have done. 'Fram' was an inspired name for the first Land-Rover – the Norwegian for 'Forward' which is the motto of Birmingham where the scheme began, and the name of Nansen's famous Arctic ship. Every week-end 'Fram' went adventuring; eight boys, with their kit in a trailer, and Mr Whitehead at the wheel. Logbook after logbook was filled – I remember going on the 300th expedition in 1959 into the Arenig Mountains. There have been many more since. 'Fram 2' was purchased; 'Fram 3' – by 1972 there were seven 'Frams' operating from various places in Britain and Northern Ireland. Irish groups using 'Fram' were met by Stanley Whitehead at Liverpool; they would drop him at his Elford home and continue to a south coast port to cross to the Continent, picking him up on their return so that he could drive 'Fram' back to Elford from Liverpool.

Frams have now travelled across the Sahara, to the Middle East, Iceland, Lapland, Turkey, all over Europe.

Elford is skirted by the River Tame, one of England's most polluted rivers, now in process of being cleansed. This cleansing has far to go however before the memory of an old inhabitant can be repeated of catching fish wholesale for human consumption with a net towed behind a cart.

Surrounded by the best-kept churchyard in the Lichfield Diocese, Elford Church is famed for its memorials, while the epitaphs around its walls read like Burke's *Peerage*, with references to the Howards, the Bagots, and those with whom they were allied, the Dukes of Norfolk, Suffolk, and Northumberland; Earls of Berkshire and Beverley; Lord Audley, and Lord Templetown. In the chantry Sir John Stanley lies unaccompanied; Sir Thomas Arderne, who restored the church in the fourteenth century, lies with his wife Matilda; while Sir William Smythe has a wife on either hand, Anne Staunton from whom he inherited the Manor of Elford, and Lady Isabella Neville who wears a coronet. What history these few names recall. Stanley abandoned

Richard III on the eve of Bosworth having, it is said, had a meeting at Elford with Henry Tudor, a meeting commemorated by the red Lancastrian roses and the Stanley portcullises in a window. Arderne was a comrade in arms of the Black Prince, and Isabella Neville was a niece of Warwick the Kingmaker. Dwarfed physically by these historic alabaster tombs, the small gritstone effigy of Sir John Stanley's grandson steals the show. Young John Stanley lies with his feet against a puppy, and in one hand holds a tennis ball while, with the other, he points to his temple where a blow from the ball killed him.

In the chancel floor are several brasses, one to a past rector, the Rev. John Sneyd, with his punning coat-of-arms blazoning a scythe, the handle of which is known as a snead. No names are more important in Elford Church than those of the Rev. Francis Paget, rector from 1835 to 1882, and his cousin, Lady Mary Howard, Lady of the Manor of Elford, who effected a complete restoration of the church. On a slab prepared before his death Paget describes himself with sickening self-abasement as 'a miserable sinner, the vilest of the vile', though he wrote books against child labour in the mines, and against the exploitation of seamstresses which landed him with a libel action. These overworked but appreciative girls clubbed together from their meagre wages and sent money for his defence. He declined any money for himself from his writings, saying it was done in parish time and ploughing it back into the church.

Across the Tame from Elford the parish of Whittington is best known for its barracks so that the churchyard has many military burials, including that of Sergeant J. B. Ford of the West Riding Regiment, who died in 1907 aged 27, his headstone adding 'also Sergeant Ellis, a comrade of the above' who died in 1942 aged 72, a happy case of comradeship spanning the years. Here, too, is the grave of Marie Cecil Birch who survived her husband, Major Birch, by 53 years, a remarkable widowhood.

Preserved in Whittington Church is a flute, a relic of days before organs drowned the singing. William Bass played the flute in the choir from 1800 to 1867, so long that one almost listens for its ghostly music today.

From Whittington across the Burton road is Alrewas, and a delightful experience as one surmounts a steep hump-backed canal bridge to be confronted with a scene straight from John Constable's Suffolk paintings. The willow-fringed Trent, wind-rippled and sun-dappled, flows from Alrewas Mill past a green waterside plot with a couple of seats. The Trent and Mersey Canal also adds immensely to the scenic amenities of the village, while barely a mile away where it is joined by the Coventry Canal, the Trent and Mersey renders Fradley Junction one of the most charming inland waterway locations in Britain.

Alrewas Church has a memorial to Clara Selwyn, daughter-in-law of that famous bishop of New Zealand and Lichfield, George Augustus Selwyn. His son, John, was a curate at Alrewas and eventually became Bishop of Melanesia, where Clara, his wife, died on Norfolk Island in 1877. John returned to Britain and became Master of Selwyn College, Cambridge. Another Alrewas curate in the mid-nineteenth-century was the Rev. Alfred Ainger, who wrote that fine hymn 'God is working his purpose out'.

The River Trent brought a cottage industry to Alrewas, its regular flooding helping in the growth of osier beds which provided material for basket making. Families engaged in this occupation included the Coates, and the Dolmans who were active in it until the Second World War.

For several months in 1973 I was intrigued by a couple of 'ginger' pigs on Mr Geoffrey Cloke's Manor Farm near Knowle in Warwickshire. Eventually he told me they were Tamworths, and that Mr Josh Holland of Edingale House, near Lichfield, had bred them – and shire horses – for many years. The sandy red Tamworth is the nearest approach to the European wild hog, hard to beat for purity of breeding, and rare enough to be thoroughly interesting though in 1884, when the National Pig Breeders' Association came into being, it was the Tamworth breeders together with breeders of the Large White and the Middle White who were responsible for its formation.

CHAPTER TWO

Lost Territory—
The Black Country

One of the most overworked and misused words in the English language today is 'jungle'. We hear of the blackboard jungle, the trades union jungle, the soccer jungle – in each of which savagery is the jungle element. If I refer to the Black Country jungle I use the word in terms of its impenetrability. No stage of Dante's 'Inferno' can be more horrible than the need to travel the Black Country by car, to stutter one's halting way along winding overcrowded roads, through streets indistinguishable one from another, and over hump-backed bridges into 'pudden-bags' petering out on tumbled slag mounds hung with smoke-encrusted hawthorn, even though one such place beside the Bentley Canal in Willenhall is Mumper's Dingle, famous as the site of Isopel Berners' encampment where George Borrow's 'Lavengro' fought the Flaming Tinman.

No direction in the Black Country lasts long enough to get going; locally-requested information involves far too many twists and turns to keep in mind while concentrating on driving a car. As in a jungle you cannot see the wood for the trees, so in the Black Country you cannot see the buildings for the bricks, though, given a vantage point such as comes here and there on the new Wolverhampton Road, there is a fascination about the sprawl of chimney stacks, cooling towers, retorts, gasometers – with the Swan Village monster predominant – gleaming storage tanks, and plumes of white smoke. Black smoke is rare; gone are the many smoke trails from railway engines.

6 *(above)   Speedwell Castle, Brewood, built to commemorate an*
unexpected victory in a horse race
7   *Himley Hall, once the stately home of the Earls of Dudley, on the*
fringe of the Black Country

An occasional eruption of sinister orange smoke from a chemical or iron works is the only noxious sign in the overall view today, but one is conscious that down there is that more insidious blanket of petroleum and diesel fumes from vehicles that move about, stop and start and reverse with as little purpose seemingly as the denizens of an ant colony.

Shanks's Pony is the most reliable means of locomotion throughout this conurbation of some 85 square miles. There is much confusion concerning the boundaries of the Black Country. In 1868, Elihu Burritt, the United States consul in Birmingham, wrote in his *Walks in the Black Country and Its Green Borderland* that 'Birmingham is the capital, manufacturing centre, and growth of the Black Country.' Phil Drabble wrote in *Black Country* (Robert Hale, 1952): 'One insult that no Black Countryman will tolerate is to be mistaken for a Brummie.' As a Brummie I have an equal abhorrence of being equated with a Black Countryman. Birmingham is, of course, outside the Black Country. So is Cannock – erroneously located there in 1973 by a London journalist to the disgust of the people of Cannock.

The Black Country stretches from Stourbridge and Halesowen in the south-west to Walsall in the north-east, and from Wolverhampton in the north-west to Smethwick in the south-east – all inclusive. In the south-west, Worcestershire claims Stourbridge with its crystal glass industry, and Halesowen with the most grotesque Black Country accent. Otherwise the area is entirely in Staffordshire, defined geologically by the ten-yard coal seam on which most of its stands, which, with iron ore, and limestone as a flux, provided the raw materials for its volcanic development in the eighteenth and nineteenth centuries.

Most Black Country towns lack definition and central points. Willenhall of the locksmiths merges with Darlaston, its chemical and giant Rubery-Owen works. Bilston, Wednesbury, Coseley, and Tipton are one mass of tinplate works, heavy and light industry, and though Wednesbury Parish Church does stand out lighthouse-like, it is no easy matter to come to it in a maze of traffic lights, road graffiti, and other impedimenta on movement hereabouts. Dudley has a certain individuality, the tree-tracery of Wren's Nest and Castle Hill forming a backdrop to the vista confronting the traveller from Birmingham. It also has a personality split between Staffordshire and

8   *Hoar Cross Church in Needwood Forest, Emily Meynell Ingram's beautiful shrine to her husband Hugo*

Worcestershire, the old borough of Dudley being an island of the latter surrounded by the former county until the 1965 re-shuffle. South of Dudley, Rowley Regis with its ragstone quarries fuses with the chain and nail-making areas of Old Hill, Cradley Heath, and Cradley, while Quarry 'Bonk' runs into Brierley Hill, where the glass-making industry spills over into Staffordshire from Stourbridge. Brierley Hill Church is another identifiable rock on this distraught sea of houses and factories, and from their higher vantage point near the western extremity of the Black Country residents of Brierley Hill have glorious distant views of the Wrekin and of the Clees and Stretton hills deep in neighbouring Shropshire.

Canals and characters, the two proliferate in the Black Country, and they came into conjunction for me in the drizzling cloud-wrack of a July dawn when I met 'Caggy' Stevens at Whimsey Bridge, Oldbury – a 'whimsey' was a pit-pumping machine. He was harnessing his dappled roan stallion 'Mac' to a towline, and soon the open boat *Trigo* was gliding gently up the cut, bound empty for Cannock Coalfield, where it would be left for filling while 'Mac' hauled back another of Caggy's boats already loaded with 24 tons of boiler coal for a Birmingham factory.

I took the tiller and as the light strengthened Caggy could be seen stepping out smartly with 'Mac', easing the towrope over obstacles. Caggy, christened Alan in 1919, looked every inch a canal boatman, his comfortable figure consorting strangely with his energetic way of life. Braces over a check shirt, sleeves rolled to the elbow, corduroy trousers and, beneath a battered narrow-brimmed trilby, a face at once kindly and shrewd – this was the man who had spent 40 years on the hard school of the canal since joining his father's boats. Beneath the bridges Mac's otherwise silent tread echoed a loud clip-clop on the tarmac, but as we turned from the High Level to the Low at Tividale Junction his muzzle was removed and he munched white clover during pauses in dropping down three locks into a ravaged landscape of jagged rubbish tips, smoking chimneys, and white-flowered elder bushes. Turning right at Dunkirk Junction, then left at the Albion turn for West Bromwich, I realised that one has to be a geometrician to lead a canal horse, and to know just where the towrope can go on the junction bridges. From the Eight Locks pub in Ryders Green Road we dropped down eight locks to Great Bridge in six furlongs.

In the last pound Caggy pointed out a wooden stump with a D incribed on it and explained: 'That's a distance post. If yo'r 'oss 'ad reached it gooin' up yo' could claim right o' way into Lock Seven against a boat comin' down. A boat lockin' down could claim Lock Eight if its 'oss were under Brickhouse Lane Bridge. There are usually distance posts before all lock flights, and on longish pounds in a flight. Many a fight they caused in old days.'

Fifteen tethering rings in a wall near the bottom lock bear witness to the horse-drawn heyday of canals. On past the pools of the derelict railway basin at Great Bridge, we entered a sulphurous smell near Hempole Lane Bridge to turn right beneath the three huge bobbins of 'Ocker Bonk' Power Station at the Tame Valley Junction where the canal was unencumbered enough for a spell of 'backering'.

'Backering', said Caggy, settling on the cabin roof, 'that's when the 'oss goes on with us resting on the boat. Mac's a good backering 'oss, an ideal boat 'oss, light-legged, and eats and sleeps well. Cost me £110 from Birmingham Corporation.'

Just on this we saw Mac's one temperamental failing as he shied and turned smartly back from a plastic sheet flapping over a cache of building bricks. Caggy tore away the sheet, put his jacket over Mac's head, and led him docilely past another billowing sheet. As we approached Newton Junction to turn into the Rushall Canal with Barr Beacon in sight we were in more open country where dozens of electricity pylons strode relentlessly towards us like robots in a space film. Working up the 'Gansey' – the first seven locks on the Rushall Canal – Caggy remembered some canal characters. There was 'Nine Lives', who helped kill a thief on the towpath with a tiller; Bill Taylor from Oldbury ('very fast, you do' arf 'av to move if he wor be'ind you'); Stabbit and Starchy, old Brummagem chaps; and 'Old Drown the Boat', who sank his boat in Perry Barr top lock and got three months.

Surprising statistics have stuck in Caggy's head, too. 'On Good Friday, 1937', he said, '80 boats loaded with coal and slack came down Rushall locks'. Today not half a dozen working boats ply the canal, but Charlie Plant, tending a tidy garden at the 'Top o' Mosses' told me there are plenty of pleasure cruisers nowadays.

A bounding breeze from Walsall swept the green fields and hawthorn hedges as we left the lock behind, and for a while only two farms were visible on a wide stretch of countryside. The Manor Arms, known as the Milk House, was left in our wake at Rushall, and up came Stonehouse Bridge where the old boatmen cracked their whips noisily to warn that they were coming round the bend. On we glided, the canal curving high above Dumble Derry, an open space where a strong wind plays havoc with a light empty boat, so that, in Caggy's inimitable words – 'We 'ave to trot we 'oss'. Opposite the old Walsall Wood Colliery Caggy pointed out a small brick building.

'That was a hovel', he said. 'The canal companies built hovels for boatmen without cabins. I've often slep' in 'em on a bag o' corn. At Benny's at Little Bloxwich we once 'ad an 'oss in as well. Them wor rough days. If yo' cor fight yo' worn't in the team. Even if yo' kep' quiet somebody 'ould tek a poke at yo!'

Walsall Wood Church and a neat cricket ground passed below us. 'When fust I come up 'ere', said Caggy, 'the ground was level with the canal. Now through mining it's sunk about ten feet'.

Turning into the Wyrley and Essington Canal at Catshill Stop we had a lunchtime drink at the 'Anchor', and in another mile reached our destination. The canal, milky at Oldbury, smoking with phosphorus at Tipton, bottle-green at West Bromwich, and weedy at Rushall, was now deep and crystal clear. With the Chasewater Reservoir dam half a mile ahead, and with reference to no one, we tied up *Trigo*, removed our belongings to boat No. 1,297, already filled with coal, harnessed up the faithful 'Mac' and started back the way we had come.

On the blustery afternoon of Easter Saturday 1973 to the strains of 'See the Conquering Hero Comes' from the Warley Senior Schools Brass Band, two 70-foot open boats emerged from the Parkhead portal of the Dudley Canal Tunnel after travelling 3,172 yards underground from the Tipton Approach Canal. Sir Frank Price, Chairman of British Waterways Board, raised the paddles of Parkhead top lock, and a canal route first available in 1792 was again open, thanks to sterling work by the Dudley Canal Trust. During the 1855 heyday of canals around 41,700 boats used the tunnel as the shortest route from the Black Country to the Severn via the Staffordshire and Worcestershire Canal. Up to the closure in 1928 of the Old Side Forge, five boats daily travelled from Harts Hill, steered from the works for long years by three generations of Mulletts – Enoch, David, and Luther – and handed over at Parkhead to the 'King of the Tunnel', Jack Wheeler. Into his seventies Jack legged boats through Dudley Tunnel, 7s.6d. full; 5s. empty; but in 1952 Jack Wheeler made his final journey with Charon as boatman, and in that same year when I first traversed the Stygian gloom of Dudley Tunnel it had almost fallen into disuse.

The tunnel ranges from vast limestone caverns, with a fossilised coral reef in Castle Mill Basin, to a bricked section called The Gaol, so narrow that it gives the impression of being squeezed through a tube of toothpaste. From the Tipton end a short section is known as Lord Ward's Tunnel, completed in 1778 by the 2nd Viscount Dudley and Ward to carry limestone from workings in Castle Hill and Wren's Nest to the Black Country as a flux in the melting of iron ore. Some 400 million years ago this area was a sediment of lime on the sea bed. In later geological ages the sea receded and coal seams formed from vegetation springing from the limestone. As prehistoric time marched on chalk and glacial deposits covered the coal. Titanic subterranean upheavals followed, and the limestone shook off its covering and reared up the outcrops of Castle Hill and Wren's Nest at Dudley. For a mere century man pitted his strength against nature, winning the Black Country's coal, iron and limestone. Wren's Nest was honey-combed until outraged nature resented these operations. Her bowels rumbled, there were roof falls, the caverns became dangerous, and the workers vacated them leaving such excavations as the Severn Sisters caves, and the Dark Cavern with its ballroom carved out of limestone, lit with gas, and accessible down the '144 Steps'.

Dudley accords civic recognition to this fossiliferous area by blazoning a trilobite on its arms.

On a site at the Tipton End of the Dudley Tunnel a group of enthu-siasts are installing a Black Country Museum to consist of a recon-structed village incorporating a row of nailers' and chain-makers' stone cottages, a fogger's warehouse, an anchor forge, a chapel, a boat-yard, and a canal bridge. Old tramcars which plied the Black Country have been collected, and 'travellers' carts' which recall the Harper, Watton, and other families from Ruiton and Gornal, who hawked salt, sand for domestic scouring, and hardware around the Midlands. From April to October they were on the road, usually with two carts, one containing their wares, the other their accommodation.

What the Black Country Museum is doing physically the Black Country Society does culturally, preserving the Black Country dialect and the stories centred around those earthy characters Anuk and Ali (Enoch and Eli). Anuk was walking along the towpath one day when he saw Ali in the canal.

' 'Elp,' I'm drownding,' shouts Ali.

'Wot's yo'r name?' bawls Anuk.

'Ali', comes the weakening reply. 'Get me out.'

'Where d'yo werk?' demands Anuk.

'Rubery-Owen', gasps Ali going down yet again. Anuk hurries to Rubery-Owen.

'Yo got a chap called Ali werks 'ere?' he asks.

'Ar', says the gatekeeper, 'but 'e aint 'ere today.'

'I know', says Anuk, ' 'e's drownded up the cut. I've cum for 'is job.'

'Yo're too late', answers the gatekeeper. 'We just gi'd it the bloke wot pushed 'im in.'

Rather more sophisticated Anuks and Alis now take their children to the zoo in Dudley Castle ruins, where sea-lions disport in what was once the moat. Ansculf, an adventurer from Picardy who came over with William the Conqueror, made Dudley the capital of a scattered barony he was granted, and built the first fortification there. The Paganels succeeded the Ansculfs, and Gervase Paganel founded the Priory, the ruins of which are a charming feature of Dudley. When the de Somerys inherited the barony through marriage the early castle was a ruin, but re-fortification began when Roger de Somery II was granted licence to crenellate after taking the side of Henry III against Simon de Montfort. A Margaret Somery married John de Sutton, bringing the Dudley estate to that family when she inherited in 1322.

In 1532 John Sutton VII succeeded to the Dudley barony and castle, a character so weak that he became known as Lord Quondam – 'once a Lord'. His grandson, John Dudley, then Viscount Lisle and Earl of

Warwick, manipulated the financial difficulties of Lord Quondam so as to gain control of Dudley Castle, where, raised to the dukedom of Northumberland, he rebuilt the residential portion, the earliest example in England of Tudor and Stuart domestic architecture. Northumberland was beheaded when he tried to put his son, Lord Guildford Dudley on the throne as husband of Lady Jane Grey, the nine-days' queen in 1553. Dudley Castle passed to the Crown, but Mary Tudor restored it to Edward Sutton, son of Lord Quondam. His son, Edward III, the last Lord Dudley of the Sutton line, married Theodosia Harington, but 'left that virtuous lady, his wife . . . and took to his home a lewd and infamous woman, a base collier's daughter, Elizabeth Tomlinson, who bore him eleven children.' One of these was Dud Dudley, famous for having invented the method of smelting iron with coal, a timely discovery, as the forests which provided the charcoal previously used were becoming denuded. Though Dud Dudley was the pioneer, it was Abraham Darby, son of a Dudley Quaker, who, a century later, applied the new smelting method with commercial success at Coalbrookdale in Shropshire.

A grand-daughter of Edward Sutton III and Theodosia, Frances, was the last of the Suttons, and her grandfather arranged her marriage with Humble Ward, the eldest son of a Cheapside goldsmith who found the money to rehabilitate the Dudley estates. In 1644 Humble Ward was created Baron Ward of Birmingham.

During the Civil War Dudley Castle was garrisoned for the King without the new baron's permission, but was captured for the Parliament by Sir William Brereton, whose son married Theodosia, Baron Ward's daughter, while the baron's heir, Edward Ward, married Brereton's daughter and eventually succeeded to his father's barony of Ward and his mother's of Dudley. With the death, unmarried, in 1740, of William, Lord Ward and Dudley, the two baronies separated. The barony of Ward with Dudley Castle and estates passed to his cousin and heir male, John Ward of Sedgley Park, later Viscount Dudley and Ward, from whose line the present earldom of Dudley has sprung, the present and fourth earl being also Viscount Ednam in Roxburghshire and Baron Ward of Birmingham. Dudley Castle suffered a great fire on 24 July 1750, but before that Himley Hall, in sylvan country west of Dudley, had become the principal home of the family. It was the 8th Baron Ward and 3rd Viscount Dudley and Ward who tidied up the castle as a ruin during his ownership in 1788–1823.

Dudley Parish Church, dedicated to Didymus – Doubting Thomas – is one of the great landmarks of the Black Country. A plaque near the pulpit introduces the Rev. Luke Booker, historian of the castle, and three of his four wives who predeceased him in 1806, 1817, and 1827, aged respectively 35, 28, and 33. Before you raise your eyebrows, just reflect that his four marriages could have arisen from filial respect. His father also married four times and had 13 children. Prepared obviously to be fruitful himself, Luke failed unhappily to multiply. 'Eight of their children like vernal flowers blossomed and died' says an inscription. Booker was Vicar of Dudley from 1812 to his death in 1835, an extensive writer and much in demand to preach charity sermons. Somewhat insensitively he had the mediaeval church demolished, and played a major role in rebuilding St Thomas's as we know it. It is said that houses were constructed at Dixon's Green of stone from the old church, some of the gravestones being used for making ovens so that loaves baked in them bore imprints from the epitaphs.

Blazoned on the headquarters of a mutual benefit society built in 1908 in Priory Street, Dudley, are clasped hands encircled by the old saying 'God helps those who help themselves'. It smacks somehow of co-opting the Almighty on to your board of directors. Eve Hill has a pub with the intriguing name 'Ye Old Struggling Man', yet having no story about it. Cuba Pit, however, that raised its pithead gear way down the Himley Road opposite the new Merryfields Estate, was opened for the production of fireclay on the day in 1898 when war ended between the United States and Spain in Cuba.

The Himley Road is liable to mining subsidence and it is this subterranean uncertainty that gives fame to the Glynne Arms at Gornal, alias the Crooked House. Approached past Baggeridge Pool along a winding lane densely hedge-fringed, with the burble of Bob's Brook for music, the Crooked House leans, heavily-buttressed, beside a field where cattle graze. This is one pub where, however you ultimately emerge, you stagger in drunkenly as the porch seems to rise at you like a ship's deck in heavy seas. Like a ship, too, the inn has a decided list from the ravaged earth below, while inside a golf ball runs 'uphill' along a ledge, a bottle rolls 'up' a table, a grandfather clock stands many degrees out of the vertical, and no one has won the licensee's proffered five shillings by managing to stand upright against a wall with heels together. Gravity is set at nought by this lopsided hostelry, called by Black Country people the Siden House.

Gornal has long been something of a joke; a synonym for gormless, one of the places where reputedly they put the pig on the wall to see the band go by. It is in fact, a fairly pleasant place, cheek by jowl with a stretch of open country, but the cost of being buried in Lower Gornal churchyard would prevent my resting quietly in the grave beneath the weight of masonry customary there – three or four layers of costly-looking Yorkshire stone between the earth and the normal surrounds and headstone. This happens elsewhere in the Black Country, particularly in Cradley Heath churchyard where Old Testament Elis, Isaacs, Obadiahs, Daniels, Neheniahs, and Rebeccas cluster so thick with memorials so ornate that I am reminded of a line from *Tilly of Bloomsbury*: 'She comes of a class which believes in a solvency during life and an extravagant funeral after death.'

Tipton has been described as the 'Venice of the Black Country', and there are still a few oldsters to whom the 'ninth of the ninth, ninety-nine' has a significance almost equal to the 'eleventh hour of the eleventh day of the eleventh month' in 1918. On 9 September 1899 Barnett's Breach occurred early on a Saturday morning when 100 yards of canal towpath caved in and the canal began emptying itself through a chasm into the pit. Two iron-boats, full of ashes, were swept through the gap and hurtled down with the torrent. They belonged to Samuel Barnett, whose Rattle Chain and Stour Valley Brick Works obtained their clay from the marlpit, in which the water rose rapidly as it poured from the canal. Another boat began to race for the breach and only by jumping ashore and cutting the towrope was the boatman able to save himself and the horse. Another, near Dudley Port Station, accelerated its pace to overtake its horse, which followed willy-nilly at an increasing canter, and again the boatman scrambled ashore to arrest the boat's headlong career by securing rope round a telegraph pole.

The marlhole, 100 yards deep and having a surface boundary of three acres, was quickly filled to the brim. Soon two miles of canal were drained, while six more miles lay muddy and lowered in depth. Locks were eventually closed above and below the breach. In Netherton Tunnel the level was lowered considerably and traffic on 40 miles of canal had to be diverted through the older Dudley Tunnel. Telegraphic communication between Dudley and Birmingham was impeded through poles being swept away. Damage to canal property was estimated up to £50,000 while the catastrophe cost Mr Barnett about £3,500.

In Lower High Street, Wednesbury, there is a public house called the 'Turk's Head', a name which, with the 'Saracen's Head', originated in the Crusades when English knights were lopping off the heads of infidel Turks. There are, however, other turk's heads than those on infidel shoulders. The rudder posts of canal boats are often decorated with a coil of rope sufficiently like a turban for them to be called turk's heads, and it is one of these that provides the sign for the Wednesbury pub. Wednesbury gets its name from Woden, but in the parish church a window depicts St Boniface, who cut down Thor's Oak in his efforts to convert the heathen Germans, and is inscribed 'In grateful commemoration of the overthrow of a heathen religion, especially the worship of a false god, Woden, and the establishment of the worship of the True God by the inhabitants of Wednesbury'. Even so, the church also pays tribute to a heathenish Black Country pastime, for instead of the customary eagle the lectern has a fighting cock.

Black Countrymen have long had a penchant for inscribing the houses they built with their names, initials, texts, odd moralising, and cynicisms, such as one on a house in Cradley, now demolished: 'This house was built by hard work. Honest men never prosper, but fools will be meddling'. One Darlaston character, the late Bob Smith, has left his mark in the name 'Favourite House' inscribed above a shop in Church Street, Darlaston. At the age of nine Bob sold newspapers and helped at week-ends in a barber's shop. He did a spell in a bakehouse at 12, moving for 1s 2d. a day to the Monway Works, Wednesbury, where, in the basic steel department, he became a leading 'teamer'. He took up clock repairing as as hobby and hairdressing as an additional trade, opening a saloon after marrying at 21. He also began framing pictures and described himself as 'Your Favourite Picture

Man'. Enabled through his sparetime activities to leave the Monway Works, Bob Smith made his move to 'Favourite House', then Darlaston's largest business premises.

On the flat roof he set up a photographic studio; down below he embarked on a delivery business with horses and carts, each with 'Favourite' painted on it. Eventually he changed to small convertible motor coaches named Favourite 1; Favourite 2; etc. A pioneer of credit sales in the Black Country, Bob Smith had as many as 3,000 customers on the never-never. Helped by his two elder sons he travelled round collecting payments which were free of any interest charges. In 1922 Bob Smith presented himself as a non-party candidate for Darlaston Urban District Council, and characteristically most of his election address was in doggerel. This document showed him keen-eyed with a waxed moustache, tall collar and bow tie and wearing a peaked chauffeur-like cap, with metal buttons on his waistcoat. He was elected and served for three years. When he retired in 1939, aged 69, the business of Bob Smith and Sons Ltd was described as 'our favourite picture men, complete house furnishers, picture framers, licensed jewellers, and toy dealers'. Bob Smith, the Favourite, died in 1956 aged 87.

This lively character would often have travelled across the Walsall Canal by inelegantly-named Bughole Bridge to Willenhall, where St Giles Church has memories of another local worthy, the Rev. William Moreton, vicar from 1795 to 1834. He was addicted to the great Black Country pastime of cock-fighting, the Old Church House having its own cockpit, while the vicar would preach with his church door open, cutting his sermon short when his cock-fighting friends passed on their way to Darlaston Fields.

Churchgoers were less enthusiastic, and the growth of nonconformity in Willenhall sprang from disgust with Moreton's interest in game birds, fighting dogs, and bull-baiting. In 1791 the vicar was even fined £5 'for sporting with a gun and two setting dogs upon the manor of H. Vernon of Hilton Park'. Moreton was declared bankrupt in 1812, and when he died in 1834 his curate, the Rev. George Fisher, preached a funeral sermon on a text from Ecclesiastes IX, 5 and 6 – 'the dead know not anything, neither have they any more a reward, for the

memory of them is forgotten'. Fisher contrived not to mention Moreton in the sermon.

In those days vicars were elected to their livings, and Fisher was
soon in the lists, issuing his election address in unseemly haste. 'My
dear friends', it began, 'the death of the Rev. William Moreton, which
took place this morning.' Fisher was vicar for 50 years and made good
much of the harm done by his predecessor to the church in Willenhall.
Nevertheless Moreton had been popular enough with the townspeople. His pedigree was unknown, and there were dark hints that
he was a 'nephew' of George III. He had an endearing habit of always
sharing his beer with his pony.

Willenhall Church accords great honour to its patronal saint. Giles
appears everywhere with the hind and the arrow which are his attributes. The vestry is a museum of old church notices – one of which
offered ten guineas reward in 1827 – 'Whereas early on Sunday morning last, some evil-disposed persons did steal and carry away the
weathercock from off the steeple . . .' The story behind this offer
beats cock-fighting, as they say. Once upon a time the people of Darlaston were alleged to have scattered corn in the churchyard to lure
down the weathercock. Their Willenhall neighbours would never let
Darlaston forget its shame, going along and mockingly strewing corn
about the churchyard. Stung to a reprisal at last, the men of Darlaston purloined Willenhall's weathercock, and it was found some years
later down a local coal pit.

Alice Johnson is a splendid Black Country character. She did not
think much of a street lamp as a present on her 79th birthday.

'What bin yo' a dooin'?' she demanded of the workman digging a
hole within a foot of her front door in Elbow Street, Old Hill. He
was, he said, installing a street lamp.

'Yo bloody b'aint', said Alice.

'Yo cor stop me', replied the indignant workman.

'Thee can put it in middle o' th'oss road', Alice conceded, 'but it
b'aint gooin' 'ere.'

Ten years later, in 1972, Alice recounted this battle of Elbow Street
blow by verbal blow with a twinkle in her eye. Elbow Street gets its
name from a right-angled bend in the middle, and Alice was born
there – 'agin the King's Yed' – one of 11 children of Enoch and Mary

Ann Partridge. Enoch and his sons were blacksmiths, while Mary Ann and Alice made nails in their own workshop as did other families in the yard.

'Them days wun grand; things wun cheap then', Alice told me. 'If yo'd cum in that yard we bin all singin', 'appy as could be.'

Elbow Street is, to be truthful, just across in Worcestershire, but Alice and her yard are typical of a comparable period in so much of the Staffordshire Black Country.

Nonconformity came to the Black Country in a bewildering variety of splinter groups which have left massive buildings dedicated to the Methodist New Connexion, the Tabernacle Methodist Church, the Wesley Reform Union; the Particular Baptists and the Ebenezer Strict Baptists. Even so, John Wesley had his detractors in the Black Country, where one verse of an irreverent song ran:

> *John Wesley had a bony 'oss*
> *As lean as ever was seen,*
> *We took him down to Hayseech Brook*
> *And shoved him yed fust in.*

Black Country houses were often well built, with archways for carts between each pair for delivering iron and collecting the out-workers' finished products. The builders took pride in their work and gave individuality to the houses on tablets incribed with the house name, street name, or initials, and date. Hours were long and life was hard, but there was a simple faith abroad in the area a century ago which led to housenames like Hope Cottage, Providence Terrace, and even a Hand of Providence pub.

In the nave of St Peter's Church, Wolverhampton, a tablet bears the profile of George Benjamin Thorneycroft, the first mayor of the town. His forebears hailed from Thorneycroft Hall, Cheshire, whence they moved eventually to an inn at Tipton where George was born in 1791. In his childhood his parents moved to Leeds, where, at Kirkstall Forge, George saw his first ironworks. At 17 he returned to his native Staffordshire, and in 1817 established a small ironworks at Tipton, but seven years later teamed up with his twin brother Edward, who had founded the Shrubbery Ironworks at Wolverhampton. Meanwhile another venture in iron had begun in the town when, in 1857, John Jones invested his £40 capital in The Corrugated Iron Company, and soon he took his brother Joseph as a partner.

This latter company prospered and in 1874 took over the Thorney-crofts' Shrubbery Ironworks and the Stour Valley Ironworks. George Thorneycroft had died in 1851; John Jones died in 1897, and his son Peter inherited the works and realised that considerable costs could be avoided by moving the Wolverhampton Corrugated Iron Company in 1905 to Ellesmere Port on the Manchester Ship Canal. The company's raw material was spelter and steel bars imported through the Mersey and conveyed to Wolverhampton by rail; 90 per cent of the finished product returning to the Mersey whence it had come. At Ellesmere Port the raw material and finished products had merely to be shipped across the Mersey in company barges. Some 2,000 Wolverhampton workers moved with the company, and Ellesmere's 4,000 population soon rose to 15,000 largely from the ironworks' impetus to local trade.

Ellesmere Port is in Cheshire, so the wheel had turned full circle, and the firm partly founded by George Benjamin Thorneycroft was back in the county of his ancestors. But for the Cullis family the circle ran in reverse direction. A Mr Cullis was one of the first Wulfrunians to move to Ellesmere Port with the firm. In March 1934 the youngest of his 12 children, Stanley, aged 17, having learned to play football with Ellesmere Port Wednesday, moved back to Wolverhampton to begin his distinguished career as player and manager with Wolverhampton Wanderers. Peter Jones built two estates for the Wolverhampton emigrés, one called Wolverham, the other having such street names as Penn Gardens, Stafford Street, and Dudley Road, while the Knot Hotel at Ellesmere Port was particularly popular when the licensee's name was John Molineux Winn, Molineux being the name of a considerable Wolverhampton family which ultimately shared it with the 'Wolves' ground.

More of Wolverhampton's industrial history is recorded across the nave at St Peter's in the brass plaque to John Marston, twice mayor, who died in 1918. The memorial, placed there by his employees at Sunbeamland, the factory he owned for nearly 50 years, records that 'he developed the whole cycle, motor-cycle, and motor-car industry of Wolverhampton.' A town's history can be read in its church memorials, and Wolverhampton was famous as a wool market before it became industrial, witness such surviving street names as Mitre Fold, Farmer's Fold, and Wheeler's Fold, while John Leveson, who died in 1575 and lies in effigy with his wife, Joyce, was 'a merchant of the staple'. His more romantic kinsman Sir Richard Leveson, postures from a pedestal with a pair of *putti* sprawling at his feet. Richard is in the armour of one of Drake's sea-dogs, for he began a distinguished naval career by fighting against the Armada, aged 18, in the *Ark Royal*. While it disproves the proposition that 'old soldiers never die', one brass in St Peter's at least records that they live to a great age. When Troop Sergeant Major John Stratford died in 1932 aged 102, his old comrades of the 14/20 Hussars who provided his memorial were able to describe him as 'the oldest soldier in the British Empire'.

Three modest men are commemorated in St Peter's. A small tile recalls a son of a Staffordshire yeoman, educated at Brewood Grammar School, Richard Hurd, 1720–1808. 'Through ability and merit he became Bishop of Lichfield and Coventry', says his inscription, and adds 'from modesty he was unwilling to accept the Archbishopric of Canterbury. The second man without normal ambition was Charles Phillips 'beloved by all for his absolute contempt of riches and his inimitable performance on the violin.' Yet this unworldly fiddler is rich – in epitaphs. He has two. David Garrick once quoted to Dr Samuel Johnson the six-line verse by a Dr Wilkes on Phillips's memorial stone in the porch. Johnson thought he could write a better, and someone was insensitive enough to add it below the earlier inscription.

Third of the trio who turned their backs on the rewards of this world is Colonel John Lane, buried in the north transept (note the sculpted group beneath the Latin). Even if the name rings no bell, here are clues – a royal crown, an oak tree, a trooper's horse, Parliamentarian pikes. For Colonel Lane of Bentley Hall, Willenhall, was the loyalist who helped Charles II escape after the Battle of Worcester in 1651, and whose daughter, Jane, took the king south as her groom on his escape to France. After the Restoration Charles did not forget the colonel, and before his death in 1667 he was offered burial among the royal tombs in Westminster Abbey, but declined the honour and lies in St Peter's.

In 1757 a marriage took place in St Peter's when the bridegroom rejoiced in the odd name of Button Gwinnett – a name for which people were to pay as much as £10,000. A Wolverhampton trader, Gwinnett emigrated to the British colony in North America after his marriage and the subsequent baptism of three daughters at St Peter's. He opened a shop at Savannah, Georgia, prospered, and was elected to Congress, which, in 1776, drew up and signed the Declaration of Independence. Next year he died of wounds suffered in a duel. So, when autograph-hunters began collecting the signatures of the 55 who signed the famous Declaration, Button Gwinnett's was the most rare, and ultimately it was worth £10,000. Then it was found that three times in 1761 Button Gwinnett had been present at meetings of subscribers to Wolverhampton Bluecoat School, and unwittingly left the school a fortune each time he signed the minute book.

Finally, writing of Wolverhampton worthies as I am in early May when 'the cherry trees are seas of bloom', I must not forget the poet Alfred Noyes, whose 'Song of England' is never long out of my mind. Though Staffordshire may have meant nothing to his poetry Noyes was born at Chapel Ash, Wolverhampton, in 1880.

The Black Country can boast another poet in Sir Henry Newbolt, born in 1862 at Bilston where his father was vicar – and Queen Mary's Grammar School, Walsall, claims at least an interest in those undying lines:

> *'There's a breathless hush in the close tonight,*
> *Ten to make, and a match to win. . . .'*

for although the close is at Clifton College, Bristol, Sir Henry, who wrote 'Vitae Lampada' and many other famous poems, was for a short while a pupil at Queen Mary's. The school maintains an annual Founder's Day tradition commemorating the grant of a charter for the school by Mary Tudor in 1554, when the headmaster, the school captain, the youngest pupil, first year boys with their masters, and

9 (above)   Barton-under-Needwood
10   Halfhead Cottage, Shallowford, left to Stafford by the author of
The Compleat Angler, and now the Izaak Walton Museum

11 *Tutbury Church with its magnificent Norman west doorway*

12 *The unhappiest occupant of Tutbury Castle was Mary, Queen of Scots, who has left a particular memory in Queen Mary's Tower*

some old scholars, process with the Dean of Westminster Abbey to Queen Mary's tomb where the school captain lays a wreath.

Walsall has more identity than most Black Country towns, and gains something of a Hanseatic appearance from the spire of its fine parish church of St Matthew soaring high above its steep cobbled approach, and drawing the eye above the busy stalls of the market. Known today for the leather industry which gives its football team the title 'The Saddlers', Walsall in the eighteenth century supplied only ancillary items for a Birmingham leather industry, its main manufacture being shoe buckles. This slumped early in the nineteenth century with the increasing use of shoelaces, and between 1818 and 1851 the number of saddlers in the town rose from four to 56. Even so, when Walsall made 25,000 sets of artillery harness during the Crimean War the metal parts were the main product, the leather work being incidental. Nevertheless, a boom in saddlery had begun, and it continued with the South African War. At the opening of the twentieth century the increase in cycle and motor transport, together with the mechanisation of the Army, threatened the trade. Fortunately for Walsall this adverse trend was offset by a great increase in the leisure use of the horse, so that saddlery became and remains a prosperous trade. Originally hides for Walsall's leather trade came from the pastures of Staffordshire and Warwickshire, but for many years foreign hides have predominated. Oak and chestnut bark for tanning came from Cannock Chase, limestone from Rushall near by, and water from the River Tame.

Walsall has – or has had – several inns named after the main saddlery or leather product in their immediate neighbourhood, the Spurmakers Arms, the Bridle Cutters Arms, the Hamemakers Arms, and the Coachmakers Arms. In the name of Jerome Road, Pleck, and in the Three Men in a Boat Inn, Stephenson Avenue, Walsall pays tribute to its native writer Jerome K. Jerome, born at Belsize House, Bradford Street. The pub sign shows the narrator of the famous story, Jerome himself, with his companions, Harris and George, in a rowing boat, while Montmorency, the dog, is leaping into the river. In case you are ever caught with a favourite quiz question, the K. in Jerome's name stands for Klapka, the name of an exiled Hungarian general who once stayed with the Jeromes in Walsall.

Walsall skyscapes are dominated by the impressive cooling towers of Birchills Power Station with their ever-changing vapours. Just north of them is an estate with a score of inventors' and scientists' names to its roads, and as many were involved with electricity the juxtaposition with the power station is not accidental. Also in Birchills, tucked away beside the canal, is St Andrew's Church, a gem in an unlikely setting. Seventy saints adorn its windows, some, such as St Phocas and St John Nepomuck, so rare that I have never seen them elsewhere.

Just beyond the outskirts of Walsall east of the Lichfield Road stands Rushall Hall, a dignified home which bears the scars of a turbulent past. Built as Rushall Castle in the fourteenth century by the Harpurs, it was held by them for Lancaster against York during the Wars of the Roses. By marriage it subsequently went to the Leighs, and Sir Edward Leigh was the incumbent when King and Parliament came to blows in the Great Civil War. A Parliamentary colonel, he was away in 1643 when Prince Rupert's Cavaliers attacked the castle. True to the fighting tradition of Civil War wives, Dame Elizabeth Leigh led a spirited defence before surrendering with 'credit and quarter'.

A Royalist garrison was set up in the castle under the Colonel Lane aforementioned from Bentley Hall, which proved a painful thorn in the Puritan flesh, commanding the route between London and the north-west, and imposing such a blockade that the Stafford Committee, Parliament's local authority, warned its friends among Manchester tradesmen not to send more merchandise to London until safer conduct could be arranged through the 'strait' between the Royalist strongholds of Rushall and Tamworth Castle. One convoy was attacked at Cannock by one of Colonel Lane's posses, and nine prisoners, 60 horses, and 55 bundles of powder and fuse were taken back to Rushall.

It became imperative for Parliament to eliminate Colonel Lane's base, and on 25 May 1644, the Earl of Denbigh encamped before Rushall with 6,000 men, outnumbering the 200 Royalists by 30 to one, while they had five guns to each one inside the castle walls. The defenders had an outpost in Rushall Church, connected to the castle by a trench with outworks. Desultory hostilities continued for five days, when, with only two fatal casualties among the contenders, Rushall capitulated to the Cromwellians.

Two more miles towards Lichfield, and St John's Church, Walsall Wood, has windows by Claude Price of Birmingham commemorating Canon James Edwards, a carpenter before he took Holy Orders, and one-time incumbent of Walsall Wood, who went as a missionary to Melanesia. Another window, by 'A. J. 1969' is an abstract, but with a miner, a whippet, and pithead gear identifiable. It commemorates James Clews, who appears also with two others of the same surname on a miner's lamp in the church, a memory of old Walsall Wood Colliery. An inscription reads '1873–1964. The miners who lost their lives. We will remember them'; and to have his name on the lamp a man must have worked underground, not necessarily died at his job.

At the same time that the buckle industry was waning in Walsall, 27-year-old Archibald Kenrick was feeling the economic draught in his business as manufacturer and plater of shoe buckles in Birmingham. So in 1791 he moved to West Bromwich and set up an iron foundry off Spon Lane, where his products included flat irons and humane mantraps. He lived at 'Springfield' in Roebuck Lane, whence he travelled to his foundry on a mule. His sons, Archibald Junr, and Timothy, joined him in the firm, which took the name of Archibald Kenrick and Sons Ltd. In 1805 Samuel, the 15-year-old son of the Rev. Timothy Kenrick of Exeter, came to work in the business. He got on so well with his cousin Marianne that he married her, but with her brothers he hit it off so poorly that in 1822 he started the rival Summit Foundry in Union Street. It failed in 1853, however, and Samuel died next year.

About 1850 John Arthur Kenrick, son of Archibald Junr, came to help his uncle Timothy manage Archibald Kenrick and Sons, of which he ultimately became chairman. He was also a director of Lloyds Bank and chairman of the local Liberal Association, when he fell under the influence of Joseph Chamberlain. To further his Liberalism, in 1878 John Arthur Kenrick bought a run-down newspaper, the *Free Press* for £103 10s., and paid £2 a week to young Frederick Thomas Jefferson, who forsook the legal profession to become editor. Thus was the firm of Kenrick and Jefferson born – international printers, envelope manufacturers, and manufacturing stationers. But before it settled down in this commercial form the *Free Press* company launched a weekly, *The Labour Tribune*, the organ of the Miners, Ironworkers, Nut and Bolt Forgers, etc. of Great Britain, which aimed to show that Labour could advocate its claims with fairness and justice. The partnership of the founders was a great success. In addition to his editorial duties Jefferson developed the jobbing printing side so prosperously that it relegated the newspapers to second place, and the *Free Press* was disposed of in 1933 for the same amount that John Arthur Kenrick paid for it.

From 1920 to his death in 1933 John Arthur's son, Alderman John Archibald Kenrick, was chairman of Kenrick and Jefferson, and joint managing director of Archibald Kenrick and Sons Ltd. He had a distinguished career on West Bromwich Council, to which he was first elected in 1906. Mayor in 1911, he became a freeman in 1933, having served on every committee of the council and been chairman of most.

The Enclosure Act of 1802 was responsible for a very rapid development of West Bromwich from the heathland which stretched on either side of Telford's Holyhead Road. Row upon row of terraced houses went up, the number doubling in the two decades up to 1831, with one pub to every 143 of the population. Perhaps the absence of piped water led to this proliferation, though in the central areas water was plentiful enough. The 4th Earl of Dartmouth had developed several collieries, among them the Terrace, the Cronehills, and Pitt Street, and the pumping machinery produced a regular supply of filtered water which was given away to the townsfolk and made excellent tea. The wild broom which grew on the heathland gave West Bromwich part of its name, and the thrushes which haunted the bushes provided the 'Throstle' of the town's emblem.

Among the exports of West Bromwich are curates. In the east window of Christ Church are three strangely-assorted coats-of-arms, of St Andrew's, Scotland; Cape Town; and Nassau in the Bahamas, and they refer to three former West Bromwich curates who became respectively Bishop C. E. Plumb of St Andrew's, Archbishop Carter of Cape Town, and Bishop H. N. Churton of Nassau. The borough library has a memorial to another much-travelled 'Throstle', David Christie Murray (1847–1907) who, as a journalist, represented *The Scotsman* and the *Chicago Times* in Europe, Australia, New Zealand,

and during the Russo-Turkish War. Nearer home, two of his scoops were the Pelsall Hall Colliery disaster in 1872 and the Black Lake pit fire at West Bromwich. He also wrote novels, of which the library keeps a complete set, though his first novel, serialised in a newspaper, became so complicated that he had to call on his experiences as a reporter and drown most of his characters in a pit disaster.

West Bromwich has an excellent sense of history as befits a borough where the Hallam Hospital is named after the family of Henry Hallam, the famous historian, who inherited Charlemont Hall, now demolished, from his father. Henry married the daughter of the Rev. Sir Abraham Elton, Vicar of West Bromwich 1782–90, and their son was the A. H. H. of Tennyson's 'In Memoriam'. At all Saints Church a headstone to Captain James Eaton, who lost an eye and an arm at Trafalgar when in command of H.M.S. *Temeraire*, has been refurbished, while the fourteenth-century Manor House, the fifteenth-century Oak House, and Asbury Cottage, the boyhood home of Francis Asbury who became the first bishop of the American Methodist Church, have been restored and preserved.

CHAPTER THREE

The Green Borderland

Staffordshire's southern extremity is an outcrop of red sandstone which until recent years provided cave dwellings where Kinver Edge drops down into Kinver itself, leaving the church perched high above the village. These sandy, bracken-covered slopes are a popular playground with Black Country folk, though the Edge is less extensive than the much quieter Highgate Common to northward. In fact this is an area of commons with Penn Common farther north still. The Staffordshire and Worcestershire Canal drops southward through the district, leaving the former county for the latter near the famous Stewponey and Foley Arms – the Stewponey said to be a corruption of Estepona, a Spanish town from which one of Wellington's Peninsular War soldiers brought back a bride to help run the inn he opened, gallantly naming it after her native town. The Rev. Sabine Baring Gould wrote a fast-moving novel *Bladys of the Stewponey*.

Enville, to westward, has the Cat Inn, with a six-day licence, the Sunday closure being dictated by traffic problems of an earlier day – horse and trap traffic which blocked the village street. The church, with a fine pinnacled tower, has a weeping chancel, a Trubshaw angel, and bench ends, one with a fine tonsured head. The gardens of Enville Hall a century ago during the 7th Earl of Stamford's time, employed a head gardener and 35 men and boys whose aggregate wages were about £100 a month. Lord Stamford – George Henry Grey – was a pioneer in the stately homes business, though without thought of gain for himself. Elihu Burritt, the peripatetic United States vice-consul in Birmingham, in his *Walks in the Black Country and its Green Borderland*, published in 1868, writes that 'On Tuesdays and

Fridays through the season all the sooty-faced and heavy-shod men of the mine, forge, and furnace in all the Black Country may come and luxuriate in these flower gardens without a farthing's charge for admission.' Burritt happily records the complete lack of vandalism on these occasions, though the Cherry Fair held in Enville on Sundays in the cherry season was notorious as 'a boisterous, roistering, ring-fighting and cock-fighting holiday with the usual amount of drunkenness and demoralisation'. Enville Wakes were also popular, and the 'Cat' still has a notice advertising the 1845 wakes which included an event calculated to upset the ineffable Race Relations Board, 'a Hurdle Race for a New Patterned Waistcoat for men and lads of any size, age, or colour – except black.'

Enville Hall is still in the Grey family, on the distaff side.

Halfpenny Green has an airfield well known for its shows. It was here in 1972 that Prince William of Gloucester was killed during an air race. Wombourn has an interesting church, with Frideswide and Longinus among the unusual saints in its windows, and there are quarries near by of intensely red sand. Kingswinford Church has a 'breeches Bible', so-called because Genesis Chapter 3 Verse 7 reads: 'They sewed figge-tree leaves together and made themselves breeches'. But it is three stately homes that most merit attention in this green borderland of the Black Country.

To many motorists Himley Hall is a long wooden fence relieved only by massive gates as they drop down from Dudley towards Shropshire, and they may wonder why wealthy earls had chosen to live so near an industrial conurbation. I wondered this, too, until in the autumn of 1966 I gatecrashed Himley Hall just before the tenancy passed from the National Coal Board to Dudley Education Department, to seek an animal graveyard, With five little headstones around me, I looked down at the hall from beneath a silver-boled beech, and saw it for the lovely place it is. Not distinguished architecturally, it is nonetheless comely and set felicitously with its lake and streams overhung with weeping willows.

It is surrounded by green pastures on which the Duke of Windsor would land his aircraft when, as Prince of Wales, he was a regular visitor to Himley. Built around 1740, Himley Hall has played a part in several lives destined for tragedy, just as its predecessor on the site, a moated half-timbered mansion, sheltered a tragic king, Charles I, who slept there on the night of 15 May 1645, a month before the Battle of Naseby finally brought his cause to ruin and the king himself that much nearer the block. On the next morning, as Charles's force left Himley, one of his soldiers met a summary fate. Refusing to march, he was strung up on a tree. 'One soldier was hanged for mutiny' was the laconic entry in the diary of Captain Symmonds, a man after my own heart who always found time in his campaigns to copy monumental inscriptions and makes notes on heraldry.

The earlier Dudleys are chronicled in the last chapter. In 1885 the 1st Earl of Dudley died, his son and heir, 18-year-old William Humble Ward, hearing of his father's death in Rio de Janeiro on a world cruise. With a vast income from the family coal mines, estates, and Jamaican plantations, and nothing particular to do, he turned for diversion to the Turf. But, getting married at 25 to Rachel Gurney, daughter of a Quaker banking family, he took up politics and a public career, which culminated as Viceroy of Ireland in 1902 and Governor-General of Australia in 1908. Always at his side in these high offices was his countess, Rachel, and they were an ever-popular pair.

Yet in 1918 came a formal separation. The earl wrote Rachel: 'The least I can do is to recognise all those years of great devotion which you gave me, and to ensure your future comfort as far as I can, and to protect you to the best of my power against misapprehension and injustice.' On 26 June 1920, Rachel arrived at the earl's seat in County Galway, Screeb Lodge. A good swimmer, she went at once with her maid to bathe, had a seizure while in the water and drowned. Four years later the earl married Gertie Millar, widow of Lionel Monckton, the composer, who wrote many songs for the Gaiety plays in which she appeared as one of the best-loved stars of musical comedy. Most of their eight years of married life, the earl and his second countess spent in their villa at Le Touquet where, in 1932, he died. After the countess's death in 1952 her jewels were sold for £32,630, but it was in search of these, thought to have been buried with her, that vandals desecrated her grave at Himley in 1965.

The 3rd Earl of Dudley had already known great personal tragedy before he succeeded in 1932. In 1919, as Viscount Ednam, he had married Lady Rosemary Leveson-Gower, a daughter of the Duke of

Sutherland. They made their home at Himley Hall, and on it Lady Ednam set the mark of her taste, so that its charm and homeliness made it a favourite with the Prince of Wales and his brother, George, Duke of Kent. On 9 December 1929, Jeremy, the nine-year-old second son of the Ednams, was killed in a cycling accident on Chelsea Embankment. Round his grave beside a stream at Himley, Lady Ednam constructed a Garden of Remembrance, but not nine months later tragedy struck again. Flying from France during a rainstorm on 21 July 1930, a Junkers aircraft crashed in a Kent orchard at Meopham. Among the passengers who lost their lives was Rosemary, Viscountess Ednam, and she was laid in her own Garden of Remembrance beside her son.

Solemnity had lifted from Himley four years later when, on 29 November 1934, the Duke of Kent arrived for his honeymoon with Princess Marina of Greece. But the marriage was not to endure. On 25 August 1942 the Duke, an air commodore in the R.A.F., took off in a Sunderland flying boat for Iceland. Shortly afterwards the aircraft hit a mountain in the north of Scotland, and all the occupants died.

In 1947 Himley Hall was sold to the National Coal Board for £45,000, but in 1966 the Board disposed of it to a consortium of the local authorities of Dudley, Warley, and Wolverhampton for £135,000. Himley Hall claims not to be haunted, but it has poignant memories far more potent than any ghost.

Poetry is unfashionable these days, but if you are lucky enough to be a poetaster I can direct you to a Mount Helicon in Staffordshire. Wightwick Manor (pronounced Wittick), like the Grecian home of the Muses, is on a hill – a red sandstone ridge which outcrops in the lane beside the Mermaid Inn, three miles out of Wolverhamption on the Bridgnorth road. A wooden bridge spans that lane from one part of the manor grounds to another, high and intimidating and built on similar lines to the bridge at Queen's College, Cambridge. At the first entrance on the left past the bridge stands the old manor house of the Wightwick family, now a lodge to Wightwick Manor which was built in 1887–93 by Theodore Mander.

The Mander family came to Wolverhampton from Warwickshire in the person of Thomas Mander, born in 1720. His son, Benjamin, a tinplate worker and japanner, inherited from his mother a house in

John Street, Wolverhampton, where his son, Charles, started a varnish works in 1803. Charles's two sons, Charles Benjamin and Samuel, went into a varnishing manufacturing business together in 1845 as Mander Bros. Theodore, builder of Wightwick Manor, was the son of Samuel. He died in 1900, aged 47, while Mayor of Wolverhampton, leaving the manor to his son, who became Sir Geoffrey Mander, M.P. for East Wolverhampton from 1929 to 1945 and chairman of the family firm for 33 years. In 1937 Sir Geoffrey presented the manor and its grounds to the National Trust, but continued to live there until his death in 1962, since when Lady Mander has continued in residence.

Theodore Mander and his cousin, Sir Charles Mander, married sisters from Nova Scotia, the Misses le Mesurier Paint, and perhaps the builder of Wightwick Manor was addressing his bride, Flora, in the couplets of Herrick on the beams beneath the barge boards on the ornate half-timbered neo-Tudor gables: 'Live, live with me, and thou shalt see the pleasures I'll prepare for thee.'

Sir Geoffrey also had his father's interest in poetry, but their great enthusiasm was for Pre-Raphaelite art, much of which is enshrined in the house. Each to his choice, and mine is for stained and painted glass far above pictures by Burne-Jones, Ford Madox Brown, Dante Gabriel Rossetti, and other portrayers of goitre-throated, consumptive women, and for poetry rather than the wallpaper by William Morris. So in the drawing-room my interest flew to a William Morris verse reproduced in glass in the bay window in which a wizard conjures up the entire window at Christmastide so: 'That through one window men beheld the spring, and through another saw the summer glow.' With it are four lights representing the four seasons, the work of that great craftsman in glass, Charles Eamer Kempe. Also in that bay window is his own coat-of-arms in glowing glass, the three wheat-sheaves, with a crest of a bird nibbling ears of wheat, explaining why he signs his church windows with a tiny wheatsheaf. The reapers' art of making sheaves is known as 'kemping'.

Around the exterior beams Herrick continues to woo Phillis with such delicious couplets as:

> *Thy feasting table shall be hills*
> *With daisies spread and daffodils.*

but I had to go to a Shakespeare concordance to identify Ulysses' lines from *Troilus and Cressida* : 'Welcome ever smiles, and farewell goes out sighing.' Shakespeare and Coleridge rub shoulders in the oak room, a real poets' corner where Swinburne contributes a cupboard and his strange folding bed, though none of his poetry. 'The Ancient Mariner' is quoted above the fireplace: 'O sleep it is a gentle thing, beloved from pole to pole', while Shakespeare comes in on a wall with 'Innocent sleep, sleep that knits up the ravelled sleeve of care.' Insomnia should be impossible in such a bedroom – unless you recall the Macbeth context of the Act 2 Scene 2 quotation, and the words immediately before: 'Sleep no more; Macbeth does murder sleep.'

Several rooms are named after their wall coverings – the Indian Bird Room, covered with a linen whose designer is unknown; the Acanthus Room with William Morris's wallpaper; and the Honeysuckle Room, where Morris's printed linen has decorated the walls since the manor was built. Although the Honeysuckle is a bedroom, the poetic reference is to waking rather than sleeping: 'Sun shall wax and star shall wane . . . and stand all ready for morn's joy.' The Great Parlour, a magnificent room with ribbed open timber ceiling and an end gallery tells the story of Orpheus and Eurydice in a frieze painted under Kempe's direction with lines from Milton *L'Allegro*. Orpheus strikes from his 'trembling lyre': 'Such strains as would have won the ear of Pluto, to have quite set free his half-regained Eurydice'.

There is no more glorious feature at Wightwick than the sumptuous oriel of this grand room. Here additional Kempe work provides 'windows before whose blazonry the diamond and the emerald fade', and in the glass can be seen Saints George, Andrew, and Patrick, various Cambridge coats-of-arms, the Wightwick family arms, and those of Wolverhampton, the Stafford Knot, and the lion of Nova Scotia. A frieze with the signs of the Zodiac surrounds Wightwick billiards room, and here too is glass painted by Morris at Leek at the works of his friend Thomas Wardle.

Wightwick Manor is open to the public on Thursday and Saturday afternoons and the lover of Ruskin, Morris, and their fraternity will find a hundred more items to please him. To his beautiful home Sir Geoffrey Mander also brought stonework from Big Ben at Westminster, displayed on a terrace against a background of trees and shrubs, including some from the gardens of William Morris at Kelmscott, Kempe at Lindfield, Burne-Jones at Rottingdean, and Ruskin at Brantwood. George V and Queen Mary planted trees there as Duke and Duchess of York in 1900, while Sir Geoffrey's breadth of mind and friendship as a Liberal M.P. is revealed in trees planted by Liberal Sir Herbert Samuel (later Lord Samuel) in 1929; by the 3rd Earl Baldwin in memory of his father, a Tory Prime Minister; and by C. R. Attlee (later Earl Attlee), the Labour Premier, in 1953.

There is more poetry about the house – Robert Browning, for instance, in typical 'Hold on, hold fast' mood. Wightwick is no moribund museum; it is a living, vivid house, and a fitting showcase for the work of men and women who had strong ideas on life and how it should be lived. Nothing better sums it up than the words of John Ruskin, carved on the panelling of the Drawing-Room: 'To watch the corn blow, or ye blossom . . . to Read, to Think, to Love, to Pray, are ye things that make men happy.'

He stands against the churchyard wall at Patshull, near Wolverhampton, on the old estate of the Legge family – the Earls of Dartmouth. His resplendent curls shelter the back of his neck from whatever northern breezes penetrate the trees behind him, trees from which each night he is serenaded by a chorus of owls. Sad of countenance, he keeps an unending sightless watch on the north wall of Patshull Church, a nameless incongruous statue in so remote a setting. Who is he?

The few who give him an identity say that he is James, Duke of Monmouth, son of Charles II and his Welsh mistress, Lucy Walter; the Protestant duke who led a rising against his Catholic uncle James II, was defeated in the last battle fought upon English soil, at Sedgemoor, Somerset, in July 1685, and beheaded ten days later.

Of one thing we can be certain. Our statue is a Knight of the Garter. The Garter is there below the left knee. On the left breast of his mantle he wears the 'George' badge, and across his chest droops the collar of his order, roses alternating with true-lovers' knots.

Lady Diana Matthews, daughter of William, 7th Earl of Dartmouth, told me: 'I have always known the statue as Monmouth, though where he came from or why he is here I don't know.'

At least Monmouth was a Knight of the Garter and he wore long curls, but the nearest he seems to have come to Patshull was in 1682, when he was arrested at Stafford after a semi-royal progress through Cheshire during which he was loudly acclaimed as a favoured successor to the reigning monarch, Charles II. He was lodged at Coleshill and at Coventry for a night or so on his journey south, to be ultimately acquitted of conspiracy by the King's Bench. Monmouth would have found scant favour with the Legge family of his day. Colonel George Legge, who was created Baron Dartmouth in 1682 by Charles II, had served James, Duke of York, brother and eventual successor to Charles, as Master of the Horse and Gentleman of the Bedchamber since 1673. Though the only Protestant in York's household, he was completely trusted and unquestionably loyal. York ascended the throne as James II in February 1685, and two years later appointed Lord Dartmouth Admiral of the Fleet to intercept William of Orange. In this, of course, Dartmouth failed, James II abdicated, and Dartmouth was sent to the Tower where he died in 1691. There seems little likelihood that the Legges would have set up Monmouth's statue at Patshull. In any case they did not come to Patshull until the growing industry of West Bromwich drove them there from Sandwell Hall in the mid-nineteenth century.

The occupants of Patshull Hall at the time of Monmouth's rising were the Astleys. Two gamecocks facing each other from ornate gateposts beside the churchyard are said to commemorate an occasion when an Astley lost the estate and won it back all in one day on cockfighting wagers. These Astleys were loyal Cavaliers during the Civil War, Patshull being attacked and captured by Roundheads in 1644. They seem unlikely to have turned against the Stuarts in the next 40 years.

In the church, against the north wall of the nave, the recumbent figures of a man and wife in alabaster have reposed since they were moved there from another church when Patshull Church was built in 1743. A note suggests that they were then laid on the altar tomb, to the side of which an inscription was added describing them as Sir John de Astley and his dame, he being a distinguished soldier who bore Edward IV's Yorkist standard and became a Knight of the Garter in 1462. But the man lying there is not wearing a Garter or any of the regalia. In fact he is wearing the S.S. collar with roses which denotes loyalty to the Lancastrian, Henry VII, while his armour and his lady's headdress are Henry VIII in period. It is conjectured that this Garterless knight is not Sir John, but a Richard Astley, who died in 1532, his wife being Joan Otleye from Pitchford, Shropshire.

Above this mysterious couple towers a mountainous marble assemblage of Jacobean monumental masonry. The central figure, standing with his hand on his sword and staring from a halo of curls that rival Monmouth's, is Sir Richard Astley who died in 1687. On either side of him are seated his two ample wives, Elizabeth Phillips and Henrietta Bodase, their eyes turned soulfully heavenward. Flanking Sir Richard above his wives are two piles of pikes, muskets and the like. Above his head two cherubs are about to garrotte him with a length of drapery, while, highest of all, two others support a coat-of-arms.

The Astleys were succeeded at Patshull by the Pigots, a memorial in the church describing the Rt Hon. George, Lord Pigot, who died in 1777, as 'the first of his family who possessed Patshull'. He was also Baron of Patshull in the Kingdom of Ireland, a title dated 1766. This just another of Patshull's mysteries. What was the association of Patshull in Staffordshire with Patshull, County Dublin?

But Monmouth remains Patshull's most absorbing mystery. Can I hazard one conjecture – that some malice placed him where he is? The north side of the churchyard is generally known as the Devil's side, where they buried suicides, unbaptised infants, and the illegitimate. And Monmouth was illegitimate.

CHAPTER FOUR

Penkridge and the River Penk

England has barely half a dozen rivers running northward. The Staffordshire Penk is one, first assuming identity at Pendeford on the northern outskirts of Wolverhampton, and pursuing a northward course for 18 miles to a confluence with the River Sow east of Stafford. Pendeford was in the thick of the recent fight against the proposed southern route of an M54 motorway from Wolverhampton to Telford in Shropshire. Among opponents of this dreadful rape of lovely and productive farmland were the occupants of Leper House Farm, Codsall, where lepers were once tended, and of The Hattons farm which had already been devastated to lay a North Sea gas pipe line. Pendeford Hall, home of the Fowler-Butler family for 400 years, was demolished in 1953.

The Penk shakes off industrial Wolverhampton in three meadowland miles to Lower Green, near Coven, and Jackson's Bridge, named after a Mr Jackson who hanged himself from a chain beneath the bridge. Somerford Park, its hall now converted into flats, lies in the angle where the Saredon Brook comes down from Cannock to join the Penk, which, thus augmented, turned a water-wheel at Somerford until 1958, pulping cattle fodder, sawing wood, and grinding corn. Today the wheel is still, and the river rushes through a sluice near a red brick barn of seven bays.

Two miles west of the Penk, in its spacious park stands Chillington Hall, home of the Giffards. Three Giffard brothers came across with

William the Conqueror from Normandy where one of them, Walter, was Count of Longueville. His son, created Earl of Buckingham, and ancestor of the first Peter Giffard of Chillington, became Justiciar of England, so by embracing the law the present Mr Peter Giffard is following a family profession more than 800 years old. Chillington was acquired in 1186 by marriage with the Corbesun family. The house of Norman times was of stone, probably a cross between a castle and a manor house. It was rebuilt in brick with many windows in Tudor times, then, in the eighteenth century the present house was built by three generations of the family. A Peter Giffard began the rebuilding in 1728 with Francis Smith, the Warwick architect, whose work survives in the drawing-room. Peter's second wife was Barbara Throckmorton of Coughton Court, Warwickshire, and both families being Roman Catholics there were several marriages between the Giffards and the Throckmortons, but the Giffards slipped away from the faith two generations ago. In Peter's time a Giffard House was built in Tup Street, Wolverhampton, now North Street, and given to the Catholic community.

Peter's son, Thomas, had 'Capability' Brown lay out the parkland at Chillington with temples beside the lake and various plantations. The son of this Thomas, another Thomas, completed Chillington Hall and gave it its major claim to architectural fame, the work of Sir John Soane, designer of the Bank of England, the famous Old Lady of Threadneedle Street. The salon at Chillington is Soane at his most elegant. Over the fireplace is carved in stone a replica of the pennant carried by Sir John Giffard when he attended Henry VIII at the Field of the Cloth of Gold. Chillington abounds – in stained glass, stone, metal, and wood carving on the great staircase – in the leopard's head and archer crest of the Giffards, which derives from a great feat of bowmanship by Sir John.

A leopard had escaped from his private zoo one morning in 1513. Armed with his crossbow and accompanied by his son, Sir John came upon the leopard about to spring on a woman and a baby.

'*Prenez haleine, tirez fort*', said the son.

Sir John did, killing the beast, and the son's advice, which means 'Take breath, pull strongly', has become the family motto, while a

13 (above)   *Staffordshire's industrial growth depended largely on canal transport*

14   *Rugeley Power Station as seen from the Trent and Mersey Canal*

rough wooden cross in a lodge garden marks the spot where the leopard fell.

The salon has an organ and a grand piano, evidence of the musical interest of Mr Peter Giffard's father, Thomas A. W. Giffard, who died in 1971 on 29 May, Oak Apple Day, a significant day for the family. Shortly after Queen Elizabeth had visited Chillington in 1575 the Giffards built Boscobel House, near by, a stone's throw across the Shropshire border, both as a hunting lodge in the Brewood Forest, and, with its secret chambers, a hiding place for Catholic priests. Several Giffards fought for Charles II at Worcester in 1651, and a Colonel Charles Giffard, escaping with the king, suggested he hide at Boscobel. It was during this period that the king had to take to the Royal Oak in Boscobel Park, thus ensuring a name for some 700 English pubs, and for Oak Apple Day – his birthday – on which in 1660 he returned triumphantly to London at the Restoration. The Penderells, retainers of the Giffards, helped Charles Stuart so loyally that he rewarded them, and their descendants are still beneficiaries under a trust with Mr Peter Giffard the sole trustee today. The fund comes from rent charges on land, some of which have been redeemed. The income is collected and an annual payment made to 20 or so beneficiaries.

Gilbert Giffard, a double agent, was the black sheep of the family. He betrayed his Jesuit friends to Elizabeth's minister, Sir Francis Walsingham, for whom he also copied letters written by Mary, Queen of Scots, who trusted him and had them smuggled out of her prison at Chartley in false bottoms of beer barrels devised by Gilbert. Simultaneously he was betraying his Protestant patrons to Spain. He died eventually in a Paris brothel.

Sir John, the bowman, is one of four Giffards whose alabaster memorials can be seen in the chancel of Brewood Church, north-east of the hall. He lies, black-bearded, between his two wives above a frieze of his 18 children, 13 in the swaddling clothes denoting they did not survive childhood. The one boy among the five who lived, Thomas, lies across the chancel between two wives. Between them they mustered only 17 children, but their survival rate was higher, 13 growing up. Also on the north side lies another John Giffard, his

15 (above)   The Abbots Bromley Horn Dance – a September custom which probably commemorates the granting to the villagers of certain rights in the Needwood Forest

16   St Nicholas Church, Abbots Bromley, peeps above the roofs at the ancient Butter Cross

Below—

recumbent wife beside him appearing pregnant – a not uncommon state of Giffard wives of the period. Fourteen children surround them, all surviving childhood, and one being the unscrupulous Gilbert. The church also has a memorial plaque to Colonel William Carless, loyal companion of Charles II during his stay up the Boscobel Oak.

Brewood (pronounced 'Brood') is a picturesque village dominated by the church which owes its massive size to the fact that in the Middle Ages the bishops of Lichfield had a manor house in the village and thus the church was used as a sub-cathedral. The Dean of Lichfield also held land and property in Brewood and this has left a legacy of place names, Deansfield, the ground of Brewood Cricket Club, Dean Street and in it Deans Gate and The Deanery, the latter having on its façade a woman's face with the tongue stuck out. Two sisters once lived, one in The Deanery, the other nearby in The Chantry, and the protruding tongue is said to have been a rude gesture from one sister to the other.

Brewood Grammar School with its Tudor foundation and modern bent towards agriculture in its curriculum, is one of several in the Midlands which rejected Dr Samuel Johnson's application for the post of usher. A prominent old boy, William Huskisson, became Colonial Secretary, and had the even greater, if more tragic, distinction of being the first person killed by a train in Britain – at the opening of the Liverpool–Manchester Railway on 15 September 1830. One of Brewood's most striking buildings is the red brick battlemented mock castle at the end of Bargate, known as Speedwell Castle. It was built by a man who owned a racehorse named Speedwell which was not running well so that the owner swore that if ever it won a race he would build a castle to celebrate, and the horse promptly won. Days when horses were familiar in Brewood streets are recalled by the old horse-trough in Stafford Street, inscribed 'To the beloved memory of Major John Edmonstone Monckton, 2nd Madras Light Cavalry, who died at Bargate, Brewood, 2 August 1891'.

In 1845 the Moncktons moved across the Penk from Somerford Hall, their home for two centuries, to Stretton Hall, some three miles downstream. As riparian owners on the river for ten miles from Wolverhampton to Congreve they dredged the entire Penk in 1857–8, and it was Mr Alan Monckton who told me that in 1896 the Penk was the fourth best trout stream in England after the Itchen, the Test, and one other, adding that a salmon was caught at Somerford Mill in 1915. Stretton Mill has an eerie atmosphere, and I could well appreciate the shock suffered by Mrs Parton, living in the mill house in November 1963 during a bad flood.

'The mill wheel had not moved for 25 years, and we used the mill for storing fodder', she told me. 'Then, one night, we were wakened by a terrible clangour – really ghostly it was. We realised that the flooded river was turning the wheel again though the paddles are gone, and by torchlight we could see terrified rats streaming out of the mill through the floors and windows, and even the roof.'

Another two miles and the Penk borders the road below Congreve Hall with its sad story of a baronetcy awarded in 1927 to a son in recognition of his father's services which became extinct when the son, Sir Geoffrey Congreve, D.S.O., was killed during an attack on the French coast on 28 July, aged 44. Sir Geoffrey had already served in the First World War, and his father, Sir Walter Congreve, knight, won the Victoria Cross in the Boer War.

At Cuttlestone Bridge, downstream of Congreve, the Penk attains the dignity of five arches, and outside Penkridge it is increased by the Church Eaton Brook. King John granted Penkridge's splendid church its charter, with a dean and four prebendaries, and bestowed the advowson on the Archbishop of Dublin, so each archbishop until the Reformation was automatically Dean of Penkridge. The screen of hammered iron in the church is much travelled. Made in Amsterdam in 1789, it became the gates of a Boer farm in South Africa. These the Hon. William Littleton, aide to the High Commissioner, shipped to Britain and gave to Penkridge Church as a chancel screen. Several Littleton memorials adorn the church, foremost being the double-decker monument to two Sir Edwards and their wives with an epitaph commendably to the point:

> *Reader! 'twas thought enough upon the tomb*
> *Of the great captain, th' enemy of Rome,*
> *To write no more but 'Here lies Hannibal',*
> *Let this suffice thee then instead of all,*

Penkridge and the River Penk

Here lye two knights, ye father and ye sonne,
Sir Edward, and Sir Edward Littleton.

The name makes a secular appearance in Penkridge at the Littleton Arms, where the sign blazons the family arms and motto: 'One God, One King.'

Across the A.449 stands the pied 'White Hart' which once afforded a night's lodging to Elizabeth I. When last I visited Penkridge the sign at the 'George and Fox' was missing. For years it showed the Prince Regent – later George IV – and his friend, Charles James Fox, the Whig leader, considering the Royal Marriage Bill aimed at extricating the prince from his matrimonial tangle. Legally married to Caroline of Brunswick an uncongenial spouse, he had undergone a clandestine wedding ceremony with Mrs Fitzherbert. There was once a 'George and Fox' in Eastgate Street, Stafford, a few doors from the 'Sheridan', which still stands. Richard Brinsley Sheridan, the playwright, was elected M.P. for Stafford in 1780, and he became a friend of Fox and the Prince Regent, so this gave the Stafford district an interest in the prince's problems.

One of the riverside meadows in Penkridge is called High Hades – the vicarage stands on it. North of the town the river becomes the close companion of the Staffordshire and Worcestershire Canal for its remaining seven miles. With them runs the M6 and east of the canal is Teddesley Park. Sir Edward Littleton, the first Lord Hatherton, turned his back on the family home, Pillaton Hall, nearer the Cannock mines, saying he found the area 'repulsive to a man of taste'. He built instead Teddesley Hall which has been called 'the ugliest house in the most beautiful park in the Midlands'. Hatherton, from which his lordship took his title, for all its proximity to mining, has a haunting quality beautifully portrayed by a Cannock writer Diana Hallchurch :

Hatherton whispers of dangling woodsmoke
tangling into acid black trees.
We wind where the grey paths lead us:
a winter place
a secret place.
Close-corsetted trees invite intrusion,

80

a shadowed pool challenged silently
soft-breaking footsteps to skirt its hollow.
Buff grey sky weighs heavily over the
flat parchment fields,
parting for a white-walled cottage and a brown tin bath.
Dogs bark.
Laughing voices balance then fall low into the well
of silence as our steps move on slowly.
We slipped by chance through the frame
between time and timelessness –
finding peace in little-known reality,
too real to be beautiful.

North of Teddesley the spires of Acton Trussell and Dunston face each other across the Penk, the canal, and the M6, and beyond them a tragic story leaves its aura over the river's last two miles. To eastward the fields rise to Acton Hill Farm. There, in March 1835, the Angel of Death was rampant. Within 11 days five children of the shepherd, Richard Burton, died, their ages between two and 17. Another son died three years later, aged 22, and two more in 1840, aged 16 and 18. Small wonder occupants of the Acton Hill farmhouse claim strange experiences – footsteps without any feet, the crying of a baby with no baby there. One visible memorial of the tragic Burton family is the stone commemorating the eight children in Baswich churchyard which looks down on the flat meadow east of Stafford.

A window in Baswich Church records the golden wedding in 1950 of Henry John and Eleanora Bostock of the family whose Lotus shoe factory rises across the meadows in Stafford. Another of Stafford's traditional industries, salt production, came into conflict with Lotus, when the shoe company's Sandon Road premises were damaged by subsidence caused by the extraction of brine from subterranean streams, as were some 1,500 properties. The outcome was the end of salt extraction from beneath the town – in 1963 the Vacuum Salt Works was producing 100,000 tons of salt annually, pumping it through pipes across the rivers Penk and Sow near their junction at Ladder Bridge.

During the terrible winter of 1947 I often travelled by road between

Stafford and Birmingham, and south of the former, for many weeks, I saw the Penk's dark waters flowing steadily while beside it the Staffordshire and Worcestershire Canal was frozen solid and white with snow settled on its ice. The 1766 Act of Parliament for the construction of this canal empowered the proprietors to raise £70,000 in 700 shares of £100 each, and an additional £30,000 if necessary, to construct a waterway 46 miles long connecting the River Severn at Stourport in Worcestershire with the Trent and Mersey Canal at Great Haywood, east of Stafford. James Brindley was the engineer, and under its earlier name, the Wolverhampton Canal, the new waterway was opened in 1772. During the previous year Dr Johnson had written how he 'crossed the Stafford Canal, one of the great efforts of human labour and contrivance which passed away on either side to lose itself in distant regions, uniting waters that nature had divided, and dividing land which nature had united'. During the canal heyday the Staffs and Worcester carried a colossal trade in Black Country hardware, with fuel from Cannock and South Staffordshire coalfields; it paid an annual dividend of 38%, and its £100 shares had a market value approaching £800. Although it suffered the inevitable decline under rail competition, this canal never came under railway control as did so many canals. Today it shares in the pleasure cruising boom, rated high among waterways in scenic value and interest. I disturbed a bittern on the towpath near Gailey in 1959, and was able to observe it closely from a bridge among rushes before continuing to Gailey Pools, the canal reservoirs where bird life remains exciting and abundant despite the M.6 which now adds its teeming traffic to that which has long thundered past Gailey on the Watling Street.

Gailey Cruisers, known throughout Midland waterways, are a memorial to a great south Staffordshire character, Ernest Thomas, who died in April 1973. Starting work in 1910 as a boat lad for his father, by 1923 he owned his first boat *Perseverance*, and, suiting his career to the name, by 1939 he had 400 working boats on local canals, and after the war became a Walsall councillor and chairman of Walsall Football Club. Ernie constructed Calf Heath Marina, embowered in 5,000 rose bushes and two dozen Walsall street lamps where the Hatherton arm leaves the main Staffs and Worcester Canal. The marina is liberally decorated with the Thomas 'coat-of-arms' –

the traditional canal roses and castles I understood, but I once asked about the whip and crossed windlasses in the other quarterings.

'My horse-drawn boats were fairly local', Ernie explained, 'and the canals had plenty of locks. There were no long pounds where the boatmen could take it easy, so they complained that the job was all bloody whip and windlass.'

Two miles from the marina Shareshill Church has a memorial tablet to the Rev. William Havergal, vicar from 1860 to 1879, whose daughter, Frances Ridley Havergal, wrote several well-loved hymns, including my own favourite 'Who is on the Lord's side?', though my preference springs from its two stirring tunes rather than the words.

South of Shareshill is Moseley Old Hall which became Charles II's refuge when Boscobel House became too risky a hiding place. The home of Thomas Whitgreave, active in the Catholic 'underground movement', it provided Charles with a more commodious priest's hole than the tiny one at Boscobel. Cromwellians were boldly turned away when they came to search Moseley Old Hall, and that same night the king had a visit from Colonel Lane, whom we left some pages back surrendering Rushall Hall to Parliamentary forces.

Among the king's companions in the flight from Worcester was one Lord Wilmot who, having left Charles at Boscobel intent on making for Swansea, put into line his own escape plan. Colonel Lane was Wilmot's friend, and Jane Lane, his sister, had been granted safe conduct to Bristol to stay with her friend, Mrs Ellen Norton of Abbot's Leigh, who was expecting a child. This pass, from the Parliamentary Governor of Stafford, also covered a manservant, and Wilmot determined to fill this role, a perfect way to break out of the dangerous Midlands. Learning, however, that the king was back at Boscobel with his Welsh project abandoned, Wilmot surrendered the escape route to him.

So Charles moved further south to the Lane home, Bentley Hall – now no more, but replaced by the Lane Arms on the Walsall–Willenhall Road – and at dawn on 10 September 1651, a cavalcade left Bentley consisting of Charles on a gelding with Jane riding pillion, Jane's cousin Henry Lascelles, and her sister and brother-in-law, Mr and Mrs Petre. The king's identity was known to Jane and Lascelles, but to the Petres and anyone else they might meet he was Will Jackson, son of a tenant of the Lanes accompanying Jane as a man-servant. Jane and the king travelled together to Trent in Dorset, where she left him with the loyal Wyndham family, and on 14 October Charles sailed for France from Shoreham, Sussex.

On regaining the throne King Charles granted the Lanes the three royal lions in their arms and offered Colonel Lane a peerage which he declined, settling instead for £2,000, £500 a year, and the monument in St Peter's Church, Wolverhampton.

CHAPTER FIVE

Burton-on-Trent and the Needwood Forest

Needwood Forest is bounded on the north by the River Dove, on the east by the Trent and Mersey Canal, on the west by the 'river country' of the Blithe valley, and on the south by the road from Yoxall to Barton-under-Needwood. Today, despite some areas of woodland, this tract bears little resemblance to a forest, and one feels, in former days, it was a chase rather than a forest. Before the Enclosures it must have been exhilarating, undulating country, well plotted with copses, coverts, and spinneys. The Enclosure Act came in 1801, before which the 9,400 acres of Needwood Forest had been a Crown possession, vested since the Accession in 1399 of Henry IV, son of John of Gaunt, Duke of Lancaster, in the Duchy of Lancaster. Disafforestation and the construction of roads came with the new Act. The Duchy's acreage was reduced to 3,225, most of the forest becoming the property of former tithe holders, freeholders, and copyholders – though the Duchy still possesses many acres around Tutbury Castle and Fauld.

The visitor will find the church at Barton-under-Needwood liberally decorated with a coat-of-arms charged with 'three violets slipped between three children's heads couped at the shoulder.' Like so many heraldic charges those three heads have a story to tell, arising in this case from Henry VII mounting a hunting expedition in Needwood Forest. Dr Plot's famous *History of Staffordshire* (1686) tells us that in a humble cottage near the spot where the church now stands a couple named Taylor had been presented with three sons at a birth, and that the triplets were shown as a rarity to the king, who ordered that care be taken of them. All three eventually prospered as doctors, but it was John Taylor who became an armiger, blazoning his own and his brothers' heads on his shield as he rose to the eminence of secretary to Henry VIII, whom he accompanied to the Field of the Cloth of Gold. Back in his native Barton he built the church, today rather fussily machicolated and pinnacled. There is a charming inspiration behind a window in the south nave wall which commemorates John Holland (1798–1876), the village's first postmaster; his daughter Elizabeth, the first postmistress, and two of his granddaughters who in turn succeeded Elizabeth. The subject of the window is the appearance of the angels to the shepherds at the first Christmas, and the text 'Behold I bring you glad tidings' recalls only the pleasant items that come through the post, forgetting the bills, rates, and tax demands.

The author who refers to inn signs is giving hostages to fortune. I swear some malicious sprite follows me round and removes those upon which I am rash enough to comment. Nevertheless I will risk mention of the 'Bell' at Barton, with a bell in a belfry on its sign, and its namesake a mile distant on the Yoxall road, with a town crier ringing his handbell in a Tudor street. In Yoxall, where the Swarbourn Brook flows beneath a prominent knoll on its journey to the Trent, and tidy ranks of slate headstones face eastward, I had to agree with the rector that the memorial to Admiral Henry Meynell is out of character with his church.

'It gives the impression', he said, 'that Almighty God, his saints and angels, are privileged to have him come among them.'

The recumbent admiral, he added, would be more in keeping with Hoar Cross Church, one of Staffordshire's many surprises, which comes suddenly on the traveller in a clearing among the trees of Needwood Forest. On this church, said to be one of the most beautiful modern churches in Britain, the Hon. Emily Meynell Ingram lavished the love, devotion, and taste of 33 years' widowhood as a memorial to her husband, Hugo Francis Meynell Ingram of Hoar Cross Hall. I was last there in mid-March when carpets of snowdrops were dying in the churchyard – the young year's first sacrifice to remorseless time. A statue of St Chad faces the road with hand uplifted to bless the passer-by. It introduces us to a feature of the church – the representation in its statues of people associated with Hoar Cross. St Chad is sculpted in the likeness of Bishop Selwyn, whom we met at Lichfield, for he it was who settled the boundaries of the new parish of Hoar Cross, and in 1876 dedicated the church to the Holy Angels.

Statues of St Basil and St Athanasius are the joint guardians of the south porch, the former a likeness of George Bodley, architect of the church; the latter of Charles, the 2nd Viscount Halifax, eldest brother of the Hon. Emily, and father of Neville Chamberlain's Foreign Minister at the outbreak of the Second World War. Another exterior statue worthy of note is that of St Stephen on the north wall. The first Christian martyr, Stephen was stoned to death, and an imaginative inscription in Latin can be translated : 'With the emblems of martyrdom we build to God's glory'. This same imagination is used inside the church. In 1888 Mrs Meynall Ingram founded and endowed a private orphanage, the Home of the Good Shepherd, in the domestic quarters of the hall. Not only is there a statue of the patron saint of orphans, Vincent de Paul, in the church – he is placed so that he faces towards the orphanage, now taken over by the Church of England Children's Society.

Perhaps the most striking portrait among the crowded gallery of saints in Hoar Cross windows is that of Edward King, Bishop of Lincoln, who is depicted as St Hugh of Lincoln with the saint's emblem of a swan. A friend of the foundress, Bishop King, preached several times in Hoar Cross Church. Another likeness is to be found in St Thomas Aquinas, the great theologian and teacher, whose flaming heart emblem denotes his love of God. He is shown with the features of a great theologian of 100 years ago, Dr Edward Pusey, leader of the Anglican Oxford Movement. Dr Pusey would never have his portrait painted – the likeness was recorded after his death.

As you enter the church take special note of the crucifix above the door. That it had a peculiarity was obvious to me – just what was not certain.

'You'll see each foot is nailed separately', the verger told me, 'instead of the usual device of crossing the feet and using one nail.'

Priceless is the only word that can be applied to the 14 Stations of the Cross at Hoar Cross. They are enclosed in wooden panels and were carved by two old craftsmen of Antwerp, and coloured by a process discovered in the Marienkirche at Danzig by Mrs Meynell Ingram while cruising in her yacht. Words are inadequate to describe the lofty magnificence of the nave and chancel. In the latter you can find carved every musical instrument mentioned in the Bible, while everywhere are choirs of angels and congregations of saints and archangels. The chantry chapel is the most intimate part of the church, housing as it does the tombs of Hugo Francis Meynell Ingram, recumbent in the uniform of the Staffordshire Yeomanry, and his widow, who built the church. Local alabaster gives a lightness and grace to both their figures, and indeed the guidebook claims that the effigy of Mrs Meynell Ingram is 'perhaps the most beautiful modern monument in England.'

Mrs Meynell Ingram's younger brother, Frederick, was almost as devoted to the church as the foundress herself. He is remembered in a strikingly beautiful memorial by Bridgeman's of Lichfield which represents him kneeling at prayer in the dress of the High Sheriff of Staffordshire.

I glanced back across the lofty nave as I was opening the door to leave the church one day when sun rays were slanting in benediction on the monuments in the chantry chapel as though in approval of this memorial raised by a woman to the man she loved and to the glory of the God in whom she believed. From the exterior the church is a symphony in warm red-brown stone with greenish tints – stone which came from Alton on the Staffordshire Churnet and Runcorn in Cheshire. But for all its beauty Hoar Cross Church has one great drawback – it is abysmally dark, so at least take a torch; at best try to have the lights switched on.

A path winds through the trees from the church to the vicarage, and to one of the tree trunks is affixed a crucifix brought home from Oberammergau by Canon Knox-Little, vicar from 1885 to 1907, a famous preacher whose eloquence drew large congregations not only to isolated Hoar Cross but to St Paul's in London, where he often preached. In Hoar Cross vicarage garden I once saw a small headstone inscribed : 'In memory of Tiny, Rhoda's dog, once the faithful attendant of Amelia, Duchess of Argyll'. Tiny died in 1903, its noble mistress having predeceased it my nine years – she became the second wife of the eighth duke in 1881, to be followed by a third after her death in 1894. Rhoda was, I believe, a daughter of the vicar.

Although the Meynell-Ingrams have gone from the hall they have left one coat-of-arms, a woman's in a lozenge shape, on the gateway, and another on the sign of the Meynell-Ingram Arms. Needwood Forest remains the home country of the Meynell Hunt – the 'Brailsford Light Horse' – whose kennels are at Sudbury, while Mrs Hugo Meynell of Hollybush Park, Newborough, and her son Nicholas Meynell are the present representatives of their family.

There is something disquieting about Housman's oft-quoted question :

Say for what were hopyards meant,
And why was Burton built on Trent?

In these pollution-conscious days it is reassuring to know that it is not the River Trent that supplies water for the renowned brews of Burton, but a number of deep wells, fed by springs seeping through deposits of gypsum that provide hard crystal-clear water ideal for brewing. Gypsum, or sulphate of lime, is the rock which gives us plaster of Paris, and polished gypsum is the alabaster of church memorials. Stretching north-west of Burton between the county boundary on the lower Dove and Needwood Forest, this Staffordshire gypsum belt rises to the wooded bluff on which stand the ruins of Tutbury Castle, with expansive views deep into Derbyshire.

Eighteen years before Clementine's father was excavating for a mine in that cavern in a Californian canyon during the '49 gold rush, there was a silver rush at Tutbury. On 1 June 1831, workmen removing gravel for an embankment near the bridge across the River Dove found some silver coins. Working upstream on the following days they found more until, on 8 June they uncovered a hoard of coins of Edward I, Edward II, and Henry III – Scottish coins, Bohemian, Polish, Flemish, and English episcopal coins. According to a history of Tutbury Castle and Priory dated 1851 : 'Upon this discovery a general scramble commenced and numbers of people soon flocked to the place. Spades had never seen busier service. Almost numberless coins, in close rows, came forth to the grateful sight of the more fortunate'.

Tutbury Church preserves a notice issued at the time forbidding any further search for the coins under pain of heavy fines. The treasure was said to belong to the Duchy of Lancaster, and it corroborated a story of 500 years earlier that Thomas, Earl of Lancaster, as he fled from Edward II in March 1321 after the Battle of Burton Bridge, deliberately hid his army's pay chest in the Dove beneath his castle at Tutbury. Doubtless Thomas intended returning one day for the money, but he was pursued by the king's henchmen, captured, and beheaded at Pontefract. With their coming to light again over 5,000 coins were picked up in one day by two men on the Derbyshire bank of the Dove, and it has been recorded that more than 100,000 were found altogether – though only 1,500 were forwarded to Duchy officials.

First built as a stronghold in Saxon times Tutbury Castle came into the hands of the Ferrers family in 1071. At the time of Domesday Book in 1086 the castle was the main residence of Henry Ferrers, who held other castles and more than 200 overlordships. In those days Tutbury was the only place in Staffordshire to have a market. Henry Ferrers' son, Robert, was created Earl of Derby in 1138. When the third earl rebelled against Henry II the king had Tutbury Castle destroyed, so that the latter part of the twelfth century witnessed a rebuilding, which included a chapel, the foundations of which have been unearthed recently by Sir Robert Somerville. The artificial mound of the castle still stands westward of the restaurant. On it one of the Ferrers family replaced the original wooden palisade with a stout stone keep known then as the Julius Tower. This has long since gone, and in 1777 Lord Vernon erected the present folly in its place, an artificial ruin to improve the view from his home at Sudbury five miles up the Dove.

Tutbury Castle came into the possession of the Duchy of Lancaster when Robert Ferrers, Earl of Derby, joined in rebellion against Henry III, who took the castle and gave it in 1266 to his younger son, Edmund, created Earl of Lancaster the following year. Thomas, the earl who lost his war chest, was Edmund's son. Thomas's brother, Henry, was also opposed to Edward II, but at a better-chosen time when the king's fortunes were slumping towards his murder in 1327. Under Edward III Henry re-possessed Tutbury Castle.

His son, another Henry, having no male issue, Tutbury went to his daughter Blanch, wife of John of Gaunt, whose name is perpetuated in the present entrance to the castle, John of Gaunt's Gateway – though it was built by the ill-fated Thomas. Nevertheless, John of Gaunt, who was promoted from earl to Duke of Lancaster, started considerable building at Tutbury. This continued under John's son, Henry Bolinbroke who, in 1399, ascended the throne as Henry IV. Thus the Duchy of Lancaster came to the Crown and Tutbury has flown the Duchy flag and remained Crown property ever since.

Between the North Tower and the chapel foundations is the site of the Queen's Lodgings, now quite obliterated, but bringing memories of the queen who gave Tutbury Castle its most romantic and tragic episode, Mary, Queen of Scots. Her subjects having turned against her, Mary, in 1568, travelled south of the Border to her cousin, Elizabeth I, for refuge. She found instead 18 years imprisonment, first at Bolton, but in February 1569, having become the focus of plots against Elizabeth, in the stricter custody of Tutbury. Even so, she was treated with some courtesies, being allowed 60 attendants. After attempts to release her had caused her removal to Wingfield, Derbyshire, and to Coventry, Mary was back at Tutbury in January 1585 under the charge of the Chancellor of the Duchy of Lancaster, Sir Ralph Sadler. He tried hard to make her life bearable, and accompanied her riding and hawking in Needwood Forest. Indoors her time was spent embroidering, but Tutbury became most irksome to her. Her accommodation was an old hunting lodge furnished in the penurious fashion of Good Queen Bess, to whom the French Ambassador complained on Mary's behalf. But Mary continued to suffer her rheumatism in 'two paltry holes with windows facing the dark surrounding walls' in unfortunate proximity to the castle privies, and at a time when 130 persons were living in the castle.

A change of warder to Sir Amyas Paulet in April 1585 brought a worsening of Mary's situation – the opening of her letters and the prevention of her almsgiving to the local poor. That December the ill-starred queen was removed from Tutbury for the last time to another Staffordshire destination, Chartley, and ultimately to

Fotheringhay, Northamptonshire, where on 8 February 1587 she was beheaded.

Both James 1, Mary's son, and Charles 1, stayed at Tutbury, but after a siege in 1646 the castle surrendered to Parliament to meet the customary fate of 'slighting', or practical destruction. So, although Tutbury Castle has been used and in part renewed since then, it is today a romantic ruin, but beside the mound is a treasure which has endured for 800 years, the Norman west front of Tutbury Priory Church, with a door among the finest in Britain. Look carefully at the second from the door of the six arches. It is unique – the only exterior arch in the country made of alabaster, the local stone. Inside the church do not fail to stand at the east end and look west at some superlative Norman architecture.

In the sixteenth and seventeenth centuries a Burton-on-Trent School of Alabasterers became famous throughout Europe for their carvings in gypsum. Then, in 1851, William White's *History and Directory of Staffordshire* included an entry 'Staton, John Clarke, Co., plaster of Paris, gypsum etc. manufacturers. Union Mill, Burton-on-Trent'. This John Clarke Staton began manufacturing plaster of Paris and floor plaster in 1833, but in the 1860s he moved from Union Mill to Shobnall Mills beside the Trent and Mersey Canal, receiving barge-loads of gypsum from Chellaston quarries in Derbyshire. By 1858 Staton had been joined by his brother-in-law William Newton, who left the family plaster business at Colton Mill, Rugeley, to become a partner in J. C. Staton and Company.

With the advent in 1848 of the North Staffordshire Railway, Staton's source of gypsum supply was changed from Chellaston to Fauld, cement and dental plaster being added to their products. During the 1870s Staton's acquired Fauld Quarry from the Orme family, and in 1879 drove an adit into the hillside from the old quarry and began 'mining' rather than quarrying gypsum. Very soon Peter Ford drove another tunnel into the gypsum belt, and in 1883 began building his own works for the manufacture of plaster and cement. By 1890 the Needwood Plaster and Cement Company had opened a third mine and works at Draycott-in-the-Clay just across the Derbyshire border.

In the 1880s Staton's Shobnall works were quite extensive, an illu-

17 *Staffordshire is a county of spacious views such as this across part of Cannock Chase*

stration on their envelopes showing three bottle-shaped kilns and four chimney stacks in line. Events were afoot in Tutbury however which were to bring about a move. Woolcombing, and later silk spinning, were traditional industries in Tutbury, giving way in the late eighteenth century to cotton. The owners of the silk mill, John Bott and Company, petitioned the king – as Duke of Lancaster – for permission to utilise common land beside the Dove for the purpose of spinning cotton. The Duchy concurred and erected a five-storey L-shaped building. Two new water turbines installed in 1880 commemorated Gladstone's return as Prime Minister in that year along with two Liberal victories in the East Staffordshire Division, being known, one as Gladstone, the other as Bass and Wiggin. Unhappily orders for cotton were falling off, and in 1888 production moved to another mill belonging to the Tutbury Mill Company upstream at Rocester. Tutbury experienced considerable unemployment, and on 5 May 1889 the *Burton Chronicle* carried a poignant letter:

Dear Sir,

I cannot help it but I must write to you. I have known you many years and have always found you to be my friend. No doubt you will wonder who I am, but do not look at my signature until you have heard my complaint. I am getting on for a hundred years, and have been a good and faithful servant. There is plenty of work in me. I am teetotaller and have been all my life, now I regret to say I am out of work. I have plenty of water to drink but nothing to eat; my poor inside has nearly gone. Why, I cannot fathom. Cannot something be done for me? I have done well for my master, and will do so again; if only set going again I would find employment for two or three hundred hands. Do all you can, dear friends. Call a meeting and try to do something for me; otherwise I shall not know how to exist.

Truly I am nearly broken hearted.

Regretfully yours,

THE OLD MILL.

This heart-cry did not go unheeded. Aware of the advantages conferred by water power, of a good sidings connection with the North

18 *Hadrian's Arch at Shugborough Hall, now the home of the Staffordshire County Museum*

Staffordshire Railway, and of the excellent buildings, Staton's took a lease of the mill in July 1890 and began production in September. In 1894, 16 weeks of frost froze the Dove solid, and former Tutbury workers now at Rocester were visited by friends who had skated the windings of the river from Tutbury. Later that same year 18 blocks of gypsum weighing up to 15 tons each were shipped to New York as alabaster pillars in Cornelius Vanderbilt's mansion. For a while at the turn of the century one Henry Spurrier occupied part of the original cotton mill buildings with a light engineering business, eventually moving to Lancashire to form the Leyland Steam Boiler Company, from which sprang Leyland Motors. Another Lancashire link with Tutbury is the ceiling of the Tower Ballroom, Blackpool – made from Staton's plaster.

Tutbury Mill closed for the manufacture of plaster in October 1968, and in the summer of 1972 the mill was demolished. Staton's is now part of British Gypsum Ltd, a subsidiary of British Plaster Boards Industries Ltd, which, at its Fauld works, concentrates on the manufacture of building plaster. As the dust has settled beside Tutbury Bridge, first of the gypsum production and later of the demolition of the mill, a new *genus loci* has risen across the river in a coffee tower at Nestlé's works which pervades the neighbourhood with appetising odours.

In 1960 Tutbury lost one of its most famous institutions, the famous steam train 'Tutbury Jennie' after 111 years on the four miles journey from Burton-on-Trent via Stretton and Rolleston. Another estimable locomotive was delayed for ten minutes at Scropton Sidings two miles west of Tutbury on 27 November 1944, thus saving the life of its driver, the late William Beck. But for those ten minutes Mr Beck, who drove one of Staton's locomotives for 38 years, would have been at Ford's Mine when it blew up in the worst explosion ever known in Britain. The mine, at Fauld, its gypsum production discontinued, was a wartime dump for 4,000 tons of R.A.F. bombs, and the explosion was heard in London and recorded on a seismograph in Switzerland. Sixty-eight were killed, some of their graves being in Tutbury churchyard. One entire farm disappeared from the face of the earth, buildings, people, and stock, leaving just an enormous crater. At Fauld House, protected from the direct blast by a hill, Mrs

Ida Hellaby heard little noise, but the sky went completely black, and she thought Judgment Day had come.

Hanbury Church, near Fauld, remembers those who died in the explosion along with the Second World War dead in a window comprised of pieces of ancient glass. It is appropriate that a church on this gypsum belt should boast the oldest alabaster effigy in England, probably the work of a local craftsmen around 1300. It depicts Sir John Hanbury, crossed-legged as a Crusader, wearing his armour and prepared for battle. In the chancel are some attractive busts of unattractive Puritan women, while round the corner in the north aisle lies the Royalist, Sir John Egerton, the King's Axe-bearer in Needwood Forest. A note explains that his sister Griselda placed Sir John here out of sight of the Puritan ladies, and he must be thankful to be spared such uncongenial company. A niche in the tower bears a statue of St Werburgh to whom the church is dedicated. Before she died, *circa* 700 A.D. at Trentham, south of the Potteries, she had expressed a wish to be buried at Hanbury. When the Trentham nuns declined to hand over her body a posse of men from Hanbury stole it despite a strong guard. It was interred at Hanbury, but in 875 fear of desecration by the Danes led to its removal to Chester, where the cathedral is dedicated to St Werburgh.

A branch factory of a Stourbridge firm brings Tutbury a glass-making industry which probably came because there was plentiful timber in Needwood Forest to fire the furnaces. When the industry arrived is uncertain, but it is on record in 1836, and today 130 are employed in the production of stemware, tumblers, and hand-made crystal ware. There is always an air of dedication in a glasshouse, an unhurried urgency in the teamwork of the craftsmen who fashion molten glass into its many shapes. The Bells, Compsons, and Nicklins are the best-known glass families in Tutbury, men with a peculiar pride in their inherited skills as they progress from bit-gatherer to foot-blower, servitor, and eventually workman – the top man in each 'chair' of glass-workers.

The church apart, Tutbury is not imposing architecturally, though the 'Dog and Partridge' lends black-and-white character to the town. To an attractive half-timbered exterior it adds an equally pleasing old-world interior, though all the fittings in the public and cocktail bars came from the liner *Reina del Pacifico* after a refit. A notorious personality of bygone Tutbury was Ann Moore, who claimed the power to subsist on little or no food, though her supposed complete abstinence was ultimately proved false. From 17 July 1807 to 9 September 1811, she claimed to be living entirely without food while many sightseers paid to look at her. Then it was discovered that relatives passed food to her by mouth when kissing her. Discredited, she slunk out of town.

An unidentified monk of Burton Abbey is credited with the discovery in the thirteenth century that water filtered through the local gypsum produced excellent ale. It was 1744 when William Worthington, a Leicestershire man, moved into Burton and established a brewery in High Street, followed very soon by William Bass, also in High Street, and several lesser brewers. The two Williams sold little of their brew locally because the Trent and Mersey Canal opened up to them an export market in the Baltic and Russia via the Trent and Hull. Worthington's first speculative shipment of ale to St Petersburg was lost to human ken for 18 months, at which his partner lost confidence and was bought out by Worthington's fiancée. Six months later came news of the cargo's safe arrival in St Petersburg and of the favour the Burton beer found in Russia, where it became widely acclaimed as *Piva Burtonski* until an adverse tariff closed the market.

Worthington and Bass then turned their attention to India, producing India Pale Ale for the delectation of eastern palates. A sailing ship bound for the East Indies with a cargo of India Pale Ale was wrecked in the Irish Sea. The ale was salvaged and sold by auction on behalf of the underwriters, thus the new brew broke into the home market and became the national drink.

As Burton's breweries expanded they posed the transport problem which was to bedevil the town for so many years. Inadequate roads and horse-drawn drays meant it was cheaper to export beer than to send it to London. With the arrival in 1829 of the Midland Railway the situation was relieved temporarily, but production increased to such a degree that new problems were raised, and congestion within Burton almost brought the town to a standstill until, in 1860, parliamentary authority was granted for loading directly into rail trucks from the brewery storehouses. Thus Burton came by the feature, the many level crossings, which converted it into a seeming dockland and for which it was to become infamous with the proliferation of cars, a situation ultimately relieved with the construction of the by-pass in the 1960s.

During this decade, too, the percentage of the working population of Burton employed in the brewery industry was reduced by amalgamations and automation from 90 to 60, and various light industries moved to old brewery sites such as the 20 acres of the Crown Industrial Estate, which formerly accommodated maltings.

In 1875 the Bass company scored a 'first' when an employee spent an uncomfortable night on the steps of the Registrar's Office in London in order to register the first ever trade mark under the new Trade Marks Act – the Bass 'triangle'. The association between the Bass brewery and the railways was so close that William's grandson, Michael Thomas Bass (1799–1884), Liberal M.P. for Derby from 1848 to 1883, befriended the railway workers in their complaint against oppressive hours in 1870, and sent an agent around the country to help organise their fight. Some years earlier he had sponsored a full enquiry into the earnings of the working class. Bass is also remembered for having introduced a parliamentary bill authorising householders to request street musicians to move away from the vicinity of their homes. Offered a baronetcy and a peerage Michael Thomas Bass declined both, but his son Michael Arthur was created a baronet in his father's own lifetime. In 1886 he was elevated to the peerage as Baron Burton, in which role he stands as a statue in front of the Gothick town hall which he presented to Burton in 1894.

Among Burton's many inns is a 'Marquis of Lorne', the second title of the dukes of Argyll and the courtesy title of their heirs. The particular Marquis of Lorne to whom pubs are dedicated was John, who became the second Duke of Argyll. He was a considerable commander under Marlborough and led the Royal Army at Sheriffmuir in 1715 against the supporters of the Old Pretender. He it was who gave us the expression 'God Bless the Duke of Argyll', used generally, but specifically by highlanders when they scratch themselves. The duke put up scratching posts for his cattle on treeless moorland, but the herdsmen found them equally efficacious against their own itches, repeating the expression as they rubbed against the posts.

Burton's patron saint is Modwena who was an abbess at Killeavy, Co. Armagh. When, in the seventh century, an English prince, Alfred, illegitimate son of King Oswin, was leaving Ireland after a visit, his host pillaged Modwena's convent to give him a parting gift. Modwena followed to obtain redress and ran Alfred to earth at Whitby where he promised to repay her. She took up residence in Whitby Abbey, but eventually set up a convent at Burton. Though she died on a visit to her brother in Scotland she was buried at Burton, thus meriting the epitaph :

> *By Ireland life, by Scotland death was given,*
> *A tomb in England, endless joy in Heaven.*

Burton has a Prince Alfred Inn. Its sign shows the famous cake-burning episode in the life of King Alfred (848–900 A.D.). Perhaps the brewery has mixed its Alfreds. Who, in any case, would refer to King Alfred as Prince Alfred? The Staffordshire Knot Inn, opposite the County Court, is also a misnomer. Correctly it is the Stafford Knot, the badge of the Stafford family.

The parish church, standing on the site of an eleventh century abbey, is dedicated to St Modwena. I found there a plaque which reminds me of the boy who stood on Felicia Hemans's 'burning deck'. It commemorates 'Pte George Robinson, 25 years a volunteer; he died of sunstroke whilst on duty with his regiment at Aldershot, August 10, 1895.' An unusual death, but less dramatic than that on 16 December 1292 of a boy, William Bond, who, working with a carpenter on the church roof, fell through to his death in front of the altar during Vespers. The church has a memorial, erected by his schoolfellows of Burton Grammar School, to Henry Corbett Gorton 'mortally wounded on Wagon Hill in the siege of Ladysmith', and another to Samuel Allsop (died 1838), 'whose ancestor Hugh de Allsop was knighted by Richard I on the Conquest of Acre.'

While Richard was swashbuckling uselessly in the Holy Land, his brother, King John, was coping with unruly barons in England – and granting Burton a fair and a weekly market, as he is shown doing above the entrance to the Market Hall. That market still survives, and on Thursdays the bull's head with a ring through the nose looks down from the Market Hall on the colourful stalls beneath a splendid chestnut outside St Modwena's, with the black and white of the 'Royal Oak' framed in its branches.

If you want to make the quickest possible journey from Dover to Calais, and without fear of sea-sickness, you must go to Burton where Dover Road and Calais Road are neighbours. From 1363 to 1558 – when Britain lost it – Calais was the wool staple port and among its wool merchants was William Wyggeston of Leicester. It was the Governors of the Wyggeston Hospital at Leicester who administered and developed the Horninglow area of Burton, hence the unexpected road names. Dame Paulet Square and Lady Paulet's Almshouses (1593) are a reminder in Burton of Elizabeth Blount, the rich widow of Sir Thomas Pope, Founder of Trinity College, Oxford. She became the second wife of Sir Hugh Paulet, whose son by his first wife was that Sir Amyas Paulet who acted as warder to Mary, Queen of Scots.

Burton beer played a large part in Mary's captivity – it could even be said to have hastened her death. A Burton brewer smuggled letters between Mary and Anthony Babington plotting the death of Elizabeth I, in false bottoms to his beer casks. He was, however, a double agent, also in the pay of Elizabeth's minister, Walsingham, and eventually the unhappy Mary made her last journey, to Fotheringhay, crossing, en route, Burton's old medieval bridge, replaced in 1864 by a 32 arch structure 470 yards long, another of Lord Burton's benefactions.

The silver eagle in the arms of Burton brings us to that great Staffordshire family, the Pagets, in whose arms it also occurs. Yet, illustrious though it is, there is in the parish church an even more famous achievement of arms – nothing less than the spear from the arms of William Shakespeare. It appears, impaled with the arms of her husband, Sir Claverhouse Graham, in the brass to the memory of Mary Newman Graham (née Whitehead) 'ninth in descent from Joan, sister of William Shakespeare of Stratford-upon-Avon.'

At Rolleston, north of Burton, the Mosley family were lords of the manor for many years, and their eagle crest gives a name to the

Spread Eagle Inn, where their arms can be seen above a fireplace, including three pickaxes. In 1928 the father of Sir Oswald Mosley was buried in Rolleston churchyard. Eighteen years earlier his father was in trouble with the villagers when he decided that the entire St Mary's aisle in the church be closed to all but his family. The parishioners showed their resentment by removing the hassocks and placing bent pins on the baronet's pew, but the Consistory Court awarded Sir Oswald 38 seats.

CHAPTER SIX

Abbots Bromley and the River Blithe

Several Staffordshire rivers flow from the northern moors south-easterly to an ultimate confluence with the Dove or the Trent. Southernmost of them, the Blithe rises near a road junction called intriguingly Cellarhead, eight miles south of Leek, and soon flows near the village of Caverswall once famed for its wakes. This accounts for the jolly, though incomprehensible, sign on the Red House Inn, depicting some uniformed bandsmen with a roundabout in the background.

A castle was first built at Caverswall 700 years ago. The present building, a 'Rest Home for Ladies', its drive sandwiched between the parish church and the Catholic church, rose when its predecessor had deteriorated into a farm. The builder, Matthew Cradock, was governor-designate of Massachusetts, of which colony he was a founder, but he was detained in England through the politics that foreshadowed the Civil War. He threatened Charles I that should he fortify the Tower of London the city would cease paying taxes, but as the antagonism between King and Parliament rose to a head Cradock died in 1641. He had made, wittingly or otherwise, his contribution to his side in building his castle with the strength of a fortress, and it became a Parliamentary stronghold during the ensuing hostilities.

Caverswall Church has memorials to the Parkers – one commonly called 'Buff Coat', and a devil-scaring corbel, half woman, half cow,

103

while in its churchyard lies Richard Plunket, sergeant of the 8th Regiment of Foot, who after 37 years' service 'obtained a pension of £40 per annum', though probably not for saving Wellington's life at Waterloo as village gossip has it.

Blythebridge changes the river's spelling, but puts it right with an inn called the 'Blithe Spirit'. At Church Leigh the river has entered gentler country, and it was September 1973 when last I visited All Saints Church in the village. Not the graceful arches of the crossing, not the Burne-Jones windows, not in fact the lovely church at all stole my thoughts, but the view. Seen from the porch the peaceful Blithe valley dreamed under the late summer sun just as it must have done in the mind's eye of the Rev. David Neaum, gazing over the south Atlantic wastes from the world's loneliest island, Tristan da Cunha, where he went as padre from Church Leigh in 1952.

Blithe comes from an Old English word meaning 'pleasant', but the river was once useful too, for at Church Farm, Gratwich, there were six sluices to irrigate King's Field, while downstream the river turned the undershot wheel at Burndhurst Mill to grind cattle feed until the 1950s. At one time this was a gathering place of shepherds for sheep dipping, and the pool below the weir had its eel traps, out-size chub, and goodly trout. Two more miles downstream at Blythe-bridge Mill the late William Henry Beeson once told me that when he kept the Blythe Inn near by they would drink river water when-ever the pump failed. This caused a Hednesford doctor who came regularly for the fishing to assure Mr Beeson that 'where a trout will live you can safely drink the water.'

On 27 October 1953 ten thousand people flocked to the little River Blithe west of Abbots Bromley to watch Queen Elizabeth the Queen Mother open the new Blithfield Reservoir which impounds 4,000,000,000 gallons of Blithe water in its 790 acres, the major work in the South Staffordshire Waterworks Company's supply area. Five million gallons daily continue to flow from the reservoir down the Blithe. A considerable acreage of Bagot Park was inundated, but the view from Blithfield Hall, home of the Bagots since Domesday, is now enhanced by vistas of lake between its parkland trees.

In the chancel of St Leonard's Church, hard by Blithfield Hall, you can read of a sad little marriage. The bells that pealed for Emily

Fitzroy and William Bagot in May 1799 were tolling for Emily's funeral in June 1800, and on New Year's Day, 1801, the story reached its tragic conclusion with the death of the baby daughter who had cost her mother's life. Look at the most elaborate of the shields on Admaston Lodge. You will probably recognise the right-hand quartering as the royal arms, but, running from the Scottish lion to the Irish harp is a baton sinister – the emblem of illegitimacy often prized by noble families. Emily's surname is the giveaway – Fitzroy, son of the king. One of her forebears was the first Duke of Grafton, the natural son of Charles ii and Barbara Villiers, the gay Duchess of Cleveland.

To the left of Emily's arms are William's, the Bagots' – two azure chevronels on a field of ermine. They can be seen, too, on the sign of the Bagot Arms in Abbots Bromley. Their supporters, a pair of goats, and the goat's head crest which gives its name to another Abbots Bromley hotel, stem from the famous Blithfield herd of black-necked goats, now much reduced, which were given to Sir John Bagot by Richard ii in thanks for the stirring hunting he had enjoyed in Bagot's Park.

The present chatelaine of Blithfield Hall is Nancy, Lady Bagot, widow of Caryl, 6th Lord Bagot. Reacting readily to a visitor's interests Lady Bagot is as quick to point out the little things as the major items; to scramble beneath bushes to disclose memorial stones in a stable wall to two coach horses, Osman and Yellow Girl, or to draw attention to a 'squint' in the churchyard wall.

'It was installed', she explained, 'rather than have heads bobbing above the wall to keep watch for the family crocodile starting from the hall. A signal was then given for the church bell to begin ringing.'

Realising my interest in epitaphs Lady Bagot pointed out one to the Rev. Thomas Townson, probably composed by the first Lord Bagot:

> Let future rectors follow if they can
> The bright example of this holy man.

The Bagots came to Blithfield in 1360 when Ralph Bagot married Elizabeth, heiress of Richard de Blithfield. He had not far to come, barely two miles from a house the site of which is marked by a squat pillar and the remains of a moat in a field to the left of the Uttoxeter road 1½ miles out of Abbots Bromley. Portraits of past Bagots adorn Blithfield's walls including Mary Bagot, one of the beauties of Charles II's court of whom it was said that she was one of very few of them who could blush, but had no reason to do so.

Blithfield is a paradise for students of heraldry, with 36 coats-of-arms over the dining-room fireplace and 18 more in the windows of the great hall. In the twelfth century a Hervey Bagot married Millicent, heiress of Robert de Stafford, and the Bagots took and continued to use the Stafford arms until, when the Staffords had fallen on sticky times as Dukes of Buckingham, the Bagots reverted to their own arms. One Lord Stafford wrote an acrimonious letter denying the Bagots' right ever to have used his arms. He said, among other things, 'Why should I change my name of Stafford for a Bag of Oats?'

Sir Charles Bagot, modelled life-size in his robes of the Order of the Bath, was British Ambassador to Washington in the early nineteenth century, in which role he concluded the Rush-Bagot Agreement, a naval disarmament treaty on the Great Lakes between the U.S.A. and Canada. Here, too, is the summons to the 2nd Lord Bagot to attend the Coronation of William IV. Some diligent postal official without fear or favour, had stamped the package 'Above Weight'.

There is a thriving Australian branch of the Bagots which came originally from Ireland, the present and 7th Lord Bagot actually living in Australia, while Nancy, Lady Bagot, is herself an Australian.

The east window of Blithfield Church, with all the lovely quality of light characteristic of Goddard and Gibbs, whose sign manual of a sailing ship is clearly seen, was recently installed to the memory of the sixth lord and his kinsman from Adelaide, Walter H. Bagot. There is antiquity, too, in the church. During the Civil War the Bagots were Royalists, Colonel Richard Bagot commanding the king's garrison in Lichfield Cathedral – he was later killed at Naseby, aged 27. Bishop Ken was hidden in Blithfield Hall, and under the choir stalls there is an engraved heart connected with him which was last seen when the box pews were replaced. A tabletop tomb in the chancel shows the incised figures of Sir Lewis Bagot with 'his three wives, their dogs and 19 children' to quote the Blithfield guidebook.

Yet, to this knight, who in 1520 accompanied Henry VIII to the Field of the Cloth of Gold, Burke's *Peerage* attributes five wives.

Such things, however, were not for a more recent Bagot, Edward Luke Henry, nephew and heir to the fourth baron. Killed on the Somme in 1916, aged 19, his epitaph says that he gave up

> *Youth's glorious hopes; the lover's ecstasy,*
> *Life's fair adventure scarcely yet begun.*
> *One gift he had, one royal gift he gave,*
> *Proud to exchange it for a soldier's grave.*

Blithfield Hall is one of the calls each year of the Abbots Bromley Horn Dancers on the Monday following the first Sunday after September 4 – St Bartholomew's Day. Traditionally the dancers kept vigil or wake in St Nicholas Church, Abbots Bromley, on St Bartholomew's Eve before taking out the horns on the saint's day for a four-day tour of local towns and villages, collecting cash for alms. The date of the dance coincides with the village's ancient 'wakes' at Barthelmy Fair, and the Monday of the dance is still known in Abbots Bromley as Wakes Monday. The horns are collected from the Hurst Chapel in the church early in the morning, and after a first performance outside the vicarage the team perambulates the parish dancing at farmsteads and cottages on an eight-miles route, returning for tea in the village, and continuing to dance as the shadows lengthen from the stout wooden legs of Abbots Bromley's market cross.

While the Horn Dance probably dates from the twelfth century when the Abbot of Bromley granted hunting rights in Needwood Forest, horn dances are prehistoric in origin. They have a fertility significance, the dancers hoping by magic to increase the number of deer for their hunting. The conjectural twelfth-century origin of the Staffordshire ceremony coincides roughly with the last occurrence of reindeer in Britain, and the horns used are those of reindeer. They are worn by six of the dancers, three sets painted white, three blue, and it is not known whence they came. Mounted on carved wooden heads, they have a hand-staff to help them round the shoulders, and the largest pair, carried by the leader, weigh 25 lb and have a span of 39 inches.

The gay rustic costume of the team is not traditional. Some 90 years back they began patching their old clothes with colours to match their horns, the costume being introduced more recently, and the present set being presented by Lady Bagot. The six hornmen wear waistcoats with a yellow flowered front and brown sleeves. Above these are sleeveless tunics, three brown, three green. Greenish knee breeches, with a pattern of oak leaves and oak apples, disappear into green stockings. 'Maid Marion', the man-woman of prehistoric fertility dances, has a blue surcoat above a yellow skirt with blue trimmings, and a white head-dress flows behind her. 'She' carries a 'collecting pipe' which looks like a bludgeon. The jester, with his customary cap and bells, is a gay figure in red and yellow. The hobby horse is predominantly brown; the two boys – one with a crossbow, the other with the triangle – and the melodeon player, wear a modified version of the horn men's costume.

Their dance is simple enough. With the trianglist and the melodeon player standing aside, the other ten move off in single file with the three white horns leading. After some serpentine twining they emerge in two rows of five facing each other, three pairs of horns, Marion paired with the jester, and the hobby horse with the crossbow boy. For a while they trip it gently, approaching and receding, the crossbow shooting the horse at each approach. Then the horns simulate a charge, but adroitly avoiding contact they pass shoulder to shoulder. Then, facing inwards again, they repeat the dance, ultimately circling and finishing by laying down the horns in a neat line.

Purists regret, and rightly, that the traditional horn dance has given way to more popular melodies. In 1924, when the dancers performed at the jubilee of Abbots Bromley's renowned girls' boarding school of St Mary and St Anne, they were asked to play the old tune. Only with difficulty was it remembered, but it was at once written down and later printed in 'The Leaflet' of the school guild. Cecil Sharp, of folk-dance fame, had previously preserved a score, and it has been suggested that it would have made a theme for a typical Vaughan Williams composition.

Joining at the age of ten, James Fowell led the dance for many of his over 60 years with the team – the family tree of the Fowells is surely a reindeer's antlers. James assumed command from his brother

Alfred, who had, in his turn, taken over from yet another brother, John. John inherited the leadership from his father, William Fowell, whose predecessor was his father, a Mr Bentley, where, having run into a name difficulty because a widowed Mrs Fowell once married a Mr Bentley, we will leave these genealogical researches, except to add that three sons of James and at least one grandson have been, or still are among the horn dancers.

The Blithe, a trout stream of renown, inspired a book by W. H. Canaway, *A Creel of Willow*, in which the river is called the 'Withy'. South of Abbots Bromley it splits, and the Little Blithe pursues a separate course of two miles before rejoining its parent stream, which has meantime run through Priory Farm with an old chapel embodied in it bearing the inscription '*Piscatoribus Sacrum* C.C. 1795', while a nearby wall incorporates the words '*Monachis et monialibus* H.M. 1140'.

Blithbury, west of the river, is noted for its pub, the 'Bull and Spectacles', the name of which has occasioned learned papers claiming its origin as 'Bullen Spectabilis' – beautiful Anne Boleyn, the bull being an old symbol of condemnation to death. Similar erudition sees the not uncommon pub name, the 'Bull and Butcher' as a corruption of Bullen (Boleyn) Butchered, but I accept the more mundane explanation of the Blithbury name as arising from a drunken prank of painting spectacles on an original 'Bull' sign.

On the last two of its 22-miles course to join the Trent near King's Bromley, the Blithe encloses between itself and the larger river the villages of Hill Ridware, Pipe Ridware, Mavesyn Ridware, and Hamstall Ridware, the 'ridware' meaning river people. King's Bromley takes its royal name from the husband of Lady Godiva, Leofric of Mercia, who died there. Hamstall Ridware has an Elizabethan gatehouse, now the entrance to a farmyard, and in its church above pastures with names such as Pearly Hills, Simpson's Hill, The Waterloos, and the Marl Flats, sloping gently to the Blithe is a memorial to Thomas Stronginthearme – an earlier Armstrong. Hill Ridware has an outstanding heraldic sign of 47 quarters at the Chadwick Arms, recalling one of the three great families ,the Mavesyns, the Cawardens, and the Chadwicks, whose memorials turn St Nicholas Church at Mavesyn Ridware into a veritable museum.

The church itself stands remote near the Trent with a gatehouse hard by, all that remains of a castle demolished around 1700. In the gatehouse Cromwell met his Council before his attack on Lichfield. Around the Trinity Chapel in the church lie the effigies of the knights, each with a verse proclaiming his deeds. The Mavesyns, who came over with the Conqueror, were known by the name of Mal-voisin, 'bad neighbour', and so Sir Robert proved to Sir William Handsacre in 1403. Their lands adjoined and they had quarrelled about a mill; furthermore Handsacre supported Percy Hotspur in his rebellion against Henry IV, while Mavesyn was a king's man. As each knight set out with his retinue to participate in the Battle of Shrewsbury they met in the River Fields, and came to single combat. Sir Robert killed Sir William, but met his own death next day at Shrewsbury, leaving two daughters as co-heiresses. The younger, Joanna married the son of Sir William Handsacre whom her father had slain; while her sister Elizabeth married Sir John Cawarden from Cheshire. Six generations later Jacosta Cawarden married Henry Chadwick, thus bringing the third of these noted families to Mavesyn Ridware. No student of history, genealogy, or heraldry should miss Mavesyn Ridware Church.

Handsacre Hall, across the Trent, has recently been demolished, but the best sections of the sixteenth-century building have gone for reconstruction to the Avoncroft Museum of Buildings near Bromsgrove in Worcestershire. The Trent and Mersey Canal runs through Handsacre, and a mile away at Armitage it has passed through the short Plum Pudding Tunnel, named after the inn beside it.

19 *Ingestre Church, thought by many to be the work of Christopher Wren, though documentary evidence was lost in a fire*

CHAPTER SEVEN

Rugeley and Cannock Chase

On Sunday, 29 April 1973, Cannock Chase saw a timely revival of a felicitous custom which had fallen into desuetude. While the Australian prime minister was returning home after breaking yet more of the few remaining ties of the old British Empire, the West Midlands branch of the Military History Society was bringing out of 20 years cold-storage the Anzac Day Service previously held at the graves of 70 New Zealanders in the military cemetery on Cannock Chase.

With Britain's fatal hospitality towards refugees, and enemies past and present, living and dead, a German cemetery had been assembled on Cannock Chase into which was collected the remains of some 6,000 Germans who died in Britain during the two world wars. They lie beneath well-kept lawns, bright with seasonal flowers, while silver birches wave their tresses above the graves and a constant requiem is sounded in the breeze from a dark background of Wagnerian conifers.

Not far distant, its significance lost on a couple of generations, is the British cemetery where, the saddest sight in Staffordshire, are the gleaming white headstones of young New Zealanders who journeyed half way across the world to help us fight a common foe, only to die in the Spanish influenza epidemic which ravaged Britain during the month of the Armistice, November 1918. Among their graves is that of 'Freda', the dog mascot of the New Zealand Rifle Brigade.

20 (above)   The gatehouse at Tixall which has seen sad and tragic scenes in the lives of Mary, Queen of Scots, Lord Aston, and Lord Stafford

21   Ingestre Hall was long the home of the Earls of Shrewsbury

During the First World War Cannock Chase was a vast military camp, which, with its Bunter pebble beds, must have had the virtue of being fairly free from mud. In mediaeval times the Chase was of far greater extent, but the sixteenth-century cutting of woodlands for charcoal, and the later development of coal mining and an iron industry, brought settlements which grew into towns, until today Cannock Chase is reduced to some 26 square miles designated as an Area of Outstanding Beauty. Of this, 7,000 acres have since 1920 been blanketed with monotonous coniferations responsible for the characteristic black skyline seen from any distance. At points the pebble beds are raped by the insatiable road-builders, and the Army still has a training ground among the heather. In the north, around Milford Common, the Cannock Chase sub-committee of Staffordshire County Council has carried out an enlightened tree-planting policy, including Scots pine, rowan, purple beech, and American red oak. A motorless zone of 1,000 acres has been designated, including the beautiful Sherbrook Valley – adder country where I always wear boots. The lucky rambler, roaming the dry gravels and pine needles of the Chase when much other countryside is waterlogged, may encounter some of the wild deer which have survived poachers and an average annual slaughter by motorists of 70 or so. Their present number is estimated at 250.

In March 1972 a new Cank Thorn was planted on Cannock Chase, a scion of the old thorn tree which traditionally marked the meeting place of the manors of Rugeley, Cannock, and Penkridge, and of three of the largest estates on the Chase – Hatherton, Lichfield, and Anglesey. The Marquis's Drive is one of the several place names which commemorate great landowners on Cannock Chase, in this case the First Marquis of Anglesey, whose park at Beaudesert is now a Scout camping ground. The Marquis lived for 40 years not with one foot, but with one leg in the grave. As Henry William Paget, Earl of Uxbridge and Beaudesert, he was commander of the horse artillery and cavalry at Waterloo. Late in the battle his leg was shattered by a cannon ball as he was riding with Wellington. Their ensuing dialogue has become historic.

'Good God, Paget, your leg's blown off', said the Duke.

'I'm damned if it isn't', was Paget's reply.

The remains of the leg were amputated at Waterloo and duly buried there with an appropriate inscription.

During his convalescence Paget was created Marquis of Anglesey, and on his return home in August 1815 his carriage was hauled by his tenants from Lichfield to Beaudesert at the head of a procession of 10,000 come to acclaim the Midlands' own hero of Waterloo. The marquis was as formidable in bed as on the battlefield – he had eight children in nine years by his first wife, Lady Caroline Villiers, and ten more by Lady Charlotte Wellesley. The Pagets scattered their limbs widespread in the service of their country, and at one Beaudesert gathering the marquis was without his leg, his brother was minus one arm, the marquis's son was on crutches with a knee wound, and a daughter had lost her left hand while with her husband at a battle in Spain.

The First Marquis of Anglesey was born in 1768 plain Henry William Bayly. His father, Henry Bayly, was heir to an obscure baronetcy, but, more important, he was a very lucky man. Despite parental objection from both sides to his marriage with Jane Champagne, a girl whose Huguenot ancestors had been smuggled out of Spain in a wine cask, he married her on 11 April 1767. Three years later, quite out of the blue, they were Lord and Lady Paget of Beaudesert Hall, Cannock Chase, blessed with wide lands and considerable possessions.

A certain William Paget, son of a humble Wednesbury man – probably a nail factor – became one of the chief advisers to Henry VIII, for whom he accomplished several diplomatic missions and as whose executor he was named. Henry rewarded him with a knighthood, with Beaudesert, and with lands belonging to the Abbey of Burton-on-Trent. In 1551 Sir William Paget was summoned to Parliament as Baron Paget of Beaudesert. Although the father of four sons, William arranged that his peerage should be transmitted through the female line should the male line ever die out, and in 1769 this happened with the death of the eighth baron unmarried. This bachelor peers' distant cousin, Caroline Paget, was Lady Bayly, mother of the lucky Henry, and though she had died in 1766 the relationship brought the Paget peerage and its perquisites to her son.

But luck had not done with him yet. Eleven years later, in 1780, he inherited vast acreages in Somerset and Dorset from an affluent landowner, Peter Walter, whose will, dated 1752, provided that his beneficiary, should his own line fail, was to be the heir of Sir Nicholas Bayly, Henry's father. Why he did this remains a mystery, but it increased the wealth and importance of Henry, the Ninth Baron Paget. On his father's death in 1782 Henry, now 38, inherited the family estates in Ireland and North Wales, including Anglesey, bringing his total territory up to 100,000 acres, rich in coal, lead and copper.

Fate held one more lucky stroke in store for Henry. The earldom of Uxbridge, created for the seventh Lord Paget, had died out with the eighth, but it was revived for the ninth, who thus faced the world as Henry, Earl of Uxbridge. He could well afford the 12 children, seven of them sons, with which Jane Champagne blessed him, one of whom became the First Marquis of Anglesey.

The breezy area of heathery moorland north from the military cemeteries is called Anson's Bank, the name commemorating George, Viscount Anson, whose voyage round the world in 1740–44 gave rise to a classic book of sea travel. Across to the north-east of the Chase, Wolseley Park and Wolseley Plain recall another famous name, that of Field-Marshal Sir Garnet (later Viscount) Wolseley. Dropping from Wolseley Plain into Abrahams Valley, off the Chase and across Weetman's Bridge, one finds the memorials of these great men in Colwich Church, where the churchyard offers a fine view southward over the Trent Valley to the bracken-clad northern hills of Cannock Chase. It is heartening to find an unfashionable patriotism expressed on the war memorial lych-gate. Not content with mentioning that England went into the First World War with lofty motives, an inscription ends unashamedly 'Long Live England'.

Inside the church a coat-of-arms in a window incorporating three snake-headed ammonites, the attributes of St Hilda, Abbess of Whitby, Yorkshire, where ammonite fossils abound, is that of the Whitby family, the window a memorial to Thomas Edward Whitby and his wife. Thomas Trubshaw, civil engineer and architect, who died in 1853, is also commemorated, his memorial being inscribed: 'The unequalled arch of Grosvenor Bridge at Chester will long remain (it is hoped) as his enduring monument.'

Here, too, is a plaque to Robert Louis Stevenson's biographer, Sir Graham Balfour, who worshipped at Colwich from 1902 to 1922, and, in the organ loft, one to Anne Margaret, who married Thomas, Viscount Anson, in 1794 – second daughter of Thomas William Coke of Holkham, Norfolk, later Earl of Leicester, whom some of us remember from our schooldays as famous in agriculture and stock rearing along with 'Turnip' Townshend.

A simple brass in the chancel, belatedly placed there 130 years after his death, is the circumnavigator's memorial. His home was Shugborough Hall, and there can be seen part of the figurehead of his ship, *Centurion*. The River Sow joins the Trent at Shugborough Park, which lies among the northern folds of Cannock Chase between Milford and Great Haywood. In 1624 William Anson, a lawyer from Dunston, bought the manor house at Shugborough, which was eventually demolished to make way for the present Georgian mansion, owned by the National Trust since 1966 and now the Staffordshire County Museum. 'Athenian' Stuart embellished the park with reproductions of Greek antiquities which gave him his nickname, and in 1795 Samuel Wyatt, elder brother of the more famous James, raised the astonishing portico of ten Ionic columns, each an oak trunk covered with slate, painted, and sanded.

Among the architectural wonders in Shugborough Park, the Triumphal Arch, which celebrated the admiral's victories and achievements, is modelled on the Arch of Adrian in Athens; and the admiral had a pillar erected with a sculpture of his favourite cat, which accompanied him on his world voyage.

Field-Marshal Wolseley is buried in St Paul's, but his memorial at Colwich lists the campaigns in which he served. Among other Wolseleys commemorated at Colwich is a Sir William who died in 1728, though the strange manner of his death is not recorded. Travelling in the Near East, Sir William acquired four Arabian horses and later had his fortune told. It was predicted that he and the horses would die of drowning. Not to tempt fate he sent the horses home separately from himself – only to perish with them while fording the Trent near Wolseley Hall in a bad thunderstorm.

Cannock is a coalfield, and its political expression is loudest in Rugeley which is well named, for its means 'red pastures', and the street names of Springfields Estate commemorate Socialist pioneers. Lovett Court and Harney Court recall Chartist leaders, while Winstanley the 'Digger', Holyoake of the Co-op, and William Morris are there, too. Aneurin Bevan, the only modern among them, deserves his place as the late husband of Jennie Lee (Baroness Lee of Asheridge), who was Labour M.P. for Cannock – including Rugeley – from 1945 to 1970. In Cannock, Ernest Bevin Street is not inappropriate on a coalfield to those who remember the Bevin Boys. Rugeley also has an Attlee Crescent, and on the Pear Tree Estate, where 800 homes built by the Coal Industry Housing Association house almost exclusively miners, benefactors of the industry are perpetuated in streets named after Keir Hardie, Lord Shaftesbury, Lord Sankey, and Humphrey Davy of the safety lamp.

Back in Springfields, Wat Tyler Close, Grindcobbe Grove, and John Ball Close recall the leaders of the Peasants' Rising in 1381. House names are not *de rigueur* on the estate, but if I lived in one of those three roads I should name my house 'Walworth', after the Lord Mayor of London who slew Wat Tyler. There were, initially, some erudite protests that Tyler and Grindcobbe were murderers, but Rugeley has murder as its main memory anyhow, as a raised white stone in St Augustine's neat spacious churchyard testifies, with its inscription 'John Parsons Cook, late of Calthorp Lodge in the County of Leicester, whose life was taken away on the night of November 22, 1855, in the 29th year of his age.'

A friend of Cook in Rugeley owned the horse Nettle which started favourite in the 1855 Oaks. A win meant a considerable fortune to the owner, but ruin otherwise, for he had backed it heavily. Nettle was leading near the post, but then came disaster. The favourite stumbled, threw the rider, and galloped off the course. Pressed by bookmakers, by moneylenders to whom he was paying £6,000 yearly in interest alone, and importuned by several of his mistresses, Nettle's owner sought other means of recouping his losses. In November 1855 he had a horse running at Shrewsbury races and went there with his friend John Parsons Cook, a young lawyer and also a racehorse owner, whose Polestar won the Shrewsbury Handicap. With £1,000 in his pocket Cook returned to Rugeley, where he stayed at the 'Talbot', now the Shrewsbury Arms. During the following week he was taken ill and died although – or because – he was attended by his fellow racehorse owner, for this was none other than Dr William Palmer, 'Prince of Poisoners', who lived in Market Street, Rugeley.

Palmer had been buying poison from Rugeley chemists and Cook's symptoms suggested poison. Palmer ordered a coffin in a great hurry and would have taken over the burial arrangement – along with Cook's £1,000 – had not the dead man's step-father demanded a post mortem. Then Dr Palmer made an elementary error. He tried to slip the coroner a tenner. Word of his poison purchases leaked out, and he was arrested and charged with the murder of Cook. This brought to a head other suspicions whispered around Rugeley. What had happened to Palmer's illegitimate daughter – to four of his five children? Did his neighbour, Dr Freer's pigs die of a poison Palmer was trying out? What caused the death in 1847 of his wealthy mother-in-law while visiting Palmer's home; of Bladen, a racing friend, who died while staying with Palmer; of Palmer's young wife whom he had insured for £13,000; and of his drunken brother Walter, also insured by Palmer for £13,000, though insurance companies had refused heavier cover?

Was it not suspicious that the doctor called in by Palmer to issue death certificates 'from natural causes' on his mother, wife, brother, and friends, was a bemused octogenarian, Dr Bamford? Rugeley was in lynch mood at Palmer's arrest and his case was removed to the Central Criminal Court in London because it was felt no Staffordshire jury would rule impartially. Thus was a precedent set for similar cases. Another outcome of the Palmer poisonings was the need for an 'insurable interest' by the proposer of an insurance policy on the life of another.

The 32-year-old Palmer's 12-day trial in May 1856 necessitated structural alterations at Old Bailey to accommodate the sensation mongers, while up to 30,000 attended his hanging outside Stafford Gaol on 14 June 1856, some travelling by special excursion train from London.

A story, probably apocryphal, is told that the townspeople were so disgusted with the notoriety Dr Palmer brought to Rugeley that they petitioned the Prime Minister, Lord Palmerston, to change the name of the town.

'Certainly', he agreed. 'Would you care in compliment to me to call it Palmerstown?'

Rugeley remains 'Red Pastures', and the enormous bobbins of its 'A' and 'B' power stations dominate a wide countryside which has, as we have seen, a horse-racing tradition. In addition to Palmer, the town had a racehorse trainer, John Porter (1838–1922), who also wrote a novel, *Kingsclere*.

Across the road in Rugeley from St Augustine's, brambles and willow-herb twine about the old church, deserted for the new last century when, at a time of expanding congregations it became too small for Rugeley's needs. Now, although the ancient fourteenth-century tower is abandoned to nesting birds, and the arcading is open to the skies above the tombs in the nave, the thirteenth-century chancel has been preserved. It contains a brass of John Weston in the clothing of Shakespearian days, and a window with, among others, the rare St Ambrose, who gave his name to honey, ambrosia, because a swarm of bees settled on his lips in his cradle and gave him eloquence. He also appears in the east window of nearby Colton Church with a beehive at his feet.

Cannock Chase is a plateau, its highest point in the south being the British fort of Castle Ring, 801 feet above sea level and 18 acres in extent, fashioned 2,000 years ago as a refuge against any invaders coming up the Vale of Trent. Like other Chase viewpoints its horizons have been seriously restricted by Forestry Commission conifers, and ironically the one gap in the dark green wall opens up a vista to Rugeley Power Station. Southward, however, the panorama is wide, if featureless, with Barr Beacon alone to break the even skyline. This was once windmill country, and the roofless stump of Gentleshaw windmill gives a name to the pub beside it, and offers a conspicuous hoarding to advertise the brew consumed. In 1952, when Upper Longdon windmill was a holiday cottage, I was taken upstairs to admire the tremendous view over much of Staffordshire, Lichfield's 'Ladies of the Vale', the Trent valley, the rugged heights of Charnwood Forest in Leicestershire, and bleak Kinder Scout in the Derbyshire Peak district.

In Hood Lane, Longdon, Hawcroft Grange incorporates an arch and door from the demolished Derby church of St Andrew. Longdon's

'Swan With Two Necks' is a pub name which corrupts the swan-upping practice of the Vintners' Company in marking Thames swans with two 'nicks' on the bill to distinguish them from the royal swans with five nicks. Nicholas, patron saint of sailors, appears in Longdon Church dressed as a bishop at the tiller of a ship in a window by the Camms of Smethwick. There is also an inscription to Captain Thomas Orme who, in 1688, having helped deny James II's Irish army landing at Portsmouth, would have suffered execution for treason had the revolution not succeeded which placed William of Orange on the throne.

Longdon Hall stands across the A.51 from the church, and on a field path north of the hall I passed, in 1971, an underground ice-house while walking towards Farewell where, at the manor, I found a donkey farm to which Bob Clay from Shareshill was delivering a baby donkey.

'I used to pick up donkeys for a fiver apiece in Ireland', he told me. 'I went over to buy horses and I'd fill any empty spaces on the return journey with donkeys. Now they cost over £20.'

Donkeys are in great demand in England – at 1971 prices a plain Jack yearling would cost £25, a plain Jenny £35 to £40, a piebald Jenny £100, and a piebald Jack £125.

A yellow azalea lent a brilliant glow to Farewell Churchyard that afternoon, and the war memorial verse sent a glow through me, harking back to less complicated days 'When Britain's flag flies wide unfurl'd, all tyrant wrongs repelling.' But a glimpse three miles distant of Lichfield's spires reminded me of Dr Johnson's dictum, too widely held today : 'Patriotism, sir, is the last refuge of a scoundrel.'

Upper Longdon is renowned for Reg. Hollinshead's racing establishment, and west of Beaudesert Park the Rawnsley or Hednesford Hills are also famous for the training of racehorses. Hednesford is an undistinguished town with a mining tradition, though its Anglesey Hotel is an imposing building with crow-stepped gables and a balcony. Local belief is that it was built as a shooting lodge by the Marquess of Anglesey's family, the Pagets, and it is a reasonable assumption that the heraldic sign blazons their arms. Not so. They are the arms of Sir Robert Peel of Drayton Bassett, one-time prime minister, and his wife Julia Floyd, and they appear, more permanently, on the façade with the date 1831.

This is an indefinite countryside with local boundaries and nomenclature ill defined. Brownhills stretches uninterestingly along the A.452; Burntwood, with a large mental hospital, has in its church a fine window of St Hubert, patron saint of sufferers from mental illness; Chasewater, a huge expanse of canal reservoir, attracts the noisier water sports. Cannock has a fine Georgian building as its Council House, setting off a large copper beech and several ordinary beeches. This was the home of a considerable literary figure, Henry Cary, born in 1872 in Gibraltar, whose great work was his translation of Dante. Leacroft Hall, along the Lichfield Road, has associations with a stormy episode of seventeenth-century history in being the birthplace of John Hough, described in a Cannock Guide as one of the famous Seven Bishops brought to trial by James II for their opposition to the Declaration of Indulgence, part of the King's attempt to promote Roman Catholicism. Yet Hough did not become a bishop – of Oxford – until 1690, and in 1715 he declined the Primacy.

In 1687–88 Hough was certainly in dispute with James II over his election as President of Magdalen College, Oxford, when the King himself, and troops, went into action to force him out of the Fellow's house. The King relented in September 1688, and confirmed Hough's presidency, one of his last acts before fleeing the country to be superseded by William III.

I have seldom seen a less interesting church than Cannock Parish Church. Just one window is worth while, of First World War soldiers receiving Communion. In their puttees, with tin hats and haversacks, they all look like portraits. The window is a memorial to 2nd-Lt Charles Loxton of the North Staffordshire Regiment, killed in action in 1915. Note the 'label' which proclaims him the eldest son in the Loxton arms in the window.

Anywhere around Cannock you may encounter a miner, for the Cannock coalfield has three collieries in operation today, Lea Hall at Rugeley, from which coal is fed direct to the power station; West Cannock Number 5, the 'Tackeroo' pit – probably a Boer War name – at Hednesford; and Littleton at Huntington, near Cannock. A labour force of 2,090 at Lea Hall, the first completely new mine planned and brought into production by the National Coal Board, produced in the year ending 31 March 1973, over 1½ million tons; West Cannock with 1,183 workers produced 426,719 tons; and Littleton's 1779 workers produced 841,403 tons. Lea Hall and Littleton collieries have underground training facilities for apprentices and trainee miners from the Valley Training Centre at Hednesford.

Just south of Cannock on an 800-acre site incorporating the Poplars opencast mining area and adjacent Kingswood, where near by residents' protests prevented the National Coal Board obtaining permission for an extension of the opencast mining, it is proposed to construct a £40 millions 'Merrie England' complex. History is to be the raw material for entertainment, and the promoters hope on peak days to attract 100,000 visitors – with all the resultant traffic chaos. As always, consciences are assuaged with statistics of the jobs that will be created, and here 5,000 are promised. In the summer of 1973 the site closely resembled a mud-coloured moonscape – the only inkling of 'Merrie England' being the little 'Robin Hood' pub where the A.34 meets the Watling Street. Alfred Noyes had a word for it in 'Sherwood' –

> *Merry, merry England, is waking as of old,*
> *With eyes of blither hazel and hair of brighter gold;*
> *For Robin Hood is here again. . . .*

Many local cynics hope he will remain the sole manifestation of this great 'spectacular'.

Great Wyrley straggles astride the Walsall-Cannock road, and rises westward of it to Cheslyn Hay or 'Wyrley Bonk'. North of the Black Country by several miles, Great Wyrley has one thing in common with it. Where the Black Country has Anuk and Ali (Enoch and Eli), Great Wyrley has 'Jellyman', hero of a peculiar brand of stories and not entirely fictitious as there are still members of the Jellyman family thereabouts.

'The first time Jellyman climbed up a ladder was down the pit.' A Jellyman story can be either a seeming paradox of this nature or something more elaborate.

The old colliery tradition still lingers in Great Wyrley with memories of such pits and names as Fair Oak; Heath Hayes, known as the 'Fair Lady'; Hawkins'; Harrison's; and Grove Pit where, on 1 October 1930 disaster struck and killed 14 miners. Many miners would walk long distances to work, from Bloxwich to Littleton Colliery for instance, but a certain Tom Bentley carried miners from Bloxwich to Harrison's Pit in a two-horse brake called Sister Dora, after Walsall's nursing heroine. Up in Cheslyn Hay a pub is dedicated to the erstwhile subterranean industry of the area, the Colliers Arms. Its heraldic sign features a safety lamp with crossed pick and spade, and two miners kneeling at their work as supporters.

The 'Wheatsheaf' at Great Wyrley was a lively pub in the days of free bread and cheese and clay pipes, with a fight most Saturday nights. In Mrs Benton's day as hostess pigs were kept to make pig's pudding, a favourite dish of the miners. Many years ago the 'Wheatsheaf' and the 'Star' had only licences for beer and porter, but their rival, the 'Swan', held a wine and spirit licence, because of which, in the days of landlord Sam Watson, it was used as a temporary mortuary in fatal accidents, not uncommon in a mining community.

Like Rugeley, Great Wyrley also had its *cause célèbre* in the Wyrley Gang of the Terror that Prowled by Night – a mystery still unsolved. For 26 years the vicar of Great Wyrley was the Rev. Shapurji Edalji, a Parsee convert to Christianity who married an English wife and succeeded her uncle in the living. In 1888 and 1892 Edalji and his family, including a teenage son, George, were plagued with anonymous letters, and later suffered from ill-natured hoaxes, throughout which trials George kept up his studies and became a successful lawyer in Birmingham.

In 1903 a horse was found disembowelled in a local field, and on the following day George Edalji was picked up by the police on suspicion of being responsible. George accounted for his movements during the evening and night of the atrocity, and corroborative evidence came from a vet. Even so, Stafford Police called a handwriting expert to say that the writing in letters threatening more killings was the 'ill-disguised' writing of George Edalji. Signed by 'G. H. Darby, Captain of the Wyrley Gang' these letters continued to arrive from various places confessing to the killing of animals, and George Edalji was charged with 'maiming and killing a horse'. A further killing after he was gaoled was considered the work of his accomplices, and though one John Henry Green made a confession he was never charged.

On 23 October 1903 George Edalji was found guilty at Stafford Quarter Sessions and sentenced to seven years imprisonment. The press was unhappy about the case and mounted a campaign which, after three years, secured Edalji's release. He then wrote Sir Arthur Conan-Doyle, who investigated the happenings and concluded that anyone so short-sighted as Edalji could not have found his way about fields at night to commit the outrage. His articles in *The Daily Telegraph* led to an inquiry which dismissed the prosecution's case, but, though given a free pardon, Edalji was never granted compensation.

The name Wyrley means the bog myrtle glade, and the bugle horns in the Great Wyrley Arms hang from a sprig of bog myrtle.

Allowing for inheritance in the female line, the lordship of the manor of Little Wyrley has changed once only since the Norman Conquest, and the present occupant of Little Wyrley Hall, Mrs Frank Wallace, is a direct successor of a Dr Phineas Fowke who inherited the manor in 1691. Among his other attributes Phineas Fowke was a mighty walker. Setting out on one occasion to walk to Edinburgh, he had put 50 miles behind him when he decided that his boots were uncomfortable. So he returned to Little Wyrley – afoot – put on another pair and set out again, this time to complete the marathon successfully. Little Wyrley Hall has many features of great interest, among them a barn dated 1664 with a great collection of big-game hunting trophies of the late Frank Wallace, hunter, author and artist. It also has a rare wind-vane, to read which one need not leave the house. It records the wind direction indoors on the ceiling above the entrance hall.

Motorways are the reverse of romantic, just miles of anonymous tarmac, their users sardined in tin boxes like souls in limbo, unrelated to the countryside through which they pass. Numbers are used instead of names, and arithmetic is the dreariest of subjects; but at least names are given to the service areas, and its name brings history to Hilton Park between Walsall and Cannock on the M.6. The landscape immediately to westward, could the motorist but appreciate it, is parkland surrounding Hilton Hall, once the home of a branch of the Vernon family. Their coat-of-arms adorns the north lodge with its punning motto *'Vernon Semper Viret'*. This is a play on the Latin tag *'Vir non semper viret'* – 'Spring does not always flourish'. As used by the family it translates 'Vernon always flourishes'.

Hilton Hall itself is a Roman Catholic retreat home, and in the grounds are the decaying remains of a tower raised by Henry Vernon in 1741 to celebrate the victory two years earlier at Portobello of his kinsman, Admiral 'Grog' Vernon. The capture of Portobello from Spain during the War of Jenkins' Ear was no major victory, but it caught the public imagination and places and pubs were named after Portobello and Vernon – the pubs most aptly, for it was Vernon who first issued rum to the Navy.

Jack of Hilton was also associated with Hilton Hall, earlier than the Vernons when the Swynnertons were lords of the manor there. Jack was a hollow brass figure of mediaeval days, a man leaning with elbow on knee. The neighbouring lord of Essington held his lands of the Swynnertons. Every New Year's Day he brought a live goose and ushered it thrice round the fire in the great hall at Hilton. Meantime Jack, filled with water and bunged up, was placed on the fire so that the steam emerged from his mouth, the 'goose step' having to be performed while this happened.

The first Derby winner, Diomed, in 1780, was trained at Hilton Park. This horse belonged to Sir Charles Bunbury, who had made a wager that his horse would beat a horse belonging to the 12th Earl of Derby – the winner to take the stakes, the loser to found and give his name to a race. So, but for Diomed being so fleet of foot, the word Bunbury might enjoy considerable currency in the English vernacular.

Back again to coal, which alternates with racehorses in this area. Essington had its own isolated group of coalpits, little ventures such as the Struggling Monkey, Nutty Stack, Dry Bread, and the Lodge Colliery 'down the Nicket', 150 feet deep and employing 16 men, which closed in 1939. Ashmore Park and High Hill were discontinued in the 1930s when water became uncontrollable. Holly Bank ceased operations in 1956, and is being reclaimed as parkland. Number 15 Pit at Holly Bank had a feature probably unique in the national coal industry, a complete pithead gear 1,000 feet underground. When a coal seam at 1,000 feet ran out its continuation was found a further

1,000 feet below, so a new shaft was sunk below ground, creating a mine within a mine.

Many Essington babies who will never go down a pit have an early introduction to the erstwhile coal industry of the locality – the font at Allen's Rough Chapel is a 4½ feet tall replica of a miner's safety lamp. At the other end of the human span, and four miles north of Essington on the Roman Watling Street west of Cannock there is a Latin inscription on an exterior beam over a window at the Four Crosses Inn. The translation is: 'You would weep if you knew you had but a month to live. You laugh when perhaps you have not a day.'

A new road in Norton Canes is called Jerome Road. It takes its name from Jerome's Pit, the local pet name for the Conduit Pit which closed 30 years or so back. In this pit the parents of Jerome K. Jerome, the writer, invested – and lost – their money, though later the pit proved profitable.

CHAPTER EIGHT

Stafford and Stone

Helen Salt had much in common with my wife – and, I suspect, wives in general. I suffer almost non-stop wifely exhortations to sell, give away, or burn my books. Not while I have breath. But William Salt predeceased his wife, Helen, and she, in 1868 'felt herself to be encumbered by the extensive collections of books, deeds, drawings, and engravings amassed by her husband' – at a cost of up to £40,000. So she proposed selling it all at Sothebys, but, by the intervention of Lord Lichfield, she gave it instead to Staffordshire – her husband's family came from Weeping Cross, Stafford, and he, a banker, specialised in the county in his archaeological pursuits. With difficulty in finding accommodation for it, the collection was left untouched at Shugborough Hall, Lord Lichfield's home, until, in 1872, Mrs Salt's nephew Thomas Salt, the town's M.P., gave the Old Bank House in Stafford's Market Square, as a home for the collection. 'Established 1872' can still be read on the building which is now occupied by the Stafford Railway Building Society, a reminder of the local locomotive building firm, W. G. Bagnall Ltd, which produced its first locomotive in 1875. The William Salt Library moved in 1918 to its present address in Eastgate Street.

Entering Stafford from the south – during working hours at the giant English Electric Company's factory unless you enjoy traffic jams – you soon see on your right St Chad's fascinating Norman church, near the brine baths. The chancel arch is magnificent, with 48 individual heads decorating five orders of carving. Pop down to the path alongside the River Sow near by, and you will see on the bridge

22 (above) *Broughton Hall, north of Eccleshall, is famed for the ghost of 'Red Stockings', a Cavalier youth*

23 *Aqualate Hall looks out across the county's largest natural lake, Aqualate Mere, equidistant between the Black Country and the Potteries*

the Stafford Knot, note not Staffordshire. It may be the county emblem, but it came to England with the Normans as the badge of the
Barons de Stafford, builders of the castle west of the town, which was
practically destroyed by Parliament during the Civil War, and is today
something of a crumbling embarrassment to the Town Council.

Across the road from the baths the Post Office was once Chetwynd
House. You will have seen the Chetwynd Arms at Brocton on your
way to Stafford with a colourful heraldic sign bearing the chevrons
and mullets of the family once of Brocton Hall. At Chetwynd House,
Richard Brinsley Sheridan, the playwright and M.P. for Stafford, often
stayed as the guest of William Horton (1750–1832), who was the
father of the boot and shoe industry in the town.

Abundant pastures to supply the hides, and the oak bark of Cannock Chase with the water of the Sow to tan them, created the right
conditions for shoemaking and attracted young Thomas Bostock
around 1814 to set up his business in Stafford. He had been apprenticed to his father in Derbyshire, where the family had made footwear
for several generations. Three of Thomas's sons were associated
with him, and by the late 1830s they were making shoes at Stafford,
Stone and Northampton. Shoemakers in those days were mainly out-
workers, supplied with material and lasts by the manufacturers.
Today the huge Stafford factory of Lotus Ltd, is one of the town's
largest employers of labour. The universally-known trade names,
Lotus and Delta, come from lotus flowers floating in the Nile Delta
of Egypt, where fine footwear was made in the days of the Pharoahs.

The patron saint of shoemakers, St Crispin, appears on the Stone
road on a pub sign. He was a skilful cobbler, content to work gratu-
itously and to preach the Christian faith, for which he was tormented
with shoemakers' awls and eventually beheaded around A.D. 290.

No sooner has Stafford laid claims to Sheridan at the Post Office
than it claims in an inscription outside the 'Swan' an association for
that hotel with George Borrow in *The Romany Rye*. He was employed
there as an ostler in 1852.

Among the decorations of the High House, Stafford's black-and-
white masterpiece in Greengate Street is a fleur-de-lys in the angle of
a scythe. An inscription explains that Richard Dorrington completed
the building in 1555, and that Charles I and Prince Rupert stayed

24   *The grounds of Alton Towers, laid out by 'Capability Brown'
above the River Churnet, abound with the follies and fancies of
John Talbot, 15th Earl of Shrewsbury*

Stafford and Stone

there in September 1642 as guests of Captain Richard Sneyd. The curved handle of a scythe is a 'snead', obviously a pun on Sneyd.

Stafford Parish Church, St Mary's, is a glorious place with windows that tell of Stafford's earlier history when, known as Bethnei, it was given in charge of St Bertelin by a King of Mercia. The strength of the pillars at the crossing can be felt almost physically, and one cannot miss the crop of 'poppy-heads' above the pew ends, carved with faces and foliage. In the north transept a memorial to the Hon. Barbara Clifford tells that 'she died after a miscarriage' in 1786, aged 39, leaving 12 children. Her husband, the Hon. Thomas Clifford, survived her 'only 10 months and 16 days' – dying, maybe, of remorse. A bust of Izaak Walton, the 'Compleat Angler', born in Stafford and baptised in the church in 1593, has bullrushes carved beneath it, a fitting symbol.

The third stone on your left from Mill Street against the churchyard wall commemorates Mr Bernard Fry, surgeon, who died on 28 January 1827, aged 40. His lengthy epitaph begins:

> When typhus in the Stafford Poor-house raged,
> Fry, like an angel, strove the bane t'expel:
> To that kind feeling which his zeal engaged
> For saving others, he a victim fell.

The Market Square is the administrative heart of Stafford – town and county – surrounded by the Shire Hall and the County Council Buildings, the Borough Hall, and the Guildhall. I have two personal memories of Stafford. In 1931 I spent a month in lodgings above a florist's shop in Salter Street when my room was so tiny, so very dark, and so permeated by a funereal scent of lilies that I lay abed with an unpleasant sense of lying in a coffin. Then, there were my days in Stafford Gaol – Sundays only I hasten to add, as a regular visiting member of a forum. We were always sure of an audience; it was marched in some 350 strong. The questions, too, were of a high standard. A disadvantage was the risk of being greeted by prisoners one had known, as happened twice in one afternoon to the acute embarrassment of one member of our brains trust.

Stafford is a railway town – as witness 'Isabel', which stands re-

132

splendent in green and polished copper opposite the station frontage. Built in 1897 for the Cliff Hill Granite Company of Markfield, Leicestershire, it was returned to Stafford in 1953 and makes an apt memorial to the 3,000 locomotives produced by Bagnall's at the Castle Engine Works. Derby, too, is a railway town, a great centre of the old Midland Railway. It was inevitable in the railway age that Stafford and Derby should be linked, and this was done with the opening on December 23 1867, of the Stafford and Uttoxeter Railway, the old 'Clog and Knocker', which ran for 13 miles through four stations built by the company, Salt, Ingestre and Weston, Chartley and Stowe, and Grindley. A fifth, Stafford Common Station, of obscure origin, had appeared on maps by 1879.

The S. and U. joined the North Staffordshire Railway at Bromshall Junction, two miles west of Uttoxeter, where the traveller to Derby continued on the N.S.R. and the Midland, or by the later Great Northern route. The early days of the S. and U. reveal an astonishing similarity with modern problems; the cost of the land was double the estimate, cash was invariably short, labour difficulties were constant and caused grievous delay. So poor was business that by 1878 the High Court of Chancery was threatening closure, but this was averted by an exchange of running powers over their various lines with the N.S.R., the Great Northern, and the L.N.W.R. Then, on 1 August 1881, came the 'Great Northern invasion of Staffordshire' when that company bought the S. and U. for £100,000. The Great Northern merged into the London and North Eastern Railway in 1923. It continued four passenger trains daily each way on the S. and U., and the goods and milk traffic, but on 3 December 1939 the passenger service was withdrawn. With nationalisation the S. and U. came under the London Midland Region in April 1951, the final blow falling on 5 March 1951 when goods traffic was ended except from Stafford to Stafford Common and the R.A.F. 16th Maintenance Unit. Salt Station had closed in 1939 – now the remaining three shut their doors.

The old line looped from Stafford northward round Hopton Heath, the scene on 19 March 1643 of a Royalist victory during the Civil War, though gained by the loss of their leader, the Earl of Northampton, whose body the defeated Roundheads surrendered for the return of their soldiers and ordnance captured in the battle.

Salt Station served also Sandon across the Trent, a feudal village
dominated by Sandon Hall and its park, the home of the Earl of
Harrowby, who is also Viscount Sandon and Baron Harrowby in
Lincolnshire. It is difficult to believe that this lovely sylvan place
cost two men their lives, yet in a duel in Hyde Park on 15 November
1712 over a law suit concerning the Sandon estate both James, 4th
Duke of Hamilton, then the owner, and Charles, Lord Mohun, a
notorious ruffian, were killed.

Sandon village clusters round the 'Dog and Doublet', colourful in
early summer with lilac and laburnum with conifers above. An old
stage-coach inn kept by one James Ballantine, it had a verse scratched
on a window:

> *Most travellers to whom these roads are known,*
> *Would rather stay at Sandon than at Stone:*
> *Good chaises, horses, treatment, and good wines*
> *They always meet with at James Ballantine's.*

It was a grandson of the duelling duke who, around 1780, sold the
Sandon estate to Nathaniel Ryder, the 1st Earl of Harrowby, who,
becoming M.P. for Tiverton at 22, was a great friend of William Pitt,
as was the 2nd Earl who became his Foreign Secretary. Pitt's Column
on a hill in Sandon Park, and Perceval's Seat, a monument to the
Prime Minister, Spencer Perceval, assassinated in the Commons in
1812, were both erected by the 2nd Earl.

A long narrow uphill lane on the fringe of the park leads to
Sandon Church, and beside it, beneath some conifers, is the Harrowby
burial ground. Here, on Easter Eve, 1956, were laid the bodies of the
5th Earl and his Countess, Mabel, who were married in 1887, the
Earl surviving 'his beloved partner of 69 years' by only three days.
His epitaph says that 'he built the central layout of Sandon village and
many farms, smallholdings, and cottages, and planted some 100,000
trees'. Of their daughter Frances, who died in 1965, her memorial
says 'She shared with her parents an immense sense of humour'.

Sandon Church has a glorious view from its west end, and inside
seven Ryder hatchments decorate the ceilings, a pulpit has a sound-
ing board, and there is an elaborately-carved screen, replete with

heraldry, dedicated in 1929 by the 5th Earl and his Countess in profound thanksgiving that their heir, Viscount Sandon, survived the First World War – unlike at least three other Ryders commemorated here. Earlier owners of Sandon Park lie in the church, including one George Digby with a ponderous verse which declares him 'The noblest tree in all the wood' and later a star 'dispensing his seraphick light'. He came of the family which produced Everard Digby, one of the executed Gunpowder Plotters, but there is an even more rabid Roman Catholic here in Hugh Erdeswick, 'the sorest and most dangerous Papist in England'. The Erdeswicks were lords of the manor of Sandon, and their monuments are the most ornate in the church.

Sampson Erdeswick the Second is the most famous of the family. Clad in a red tunic and cloak, he shares a huge monument with his two wives wearing black dresses and white ruffs. The second wife was the mother, by her first marriage, of the ill-fated Everard Digby. A considerable scholar, Sampson's hobbies were genealogy and heraldry, and in some explanatory words in the church 'he found himself free to work his will on the chancel, and thus he set about a unique and extraordinarily-ambitious scheme of family and local history, first enriching the tombs of his grandfathers by adding, in heraldic form, shields which in pictorial form record the marriages of those buried in the tombs with family trees springing from them.' Sampson died in 1603 having produced in his *Survey of Staffordshire* the first county history. The church notes continue : 'This enthusiastic man raised his own magnificent monument to be a memorial to himself and a key to his wall painting.'

Near the old Salt Station an elderly resident once reminisced to me about the old 'Clog and Knocker' in its heyday.

'Lots of people used to come into the country by train for an evening drink at the 'Holly Bush', he told me. 'The last train returned from Uttoxeter near closing time – the Boozers' Train we called it – and they would sit drinking until they could hear it. Then there'd be a mad rush for the station. But the milk train was even more exciting. Horse-drawn floats full of churns came from farms for miles around. The train crew knew who to expect, and if some were late the engine would stand there hooting to hurry them up. Then round the bend they'd come, charging like a chariot race up the station drive into the milk bay.'

The line crossed the Trent into Weston and Ingestre Station, which stood in the village of Weston nearly two miles north of Ingestre Hall, the old home of the Talbots, the Earls of Shrewsbury. Weston has an exceptionally large village green and a fine sign at the Saracen's Head.

The first engine owned by the S. and U. Railway was a light tank named 'Shrewsbury and Talbot', but it crashed on Hopton Bank on 1 February 1873 killing its crew. Ingestre Hall, surrounded by spacious agricultural and park land, is no longer the home of the Talbots – it was bought by West Bromwich as an art centre for its schoolchildren when the 21st Earl sold it in the mid-1960s. A fire in 1882 damaged the Jacobean pile, but the restorers left a handsome highly-fenestrated building with massive bays, roof balustrades, and a central ogee-shaped dome. The fire destroyed documents which could have proved that the adjacent church was designed by Christopher Wren for the earlier owner of Ingestre, Walter Chetwynd. The oaken chancel screen and pulpit are said to have been carved by Grinling Gibbons. Marcus Whiffen in *Stuart and Georgian Churches* writes, however, that 'he quite certainly never executed a single piece of wood carving for any church outside London', but he does say that Ingestre is one of the only two churches outside London whose claims to be designed by Wren 'will bear scrutiny', the other being at Farley, Wiltshire. Dr Robert Plot, the Staffordshire historian, was secretary of the Royal Society during Wren's presidency, and it is suggested that Plot's account of Ingestre Church may have come from Wren himself.

Two miles south of Ingestre stands an ornate domed and turreted Tudor gatehouse with Doric, Ionic, and Corinthian columns in the windows of its three storeys. It has outlasted two halls to which it gave access, one Tudor, the other Georgian, demolished in 1927. In 1586 Mary, Queen of Scots, arrived at Tixall from nearby Chartley, her retinue gaily caparisoned for a hunt. The Babington Plot had just been broken, and Mary was implicated, so she was lured to Tixall where, for 17 days, she was imprisoned while her apartments at Chartley were searched. The evidence found there was fatal, and when Mary rode out of that gatehouse again, telling the poor people who had gathered that she could not dispense alms because 'I am a beggar too; all is taken from me', she was taking her first steps towards the headsman's axe at Fotheringhay on 8 February 1587.

Another famous conspiracy, the Titus Oates Plot, was to cast its shadow over Tixall when, in 1678, Oates involved the steward Stephen Dugdale who swore that his master, Lord Aston, and Lord Stafford were conspiring to murder Charles II. Aston was sent to the Tower for seven years until the exposure of Oates's perjury, when he was released, to defend Chester Castle for James II before retiring to Tixall. Stafford's fate was more brutal. Dugdale vowed that, beneath the Tixall gatehouse arch, Stafford had offered him £500 to kill the king; unsupported testimony, but sufficient to send the 66-year-old Stafford to the block. When Oates was discredited, Stafford's widow was created Countess of Stafford for life, and her son was given the earldom of Stafford, which lasted through four holders. The Stafford title today is a barony, the 14th Baron, Basil Francis Nicholas Fitzherbert, residing at Swynnerton Park, Stone.

Chartley and Stowe Station, two miles on from Weston and Ingestre, stood just north of Stowe Church – it still does, converted into a residence. After its closure the station hit the headlines once when someone purloined the 'Gents', an unusual antique structure matched only by one at Mow Cop Station. Half a mile from the station the ruins are visible on their hilltop of Chartley Castle where Mary, Queen of Scots, was brought prisoner in December 1585, to be involved in the false-bottomed beer barrel episode already recounted in Chapter 5. Two round stone towers are all that remain of the castle, built early in the thirteenth century by Ranulph, 6th Earl of Chester, a brother-in-law of William de Ferrers, Earl of Derby, both of them witnesses of the will of King John. Ferrers inherited Chartley Castle at Ranulph's death, and it stayed with his family until 1461 when the Ferrers heiress married Sir Walter Devereux who died beside Richard III at Bosworth Field. His great grandson was the first Earl of Essex, a courtier of Elizabeth I, and after his death his home was selected, against the wishes of his 18-year-old son and heir as the prison of Mary, Queen of Scots. This young man, the 2nd Earl of Essex, became a favourite of Elizabeth, but outgrowing her affection for him she had him beheaded. Chartley then passed to his son,

Robert Devereux who, as the 3rd Earl of Essex, became the famous Cromwellian leader. With his death in 1646 his sister's grandson, Sir Robert Shirley, inherited Chartley, and his son was created Lord Chartley by Charles II. The Shirleys, descended from a family of Ettington, Warwickshire, trace their descent back to Saxon days, though the Chartley branch, ennobled as the Earls Ferrers, used another family seat, at Staunton Harold, Leicestershire.

Late in the eighteenth century there was a disastrous fire at Chartley, necessitating re-building, but the Shirleys remained in possession until the early 1900s. Also gone are the Chartley cattle, white beasts with black ears and branching horns descended from the primitive English aurochs which were first domesticated by the Romans. The Chartley herd, never quite tame, roamed the park for 700 years until, in the time of the last Shirley, it was almost wiped out with tuberculosis. The survivors were moved to Woburn Abbey, where they can still be seen by visitors to the Duke of Bedford's seat.

Stowe Church is remarkable for memorials to a father and son both holders of the Victoria Cross. Mention is made in Chapter 4 of the baronetcy conferred on Sir Geoffrey Congreve – subsequently killed in the Second World War – in recognition of the services of his father, Sir Walter Congreve, who won the Victoria Cross in the Boer War. Geoffrey was a younger son – his elder brother, William La Touche Congreve, had won his Victoria Cross in the First World War, being killed in action on the Somme, aged 25, in 1916, and he, with his father, is commemorated in Stowe Church.

The old 'Clog and Knocker' moved on another two miles to Grindley Station and then across the River Blithe and through the 321 yards of the Locksley Tunnel to join the main line at Bromshall Junction. Why is it, that with the nearby village spelled Bramshall, the junction is known and written as Bromshall?

North-west of Stafford, across the M6 Motorway, is the home country of Izaak Walton, where he sought the 'chavender or chub' and other species in the River Sow and its tributaries such as the Meece Brook. Today his juvenile devotees favour such places as Shaky Bridge on the Sow near Seighford, a village of some antiquity with a Norman chancel arch to its church, the Holly Bush Inn bearing the date 1675, and Seighford Hall Hotel, the black and white ancestral home of the Elde family, still represented in the village. In 1559 Elizabeth I gave the hall to Richard Elde, paymaster to her forces in Ulster, and a visit she is said to have made is commemorated by her coat-of-arms over the fireplace in the residents' lounge. A more domestic touch is the ghost said to be that of a one-time governess at the hall, which always appeared on the appointment of a new governess.

There are two hatchments of the Eldes in Seighford chancel. Of the tomb of Sir William Bowyer and his lady, who lived in the reign of Elizabeth I, the vicar told me something I had not known before. In common with many tombs it has the couple's six children around it.

'You will see two of the girls have their hands clasped in their laps', said the vicar. 'Two others hold them raised in prayer, and I have been told that the symbolism is that the ones with clasped hands were married, while the other two are praying for husbands.'

Walton is most often associated with more spectacular scenes like Dovedale, Wolfscote and Beresford Dales, the territory of his angling friend, Charles Cotton. Izaak himself fished the lesser streams of Staffordshire, and at Shallowford, three miles north of Seighford, his cottage is preserved as a museum by Stafford Borough Council. A long, low, black-and-white building, pretty with flowers, its well-tended lawn stretches to the busy railway alongside the Meece Brook. Its name, Halfhead Cottage, is a corruption of 'half hide' – a hide was about 120 acres, and possibly the farm on which the cottage stood was about 60 acres.

The visitor learns from the museum that there was more than angling and contemplation to Izaak Walton. Born on 9 August 1593, he was apprenticed in London and became a free brother of the Ironmongers Company, though he may never have been an ironmonger. In 1614 he owned 'half a draper's shop' in Fleet Street, so perhaps it was inevitable that he turned to writing – the lives of worthies such as John Donne who was vicar of St Dunstan's, nearby. In 1653 came *The Compleat Angler*.

Walton had retired from business and was often at Halfhead Farm. Izaak married in turn two women related to famous bishops – Cranmer and Ken – himself became steward in 1660 to Dr George Morley, Bishop of Worcester, and moved with him to his new see of

Winchester. The Compleat Angler finally hung up his fishing boots at the ripe old age of 90 in 1683 and is buried in Winchester Cathedral. When last I visited the museum in August 1971 the custodian was 89-year-old James Popple, a surname that would have pleased Walton – it means a ripple on the water.

Stone, six miles north of Stafford, is a canal centre and a brewery town. The Trent and Mersey Canal still brings work there through the Canal Cruising Company Ltd, where, in three dry docks, four standard cruisers are made most years, while boats such as *Erminilda*, named after a queen of Mercia, wife of King Wulfhere, can be hired. Stone is exceptionally well placed for travel on the Cheshire canals, the Llangollen Canal, and southward. In the canal company office there is a magnificent framed map entitled 'The Voyage of the Mancunian, August 27 to September 10, 1955', which depicts in graphic colour the 436 miles travelled by a Leeds Grammar School party via the Trent and Mersey, Coventry, and Oxford Canals, and the Thames to London, returning largely by the Grand Union Canal and through Birmingham. Painted by the school art master, the map incorporates 30 civic coats-of-arms and charming vignettes of places visited.

Joule's Brewery, of which Stone's streets are pleasantly redolent along with the mouth-watering bakery smell from the Scotch Brook Restaurant, used the canal as its early means of transport, its fleet of boats co-operating with the Wedgwood fleet in moving their different products of ale and earthenware. Joule's red cross trade mark is a memory that twelfth-century monks were Stone's first brewers, the trade being revived in 1719 in the High Street. Francis Joule from Youlgreave, Derbyshire, took over in 1785, followed by his son John, who became a magistrate, died at Meaford Old Hall in 1875, and has a memorial in Stone Church.

Stone's High Street, where 38 coaches a day once pulled up at the bow-windowed Crown Hotel with its white portico, is now a one-way thoroughfare, particularly dangerous to pedestrians of a 'Keep Left' generation who might inadvertently step off the offside pavement with backs to traffic travelling far too quickly down this narrow street. Cumberland House in the High Street is a reminder that in 1745, when 'Bonnie Prince Charlie' and his Scots reached Derby, the

Duke of Cumberland, seeking to engage them with the Crown forces, made his headquarters in Stone.

The traditional Staffordshire footwear industry, along with the manufacture of scientific glassware, is still strong in Stone. A single boot and shoe manufacturer in 1787 had become 16 in 1851 when some 500 homes produced items for shoes and boots, an outwork system which ended with the establishment of factories. A slump in 1892 left 300 operatives unemployed.

Roman Catholicism has always been active in and around Stone. Aston Hall, just southward, belonged to the Fitzherberts, whose resident priests had tended the relics of St Chad in several of their homes, and there in 1837 a richly-decorated casket was found in the chapel. It contained relics of saints, and four large bones were accepted by Pope Gregory xvi as the remains of St Chad. Birmingham's new Roman Catholic cathedral was about to be dedicated, so the bones were installed there and there they remain. In 1889 St Chad's Cathedral gave Stone a *quid pro quo*. William Bernard Ullathorne, who as a mission priest in Australia had worked hard for better conditions for the Botany Bay convicts, became the first Roman Catholic Bishop of Birmingham, and upon his death he was taken to Stone for burial in St Dominic's Priory Church.

Kenilworth Priory in Warwickshire controlled Stone's mediaeval abbey from its inception, and during the thirteenth-century Barons Wars, when Simon de Montfort was custodian of Kenilworth Castle, his enemies, the royalist forces of Henry iii, attacked Stone. Stone's other Warwickshire association is a remarkable one. Richard Barnfield was buried at the parish church, St Michael's, in 1627, but in the rebuilding of 1750 and the transformation of the churchyard into expansive lawns, his grave has been lost. He was a poet in his earlier years, and two of his poems became attributed to Shakespeare, whose work they were thought to be until comparatively recently.

I must protest at Stone's canonisation of Ruffin and Wulfhade, the sons of King Wulfhere, murdered by their father because of their conversion to Christianity. They are entitled to the martyrs' palms, but not to the haloes they are given, or their description as saints in a window at St Michael's. Burston Church, nearby, is dedicated to St Ruffin, and the earlier dedication of St Michael's itself was St Mary and St Wulfhade. The rector agreed with me that this must be some unofficial 'canonisation' arising from the circumstance of their having been murdered and buried near the site of the church.

The great name in Stone Church is that of Admiral Sir John Jervis, Earl St Vincent, who was born at Meaford Hall, and died in 1823 to be buried in the mausoleum east of the church. His bust by Chantrey, a portrait painted by one of his officers in *Foudroyant*, from which he boarded and captured the French warship *La Pégase* in 1782, and a sanctuary window celebrating the centenary of his greatest victory, over the Spanish fleet off Cape St Vincent in 1797 – these are some of the features of the church. The commendable brevity of his motto, 'Thus', contrasts with the lengthy inscription on his memorial tablet. This recalls his part as commander of the *Porcupine* in 1759 at the taking of Quebec and the conquest of Canada, and how, as First Lord of the Admiralty, he fought again 'Fraud, Peculation, and Profucion in the administration of the country's finances'.

You will search Burke's *Peerage* in vain for an Earl St Vincent today. The earldom died with the admiral in default of male issue, but the viscounty passed to a nephew. Like the earl, the 4th Viscount, John Edward Leveson Jervis, also served in ships – of sorts – the ships of the desert, the Heavy Camel Corps, and he died of wounds at Abuklea in the Sudan in 1885, his aunt, Lady Forester of Meaford Hall, erecting a new chancel and organ chamber to his memory.

In secular terms Stone remembers its associations in some of its street names. Forester and Jervis roads are off Priory Road, along with Dewint Road – a memory of a Stone landscape artist, Peter De Wint (1784–1849). Here, too, are Sutherland and Gower roads, the dukedom and the earldom of the great family who are also marquises of Stafford and viscounts Trentham. One of their family names gives its name to Granville Square, Stone, bounded in part by the old-world thatched 'Crown and Anchor' and the Post Office, where a graceful plane tree casts its shade on the war memorial.

CHAPTER NINE

Eccleshall and the Woodland Quarter

Autherley Junction is a name little known to the man in the street, but to canal travellers it is the 'Clapham Junction' where boats which have locked down from the Birmingham Canal and the Black Country find a contrast as fantastic as any pantomime transformation scene. These boats have come laboriously down 21 locks from Wolverhampton to the Staffordshire and Worcestershire Canal at Aldersley Junction, turned right, and within a mile reached Autherley, the portal to 80 miles of tranquil beauty on the Shropshire Union Canal, the first 25 of these miles being in Staffordshire, where they reveal a pastoral peace little suspected in this county. For 80 miles from Autherley Junction the 'Shroppy' strikes northward to Ellesmere Port on the Manchester Ship Canal, and several times in the early 1950s I did that journey with boatman Leslie Berridge and his family, dossing in the 'hay loft' of the butty *Kubina* for three nights each way, and by day taking my turn at the tiller of the motor-boat *Towy*. We travelled from the Tar Distillers at Oldbury empty, and returned with 45 tons of crude tar from the oil refinery at Stanlow beside the Manchester Ship Canal. This waterborne tar traffic is finished, but the 'Shroppy' is one of Britain's most popular canals with pleasure boats, and their navigators enjoy the same rural felicity that I recorded 20 years ago in my canal logbook:

'The Shropshire Union Canal was formed in the mid-1840s by the amalgamation of the Ellesmere and Chester Canal, the Birmingham

Eccleshall and the Woodland Quarter

and Liverpool Junction, the Shrewsbury Canal, and two parts of the Montgomeryshire Canal, and it was the Birmingham and Liverpool Junction section we were now travelling, authorised in 1826 to reduce the distance and lockage between Birmingham and Liverpool to 94 miles with 69 locks, as against 114 miles and 99 locks via the Trent and Mersey Canal. To our right aircraft glistened in the sun on Wolverhampton Municipal Airport, and far beyond, across the valley of the Penk, was the dark horizon of Cannock Chase, always sombre, while over the hedge on our left potato pickers were busy in the fields. It was becoming an expansive afternoon with a bounding breeze from the north-west, a benign sun, and tumbled cumulo-stratus cloud. Already, far inland though we were, seagulls were flying along the line of the canal, and lapwings hurried about the stubble and gambolled in the wind. Golden domes of wheat fields alternated with the shining green of sugar beet, and as we approached Brewood the canal narrowed with larch and silver birch bordering either bank. This was a foretaste of the deep narrow cuttings which alternate with long stretches of broader canal high on embankments. Just short of Brewood an ornamental balustered bridge carried the drive to Chillington Hall across the canal, and as we emerged into the open again Brewood was visible to our right across a meadow where black and white Friesian cattle matched a magpie cottage or two before a red row of houses sloped up to the church spire.

Barely more than a mile and we were crossing the Watling Street, high on Telford's fine aqueduct, dated 1832, with the Aqueduct Inn beside it. Nearby a canal signpost read 'Autherley 6, Nantwich 33'. With only about 20 miles behind us from Oldbury we were having an early night, and in two miles more we tied up at Wheaton Aston lock at 6.30 p.m. Here the first job was a counting of heads to make sure the six children were all present. The wear and tear on Mrs Berridge's nerves is considerable, and from time to time, not having noticed one of her brood for some time, she would raise a shrill enquiry until he emerged from somewhere. I was the only swimmer aboard, but Les is a past master at fishing young Leslie out of the cut on a boathook.

Our companions for the night, tied up before us, were the Walters family aboard Thomas Clayton's *Ribble* and *Forth*. In addition to

144

their complement of small children they had on their decks a diminutive hen coop with a couple of Plymouth Rocks, and a kennel with a nondescript mongrel. Throughout the day there had been incessant cups of tea on our boats; hunks of bread and cheese had sustained us after the tussle with the Wolverhampton locks, and now came an evening meal of bacon and beans eaten on the cabin roof in the cheerful glow of a westering sun. A mile or so to eastward this lit up the square tower of Lapley Church so invitingly that I set out to inspect it. Across fields I tramped among the stubble of recently-stooked barley, through bracken neck high, over green pastures with lengthening shadows to the crunching of cows as they cropped the grass. Once a whirring covey of partridges erupted from the corn, and I came at last to winding lanes which took me through the village to the church.

From the porch I looked back over much of Staffordshire and all Shropshire, stretched towards the sunset with the Wrekin dark and prominent. The even upland skyline of Cannock Chase closed the east behind the church. I wondered if the striking white memorial in the churchyard referred to the earthly or heavenly habitat of the deceased – William Bickford of Paradise, who died in 1896. I could see no such placename on the Stafford One-Inch map. The tower is half way along the length of Lapley Church, and on buttresses to north and south it bore the names, Edward Berree and William Tonck – C.W.1637. The C.W. obviously identifies the couple as churchwardens when the tower was buttressed. The mediaeval Dutch font, carved with biblical scenes, was probably thrown out of the church by Cromwellians, for it was found around 1850 doing duty as a drinking trough in a farmyard and restored to its rightful position on a modern shaft and base. An enormous charity board in the nave recorded a benefaction by Edward Perkes in 1662 when he 'gave £1 a year for ever to the poore of Lapley, to be paid out of a meadow calling Stinking Lake'. In the sanctuary are plaques to members of two local families, the Vaughans and the Hartleys, who have given their names respectively to the pubs in Lapley and Wheaton Aston, each with a heraldic sign.

I left the church to the clangour of its bells as the ringers put in some practice. The sun, to right of the Wrekin, was sinking into an ominous cloud-bank, with an equally evil canopy of blue-black clouds above. By the time I reached the boats there was a clear amber sky in the west and the inky stratus had turned grey with orange and red wisps at the zenith, and there were two moons, both gibbous, one in the sky, the other in the canal.

The Berridges had adjourned to the Hartley Arms, and I followed them. There débâcle overtook me. I had never played darts but Les encouraged me to give him several games and though defeated I was not dishonoured. Then Mr Walters took him on and it was suggested that 'the writing gentleman' might keep the score. This necessitated subtracting the players' initial scores from 301, and continuing to subtract successive scores from the remainder. Painfully I bent to my task, helped by the chalk and blackboard, but the boatmen, with whom education is not a strong suit, regarded me with astonishment and proceeded to do this arithmetic in their heads in the twinkling of an eye. Leaving them to it, and Mrs Berridge to a cosy chat with Mrs Walters over two bottles of stout, I picked my way back to the boats by the light of my torch which was my sole illumination in the 'hay loft' as I struggled into pyjamas, pulled my trousers, socks, and pullover over them, and resigned myself to a sleepless night in my two blankets. My fears were realised, and the melancholy tremolo of the owls gave place to early cock-crow before I contrived an hour's slumber.

The square of starry sky seen through my hatch had become pearly-grey when I was awakened by dull thuds and rumblings, and a buoyancy about *Kubina* which suggested that Les was astir. It was not quite 5 a.m., but I was not sorry to get up. There was mist on the water and a suspicion of sunshine. With much spluttering from the engines of *Ribble* and *Towy* we were off, a big day of nearly 50 miles before us. A golden sun had come up over Cannock Chase, and its rays, slanting from beneath mother-of-pearl cloudlets, threw long shadows from tree and hedgerow on the low sea of mist covering the pastures until it looked like icebound flood water. So dense was the mist, and so even, that only the tops of the corn stooks were visible above it, and in a cutting tall ashes thrust their topmost branches into the sunlight. Then Les gave me the tiller, and with instructions to slow down two boats' lengths before the frequent

25   *The garish Roman Catholic church at Cheadle is a*
masterpiece of Pugin

accommodation bridges, he went astern leaving me sole custodian of
Towy.

The village of Gnosall has a deep cutting where ash and sycamores
meet overhead to form a tunnel of greenery, and a more authentic
tunnel 100 yards long, cut through the red sandstone, its walls
jagged, natural, and unbricked. It also has a ghost. Georgina Jackson's
collection of folklore tells us that on 21 January 1879 a labourer was
attacked at Gnosall canal bridge by a black creature with great white
eyes which a policeman readily identified as the ghostly 'man-monkey'
said to haunt the spot since a man was drowned in the canal there.
Imaginations might well run rife at Gnosall however, with the
Boat Inn at one bridge and the 'Navigation' at the next, only 300
yards away. We cruised out of Gnosall above the Norbury valley
on an embankment a mile long with stop locks at each end to im-
pound the water should a breach occur. At Norbury Junction, where
there is a maintenance depot, the Newport Canal branched to the
left for its pleasant four miles to Newport in Shropshire. Traffic
no longer used the Newport branch from Norbury, and the top
lock behind the junction bridge had been converted into a dry
dock.

Another of the now familiar narrow cuttings carried us, at the
Eccleshall road bridge, beneath the shortest telegraph pole on the
Shropshire Union. Telegraph wires run along the towpath and are
enabled to zigzag beneath the lofty arch of this bridge by the construction of a second lower arch on which stands just the cross trees
of a telegraph pole. While we breakfasted we saw three kingfishers,
the tower of High Offley Church came into view on a hill a mile
to our right, and soon we had a first glimpse of Cadbury's Knighton
factory, where I saw hundreds of milk churns on a loading bay back
in the works. After a morning walk along the towpath north of
Knighton I perched astride *Towy's* nose, the red stud sticking in my
stomach and my shadow thrown before me as we travelled through
plains and ploughlands where I rejoiced to see conical stooks rather
than the oblong bales which bespeak mechanical harvesting. Substan-
tial red farms glided past, and all the time distance was ticking off
slowly but surely, a milepost 'Autherley 22' proclaiming that we had
passed out of Staffordshire.'

*26   Some of the kilns still remain in the Potteries despite intense
redevelopment of its derelict industrial areas*

A June morning in 1972 found me in Lapley again, abandoning my car to go walking. The story of Lapley Church begins in 1061 when Aldred, Archbishop of York, went on a pilgrimage to Rome, taking with him many noble Englishmen, among them Burchard, youngest son of Algar, Earl of Mercia, and a grandson of Lady Godiva. Returning home from Rome Burchard became mortally ill and was nursed by the monks of St Remigius at Rheims. Before his death he requested that he be buried in the abbey at Rheims, promising in return that certain lands around Lapley should be put at the disposal of the Abbot of Rheims. Earl Algar, with the consent of Edward the Confessor, fulfilled his dying son's promise, and accordingly, around 1063, Benedictine monks from the abbey of St Remigius formed a cell at Lapley and built a church and priory. The abbots of Rheims, through their representatives the Priors of Lapley, became Lords of the Manor of Lapley, which they held until the dissolution of alien priories by Henry v in 1414, when the lands and property were transferred to an English college at Tong, Shropshire. After 1414, therefore, the church became the parish church of Lapley.

Walking the towpath of the canal I had cruised 20 years earlier, with the sun warm on my back and a riot of assorted vetches underfoot, my intention was to investigate Joan Eaton's Cross between the canal and Church Eaton. So I left the towpath at High Onn Wharf, where the waters of St Edith's Well are said to have curative properties in eye ailments. Joan Eaton's Cross turned out to be merely a triangle of grass at a lane junction where Joan, a witch, was supposedly burned. No sign of any memorial cross remains. Her speciality was the customary witch's trick of milking the cows dry, and a farmer from Red House Farm, Little Onn, challenged her to milk his prolific dun cow dry, a feat never before accomplished. The cow was tethered, and Joan, seated on a milking stool, began milking the beast through a riddle. Try as she could, the cow continued to give milk until, tiring of the performance, it kicked the witch off her stool, uprooted the tethering stake and ran away – leaving the imprint of one hoof on a large glacial boulder nearby. The cow ran to Worcester over 30 miles distant where it was buried near the cathedral, and the outraged witch put a curse on Red House Farm, saying that if ever the stone was removed all the cattle would die. A sequel to this curse was that when a Colonel Ashton did have the stone removed all the Red House Farm cattle died.

At Bradley where in June the creeper-covered church tower rises like a cliff from the foam of a glorious white chestnut tree, the screen is worth seeing, but it was the Webb Stone, marked in Gothic on the map, which drew me to the village. Taller than the Red House stone it has much the same story, that a farmer at White House Farm once moved it and all his cattle died, so he replaced it where it now stands beside a bungalow. Spinsters are expected to bow to it as they pass on pain of never marrying, and it is said to turn completely round at one minute to midnight. Pleasant field paths and a hop, skip, and jump over the Whiston Brook took me back to my car at Lapley after a gentle 12 miles afoot.

West of the 'Shroppy' Staffordshire marches with Shropshire through delightful pastoral countryside down the valley of the Back Brook from Weston-under-Lizard, on the ubiquitous Watling Street, to Forton. Among the few habitations in the area is Wrestlers Farm, once Wrestlers Inn, famed for gaming, cockfighting – and wrestling.

The 'Lizard' at Weston derives from 'lazar', a leper, and Lizard Hill just across in Shropshire once housed a leper colony. Weston Park is the home of the Earl of Bradford, and the church is within it, adjacent to Weston Hall. Dedicated to St Andrew, it has the only window I know depicting him crucified on his diagonal cross. It also has a memorial to two daughters of the 3rd Earl, Lady Lucy Caroline and Lady Charlotte Anne Bridgeman, who lost their lives in 1858 when, on retiring after dinner, Lucy somehow set fire to her clothes, and as Charlotte tried to beat out the flames both girls perished. Neighbouring Blymhill Church with its unusual and picturesque dormer windows, the living of which is in the patronage of the Earls of Bradford, has four windows to the sisters' memory with an inscription that they 'were snatched away in the prime of life by the awful effects of fire'.

In 1619 John Bridgeman, son of a Devon family, became Bishop of Chester. Five generations later his descendants came to Weston Park where, in 1815, one of them raised an obelisk to Wellington's victory at Waterloo and was himself raised to the Earldom of Bradford and the Viscounty of Newport, lapsed titles revived from the Newport family into which the Bridgemans had married. The bishop's eldest surviving son was called Orlando, a name retained in the family down to the present and 6th Earl. The first Orlando was a Royalist; he was the first baronet created by Charles II after the Restoration, and he presided at the trial of the Regicides. In the year that Orlando received his baronetcy his heir, John, had been nominated as a Knight of the Royal Oak, a new branch of knighthood conceived by Charles II to commemorate his Boscobel Oak escapade, but wisely abandoned rather than perpetuate old strife. In 1719 John's grandson, Orlando, married Lady Anne Newport, through which marriage the present Weston estates passed eventually to the Bridgemans. Anne did not succeed to them because her brother, the last Earl of Bradford of an earlier creation, survived her. In fact, her husband was nearly the last in the direct Bridgeman male line, for, when the birth of their heir was near their London house collapsed, Anne being moved out with only moments to spare.

She died in 1752 and her husband ten years later, his estates passing to his sister Diana, Countess of Mountrath, and to Henry Bridgeman, whose birth had almost been prevented in the house collapse. They joined in a deed of partition, two lots being agreed upon – Weston, and the Newport's Walsall properties. The countess drew Walsall, where there is now a Bradford Arms in Milton Street and a Mountrath Street in Chuckery, Henry Bridgeman, drawing Weston, spent £12,000 on the estate, and in 1794 he was created Baron Bradford. It was his son, Orlando, who became the first earl of the present line. He married the Hon. Lucy Byng of Tong Castle, just inside Shropshire, and their son George, the 2nd Earl, added Tong Castle – now demolished – and 3,000 acres to the Weston estate.

It was written of Weston as long ago as 1817: 'The whole farming concern is conducted in a masterly style', and this is very much the case under the present and 6th Earl, George Michael Orlando Bridgeman, who succeeded in 1957. On his 15,000 acres at Weston he has some 70 tenant farmers, but farms much of the estate himself. During last century the ploughing at Weston was done by a famous line of Suffolk Punches and an equally noteworthy family of ploughmen – John Gee, killed by a wagon in 1843, his son, and three grandsons.

Aqualate Mere is said to be the largest natural lake in private ownership in England, and it came into my view one morning in 1972 like a cluster of sapphires in a ring as it sparkled through the autumn gold of the trees. There was gold, too, in the reed fringe, waving in a playful wind to the blue skies above. Standing among the green parkland was a gracious red mansion with twisted Tudor chimneys and a white cupola crowning its stable block. A mile away, round the flank of the lake, rose 'a decent church that topt the neighbouring hill' just where it wanted a church to complete the felicity of the scene, which might have been in the lovely Irish lakeland of Oliver Goldsmith's native County Longford. It was, in fact, about equidistant between the Staffordshire Potteries and the Black Country.

Aqualate Hall has been the home of the lords of the manor of Mere these several centuries. The church in this delectable landscape is All Saints, Forton, where a list of these lords begins with the Saxon Earls of Mercia and continues through the Norman kings to the de Somerys and the de Botetourts to the Butlers who, as Earls of Ormond in Ireland, forfeited the manor in 1461 when the fifth earl was beheaded by the Yorkists after the Battle of Towton. The manor was returned to his brother, John, in 1475 by Edward IV who, though a Yorkist himself, said of John Butler 'if good breeding and liberal qualities were lost in the world, they might all be found in the Earl of Ormond.'

In 1535 Thomas Skrymsher of the adjacent parish of Norbury bought the manor of Mere, and one of his successors built Forton Hall beside the church in 1665 – the initials G.A.S. are above the door. From the Skrymshers the manor passed by marriage to the Baldwyns, and it was sold to Sir Thomas Fletcher, Bart, of Betley Court, Staffordshire. His heir, the second baronet, had assumed the additional surname of Boughey (pronounced Bowie) on inheriting the estates of a cousin, so, on the death of Sir Thomas in 1812 the Boughey name came to Aqualate Hall in the person of Sir John Fenton Boughey. The line of Boughey baronets has moved to Ringmer in Sussex, and the last of the Bougheys of Aqualate, Mrs John Wollaston Greene, died in March 1973, aged 95. A daughter of the fifth baronet, the Rev. Sir George Boughey, Rector of Forton for 45 years from 1863 to 1908, this gracious lady spoke to me of her home shortly after her 93rd birthday, of the Roman origin of the name, Aqualate – the broad water – of the Elizabethan hall and of the new wing designed for her great-grandfather by Nash. Mrs Greene continued:

'One day when I was young and down south I overlooked a head-line about a mansion fire and had a premonition that it was Aqualate. Reading that it was, I thought the end of the world had come, but it was only the new wing, and now that I have to run the house I realise the fire was a blessing.'

Mrs Greene's grandfather was the third baronet, and the title descended through five of his sons. The Boughey motto, which trans-lates as 'Neither seek nor despise distinction' can be seen on several coats-of-arms in Forton Church, where you will learn, too, that those with the greatest stake in the country are not unready to die for it. One tablet honours three Bougheys who died in the Second World War, one at sea, one over Tobruk in the air, and Mary Ursula Boughey a Junior Commander in the A.T.S. who died on active service aged 25. The First World War had been equally disastrous for the family, with one lost at Jutland, one at Ypres, and a third when the S.S. *Leinster* was torpedoed in the Irish Sea. Earlier military Bougheys had served in India, and there are memorial tablets at Forton to three of the family and its offshoots in Victoria's reign, officers who fought in such places as Bhutan, Afghanistan, and Amritsar. The long-serving rector, Sir George, is commemorated – and for his entire 45 years as rector one Mark Whitmore sang in the choir. Boy and man he was a chorister for 68 years, all but nine of the 77 he lived.

It is the earlier Skrymshers who have left the grandest monument in Forton Church. Thomas Skrymsher, who bought the manor of Mere in 1535, did so probably because his father had been disinherited of the main family residence and estate at Norbury only four miles from Aqualate. Thomas's grandson, Sir Thomas Skrymsher, built the first hall at Aqualate. and he lies in effigy with his wife, Anne Sneyd of Keele, Staffordshire, on a sumptuous tomb, their five sons and four daughters kneeling below in a prayerful frieze. Anne's coat-of-arms, impaled with the three 'mouches' or flies of her husband, is a heraldic pun on her surname – a 'snead' or scythe handle.

Immediately below the rood screen at Forton is a stone to Richard Awnsham, one of those stones often seen which have more to say of someone other than the person they commemorate. Richard 'served several lords of the manor as steward for more than 40 years', but his epitaph goes on to tell that he was grandson of the Rev. R. Awnsham, Rector of Hopesay, who was ejected 'by the prevailing faction in 1644' for supporting Charles I, and only restored to his parish after a long imprisonment.

Half a mile north-east of Forton the map indicates a 'monument'. It is conical, 30 feet tall, has a door and a chamber at ground level, and is, in fact, the base of a windmill. There was once a water mill on a nearby stream. Early in the eighteenth century some work upstream by the landowner caused the water level to fall so that the mill became useless. The landowner thereupon built a windmill for the miller on higher ground above Forton. Before long the miller left, and rather than have a derelict windmill the landlord decapitated it, embellishing the base with a conical cap and a large stone ball which has since fallen.

There is a farm east of Aqualate Mere called Guild of Monks from which, I was told locally, a tunnel ran to Forton Church. Why, I wonder, and how were such major engineering feats performed? Were our ancestors all troglodytes? Will this fixation on secret tunnels never die? This one at Forton, did it ever exist, would have run nearly three miles through marshy terrain only recently reclaimed for pasture, country still rich in snipe and herons – from a heronry in Fairchild Covert.

Adbaston, across the 'Shroppy', has a Haberdashers' Arms, an unexpected name for a country pub, deriving from the Company of Haberdashers being extensive landowners in the area. Above the door of Adbaston Church is a memorial to William Wakeley 'late of the Outlands in this parish, who died 28 November 1714, aged 125 years'. Such longevity deserves the second memorial I have seen to William Wakeley in Shifnal Church, Shropshire, where he was baptised, which records that he lived through eight reigns.

The most striking thing in Adbaston Church is an ornate hatchment, one of the diamond-shaped funeral boards bearing a coat-of-arms. The supporters on this one are two ancient sailors in blue tunics and yellow skirts, the arms being those of the Whitworth family of Batchacre Hall, and the sailors stemming from an Admiral

Richard Whitworth. So keen was he on the Navy that on retirement he established a miniature battle fleet in his grounds. To do this he had to dam the Lonco Brook, the county boundary hereabouts, to make a lake. The riparian owners downstream naturally complained of this interference with their head of water, especially Thomas Bowker of Weston Jones Mill. The admiral was taken to court, and at Stafford Assizes on 22 May 1780 Bowker recovered £232 damages, the admiral being ordered to remove his weirs. As late as 1806 there is evidence of Bowker and a friend destroying a stop lock erected by the redoubtable admiral on the Lonco Brook.

North of Adbaston, in the 'Woodland Quarter' of Staffordshire, the scenery is not unlike many a Welsh Border valley, with considerable afforestation on the little hills of Bishop's Wood. One of the most surprising things about Staffordshire is how close it approaches to Wales – from its westernmost salient near Market Drayton, it is scarcely a dozen miles across Shropshire into Maelor Saesneg, the 'Saxon Hundred', that once detached portion of Flintshire.

Croxton has a memorial to a sailor who was in the crew of the *Northumberland* as it carried Napoleon to exile on St Helena. Two and a half miles on along the B.5026 is isolated Broughton Church, on no account to be missed, cluttered with box pews so tall that as the unseen congregation rises from prayer it bears some resemblance to the Day of Resurrection. Immediately across the road, at the black-and-white Elizabethan Broughton Hall, and a mile distant at Charnes Hall, there are said to be spirits which cannot await that dread occasion in patience, for each has a harrowing tale of haunting.

Broughton Hall was occupied in 1952 by the Franciscan Missionaries of St Joseph. Three centuries earlier it was Royalist in the Civil War, and when, one day, a group of Roundheads rode down the drive, the young heir taunted them from the long gallery window on the fourth storey. 'I am for the King', he shouted, to be shot dead for his loyalty, crawling into a room adjoining the gallery where his blood left a stain on the floor until some reconstruction work in 1926. The boy was wearing red stockings when he died, and his sad ghost – also with red stockings – is said to have been seen in the long gallery and elsewhere. A guest once apologised for arriving without fancy dress at a party, explaining that not until she saw a young man in cavalier clothes and red stockings did she realise that it was a fancy-dress occasion. At another party, playing hide and seek, a girl visitor saw 'Red Stockings' at the long gallery window, and to look through those leaded panes as sunset lengthens the shadows of the trees in the drive at Broughton Hall is to experience an atmosphere ripe for a haunting. At the end of the Civil War Broughton Hall gave Izaak Walton the one event of a tranquil life more stirring than landing an outsize fish. The 'Compleat Angler' was a Royalist sympathiser, though not suspected by the Roundheads of active participation in the war, and visiting his Staffordshire home he met George Barlow of Broughton Hall and received from him a jewel left there by a Colonel Blagg who had been entrusted with it by Charles II during his escape from Worcester. Blagg had hidden awhile at Broughton, but was captured soon after and taken to the Tower of London, eventually escaping, contacting Walton in London, retrieving the jewel, and restoring it to Charles in France.

A gracious William-and-Mary residence, Charnes Hall, stands in its parkland across the road from the dark conifers of Chapel Wood. One dark night a woman's figure staggered from among those trees, blood from an almost severed finger dripping on to the white shroud she wore. In the grounds of Charnes Hall she rapped feebly on a ground-floor window, and when the shutters were drawn back and the window opened, she murmured to the man whose face appeared : 'Let me in husband : I am very cold.' Aghast, the husband rushed out to aid his wife – who had been buried only that morning. She recovered from the fearful ordeal of premature burial and lived many more years before her ultimate interment at Eccleshall. But her spirit never knew rest, and her ghost, rustling with silk, is said to haunt Charnes Hall searching for a ring she lost during her day in the tomb in Chapel Wood.

This macabre event happened more than 300 years ago, when the young wife of one of the Yonges of Charnes Hall was thought to be mortally ill. She had the servants brought to her bedside to bid them farewell, and a coachman saw that she still wore a valuable ring. Assuming that it would not be removed at her death, he bribed the sexton of the chapel to leave the vault open after the funeral. That night, when the coachman opened the coffin and tried to remove the ring he could not make it budge, so with his knife he tried to amputate the finger. Judge of his horror when the finger spurted blood, and the 'corpse' sat up in her coffin. He decamped at great speed, and Mrs Yonge made her uncertain way back to the home from which she had been carried as dead that morning.

Charnes Hall is a thoroughly wholesome place, and the haunted room is known ordinarily-enough as the 'main spare room'. One feature is an internal passage from one side of the hall to the other, and it is here, at dusk, with the sigh of the wind across the elevated grounds of the hall, that I might imagine the rustling of silk – or of a shroud.

The epitaph hunter will find rich reward at Broughton. In the centre aisle of the church a brass to Willyam Ingram, who died in 1634, begins:

> *Here lies the first whom Death translated*
> *After this church was consecrated:*
> *The first pastor here installed,*
> *And Mr Willyam Ingram called. . . .*

In the churchyard Mrs Elizabeth Broughton made a Shakespearian plea on her seventeenth-century gravestone that posterity 'forbeare to stir my bones', a request repeated in not dissimilar words a century later by one Thomas Nevill. Another parishioner was more forth-right:

> *John Sutton was my name,*
> *England is my nation;*
> *Fair Oak was my dwelling place*
> *And Christ is my salvation.*

North-west of Broughton at Loggerheads crossroads there is an inn with an intriguing name, the 'Three Loggerheads'. It once had an equally intriguing sign, which, alas, some insensitive brewery official has replaced with an ordinary one. A loggerhead is a fool. The old sign depicted two loggerheads, clowns, or fools – the implication being that the onlooker was the third, a harmless witticism. Now the sign itself bears the three loggerheads.

Prehistory and history have left their mark in this corner of Staffordshire which presses to within ten miles of Wales. Almost on the Shropshire border two stones in a field, pierced in prehistoric times, are known as the Devil's Ring and the Devil's Finger, and on 23 September 1459 the Battle of Blore Heath was fought hereabouts during the War of the Roses, an engagement much better 'documented' in the surrounding countryside than many bigger battles.

Lord Audley, the Lancastrian leader, with an army of 10,000, had been ordered by Queen Margaret to intercept the Earl of Salisbury and his Yorkists who were marching from Yorkshire to Ludlow. From a strong position south of Hemp Mill Brook, Audley allowed himself to be lured by a feint retreat of the enemy. He was killed after crossing the brook, and a cross in the field marks the spot where he fell. His army was defeated, with 2,400 Lancastrians dead. Margaret watched the rout of her forces from the tower of Mucklestone Church, at the base of which she now appears in a window with her husband, Henry VI. Descending from her tower, she fled on horseback to Eccleshall, the horseshoes having been reversed, we are told, by a blacksmith named Skelhorn who lived opposite the church. The anvil is preserved in Mucklestone churchyard, and alongside it is a cross to Mary Skelhorn, schoolmistress of Mucklestone for 25 years, who died on 10 November 1876. Perhaps she could be pardoned some little pride when the history lesson came round to the War of the Roses and she recounted the part played by her ancestor in saving the queen.

In 1356 David Kynric was returning to his Flintshire home after serving with the Black Prince in the French wars when he lost his way in the Needwood Forest, then more extensive than it is today. Emerging ultimately he came upon a church and vowed to rebuild it, which he did. I came upon the church of St John the Baptist at Ashley, two miles east of Loggerheads, equally fortuitously and therefore with a gratifying sense of discovery, never having read of the splendid features which surely entitle it to showplace status. It first impressed through the shining brass of its many candelabra, but its most charming and colourful attraction is the loving and skilful embroidery of the many kneelers, comparable with Gloucester Cathedral and Lacock Church, Wiltshire, in this new and acceptable branch of church art. From dubious modern local institutions such as Keele University to ancient associations such as Kynric's friendship with the Black Prince, from Space Age rockets to country farmyard scenes, from Lichfield's time-honoured cathedral to the nineteenth-century church of Hoar Cross, all have been wrought by the needlewomen of Ashley.

The village had a church in 1205, for King John presented it to the Canons Regular of Motesfunt Abbey, Normandy. In the mid-thirteenth century, building was still in progress under Philip de Bromley who received a knighthood for participating in the rebuilding of Westminster Abbey. As lords of the manor of Ashley the Bromleys had to attend with four men and a net when bishops of Lichfield were hunting in Bishops Wood, a name still on the map though much of the woodland is gone.

The Gerards, related to the Bromleys, became lords of Ashley, and they provided the church with a monument 'perhaps the largest Elizabethan monument of any church or cathedral in England', fashioned by the famous Burton alabaster masons. Prone upon it are the effigies of Sir Gilbert Gerard, who died in 1592, and his wife Anne, while kneeling at their head and feet are Thomas, their elder son, and Ratcliffe, the younger. In 1617 James I visited Thomas, whom he ennobled, at Gerrards Bromley, the mansion built by his father, and described by Dr Plot, the Staffordshire historian, as the finest house in the county. It was demolished around 1750, but King James's visit is still commemorated at Ashley in the name of Sovereign Lane. American visitors to Ashley Church will be pleased to find, quartered on the Gerard arms above the monument, the mullets and bars – stars and stripes of the Washingtons of Sulgrave, Northamptonshire, with whom the Gerards were allied by marriage.

The south chapel at Ashley is Kinnersley territory, with a breathtaking Chantrey sculpture of Thomas Kinnersley of Clough Hall who died in 1819. The folded wings of the angels on another monument give them the appearance of invalids seated in Bath chairs, but Ashley's one error is surely the huge reredos which obliterates the east windows and darkens this exciting church. Today the patrons of the

Ashley living are the Meynell Trustees, and the village inn, the Meynell Arms, has a fine heraldic sign.

Around 1650 Jane, Lady Gerard, discovered sulphur springs at the family hunting lodge of Willoughbridge, and Dr Plot computes 'that there are not less than sixty copious springs rising within ten yards square.' Lady Gerard built several bath houses and a well house, but only the latter remains. Jane's husband had a black servant, and it is recorded in Ashley Church Registers: '6th April 1668. There was buried Laurence of unknown surname, an African by nationality, a Christian by profession.' Unfortunately, unlike the churchyards of Henbury, Bristol, and Oxhill, Warwickshire, Ashley has lost sight of the black servant's grave.

From my schooldays I remember an essay by A. G. Gardiner, 'On Choosing a Name', in which he warns that 'the child has to bear the burden of your momentary impulse if you name it Inkerman Jones, Kitchener Smith, or Milton Spinks'. 'Perhaps', Gardiner wrote, 'Milton Spinks grows up bow-legged and commonplace – all Spinks and no Milton.'

I suspect that Augustus Caesar Venables never achieved anything commensurate with his name, of which I am aware only because his 'relict', Elizabeth, has a memorial tablet in the exterior east wall of Eccleshall Church, which records that she was 'born the 6th April 1748, old style' – four years before the 'new style' calendar lost us the 11 days.

Eccleshall, the one sizable townlet in this sparsely-populated portion of Staffordshire, is a pleasant place, with a wide main street where the pavements have cobbled verges, and two loyal pubs, the 'Crown' and the 'Royal Oak', throw out arcades across the pavement next door to each other. The 'eccles' element in the name indicates a church, and Eccleshall was long the seat of the bishops of Lichfield, five of whom lie buried in the large church, while in the town at least two modern residential courts are named after Bishops Selwyn and Lonsdale. Bishop William Overton (1580–1609), is said on an explanatory note 'to have composed his own epitaph'. Unfortunately this does not appear, because the note describes him as 'a man of hard and avaricious nature', and one would welcome his self-appraisal. James Bayley, buried in the churchyard, died in 1836 having served five bishops for 60 years 9 months and 17 days as keeper and wood-man. He also fished Copmore Pool for 45 years. Yet to me the most remarkable thing about Mr Bayley is his age at death as given on his headstone. Sorrowing relatives almost always wring another year out of their long-lived forebears, and it is astonishing that James Bayley's age is given as a mere '99 years', when they might have inscribed instead 'in his 100th year'.

The bishops eventually moved to Lichfield, but a particularly holy aura continued at Eccleshall in the latter nineteenth century with an incumbent named Good and a churchwarden named Blest.

It was Bishop Walter Langton, Bishop of Lichfield from 1297 to 1321, who largely built moated Eccleshall Castle – Lord High Treasurer of England under Edward I, he was thrown into prison by Edward II, but later restored to his office. Bishop Wright held the castle for Charles I while Parliamentary forces garrisoned Eccleshall Church. Late in 1643 the Royalists took the town and for a while besieged their enemies in the church until Parliamentary reinforcements from Stafford turned the tables and captured the castle, which was thereafter dismantled. Later it was restored as the bishops' manor house until the nineteenth century when the residence was de-molished.

CHAPTER TEN

Cheadle and the Churnet Valley

A local philologist once wrote of Uttoxeter that its pronunciation indicates the kind of person one is. The standard pronunciation, he declared, as used by clergy, lawyers, bank managers, policemen and tax-gatherers – and this author – is 'Yootoxeter'. Wives, womenfolk, and elder sons of these people say 'Uxeter', the 'Ux' being stressed but with a genteel 'Ax' inflection. But what used to be known as the working classes, the glorious company of railway porters, poachers, and punters on the local racecourse, still say in obstinate felicity 'Utchiter' with a full-throated 'Utch'. A splinter group, the boys from Smallwood Manor, the prep school for Denstone College, call the town just plain 'Ug', and, whichever your category, it means 'Wittuc's heathery place'.

Above the west bank of the Dove, where that river forms the boundary with Derbyshire, Uttoxeter is a town of 10,000 population. It has a most popular racecourse, and a poignant association with a penitent Dr Samuel Johnson, who once stood in the market place in his old age for an hour, bareheaded in heavy rain, in atonement for his youthful refusal to man his father's bookstall there. The penance, which was enacted on the fiftieth anniversary of the 'breach of filial piety', is captured in relief on a memorial on the spot.

The tower of Uttoxeter Church survives from the building designed between 1325 and 1350 by a man once described as 'the greatest English architect', Henry Yevele, son of a Uttoxeter freeholder. Among his works are the nave of Westminster Abbey and of Canterbury

Cathedral. In 1828 the church was rebuilt in neo-Gothick, and along with other memorial tablets it has one to George Henry Tortoishell, head of the Church of England Boys' School for 41 years – the unusual surname occurs again on Denstone war memorial with Corporal J. H. Tortoishell.

The River Churnet flows some 25 miles from the moorlands north-west of Leek to its confluence with the Dove between Uttoxeter and Rocester. For some 200 years it had the companionship over part of its length of the Froghall–Uttoxeter Canal, and of the Macclesfield–Uttoxeter branch of the North Staffordshire Railway, the famous 'Knotty', so called from its Stafford Knot emblem worn on locomotives of crimson lake. The canal, which reached Uttoxeter in 1811, had James Rennie as its engineer, and its purpose was to provide an outlet for the products of Cheadle Copper and Brass Works at Oakamoor and Alton, for the coal of the Cheadle and Kingsley Moor coalfield, and for lime for agricultural purposes.

The railway came to the Churnet Valley in 1849 in a period when no fewer than 24 railway companies had been promoted in north Staffordshire, which would have turned the area into a veritable octopus of metal tentacles. A. W. Pugin, better known for his ecclesiastical architecture, designed some stations on the Churnet Valley line, notably Alton, where he worked for John Talbot, 16th Earl of Shrewsbury, on enlargements at Alton Towers. In 1923 the 'Knotty' became part of the London, Midland and Scottish Railway, and operations ceased in the Churnet Valley in 1964/5. Uttoxeter once had as many as three railways stations, but these were closed in 1881 when the present station was built, and the town still has rail communications with Stoke-on-Trent and Derby. The White Hart Hotel has a striking portico, while the 'White Horse' has incorporated four wagon wheels into its entrance porch.

Rocester – pronounced Roaster – lives in my mind for the epitaph in its churchyard to Ellen Moreton:

> *Thirty-five years I lived a maid,*
> *Nine months I was a wife;*
> *Ten days the mother of two babes –*
> *And then I lost my life.*

27   *In the stone wall country above Alstonfield looking towards*
Steep Low

Buried with her in 1812 were her infant daughters Mary and Martha. What a human story. At 35 Ellen is 'on the shelf', but no! romance comes late. She wants a child as soon as possible, has twins, they die and she dies. An unusual forename to vie with Charity, Prudence, Faith and the other virtues can be seen at Rocester – Mrs Temperance Hainsworth.

I remember walking into the century-old mill at Churnet Bridge, Rocester, one day in 1961 and watching the production of potters' clay from Norwegian felspar, flint from France, china clay from Cornwall, and even an ingredient from Australia. The final product was supplied to the Potteries and exported among other places to Genoa and the United States.

But primarily this is Bamford territory. Just after the last war, on a capital of 50 shillings, Joseph C. Bamford began making farm trailers which he sold at local markets. By 1960 his firm's sales were £2·8 millions, and four years later he was giving away a £250,000 tax-free bonus to his 500 workers. In 1970 when Joseph Bamford won the annual Market Award of the Institute of Marketing, he was chairman of a group of companies, mainly concerned with excavation and earth-shifting machinery, looking forward to £30 millions sale in that year. A millionaire, who travels the world in his firm's executive jet, he had built for him at Southampton in 1967 a 357-tons yacht, thought to be the largest aluminium yacht in the world. At the approach to Rocester the firm has landscaped its premises most attractively with neatly-cut grassy mounds and a large fishing lake.

Mr Bamford's residence is the romantically-situated Wootton Lodge, north of Rocester, built early in the seventeenth century for Sir Richard Fleetwood, whose emblem of baronetcy, the Red Hand of Ulster, appears on the entrance. He was one of the original baronets created by James I, but during the Civil War he had the ignominy of being marched from his home roped to two of his sons and 70 of his retainers by Parliamentarians who had captured the lodge with guns sited on what is still known as Cromwell's Battery.

Rocester is the Rosseter of George Eliot's novel *Adam Bede*, and my churchyard researches there have revealed several Salts, one of the local names in the book – 'Sandy' Jim Salt, a carpenter colleague of Adam. George Eliot was born Mary Ann Evans near Nuneaton in 1819.

Warwickshire by birth, she set her greatest novel on the border of Staffordshire and Derbyshire, which she called Loamshire and Stonyshire respectively. She treated names with contempt, changing not only her name but its sex in the hope that her novels would attract more attention coming from a 'masculine' author.

Many of her characters were portraits of living people, though usually she gave them fictitious names. Occasionally, as with Bartle Massey, the schoolmaster in *Adam Bede*, she used a real person with his real name. Elsewhere she took a local name and invented the character, as in Will Maskery, the drunken wheelwright turned Methodist. Her place-names are fictitious but refer to real places, though here again she clouds the issue. Her Oakbourne barely conceals Ashbourne and, in the same area, Dovedale assumes greater nobility as Eagledale. But you have to be in the know to identify the actual village of Ellastone as the Hayslope of *Adam Bede*. Then again, George Eliot is not above transporting a farm, lock, stock, and Barney's bull, some 40 miles, as she does her Hall Farm, from Corley near Coventry to Hayslope. She has also a bad habit of giving wrong distances between her places, making the confusion even greater. Thus it was, some years ago, driving to the scenes of *Adam Bede*, I passed unknowingly through the first George Eliot town, Uttoxeter. I had thought Treddleston, her market town three miles from Hayslope, to be Alton, only to learn, too late, that it was Uttoxeter. This is not three but seven miles from Ellastone where the Bedes lived – a tidy stagger for Thias, Adam's father, back from the '*Wagon Overthrown*' where he passed so much of the time he should have spent making coffins.

Ellastone still has a charming Adam Bede Cottage where the garden walls are distinguished by stone pinnacles, and where I was shown wood carvings said to be the work of George Eliot's father, Robert Evans, who once lived there. His parents, George and Mary Evans – the Matthias and Lisbeth Bede of the novel – lie buried in Norbury churchyard, only a stone's throw across the River Dove in Derbyshire. The carving at Adam Bede Cottage takes the form of decoration on the gables, and, inside, on cupboards, filigree over a window, and two exquisite corbels, one representing a preacher, the other an unidentified character bowed down with sorrow.

It is uncertain whether any Ellastone workshop supplied George Eliot with her original of Jonathan's Burge's carpenter shop in *Adam Bede* where Adam and Seth are introduced in the first chapter at work among 'a scent of pinewood from a tent-like pile of planks outside the open door.' In *Adam Bede* the Hayslope pub is the Donnithorne Arms, after Squire Donnithorne, and its Ellastone original was the Bromley-Davenport Arms, once kept by a cousin of George Eliot, yet another Evans. The small 'farmyard and stockyard' flanking the Donnithorne Arms can still be seen, though the old inn, imposing in a grey sort of county gaol way as it dominates the village steet. left the licensed trade some years ago. It became an antiques business known as Ellastone Old House – the occupant told me she turned down suggestions to call it 'Donnithorne', having no love for George Eliot's work. Next door to the Bromley-Davenport Arms was another inn, the Duncombe Arms, and 14 years ago I remember calling when they were kept respectively and separately by a man and his wife, though they both slept in the 'Duncombe'.

Ellastone once basked in brighter limelight than that beamed on it by George Eliot when a film, *Blanche Fury*, was made there starring Valerie Hobson and Stewart Granger.

So one way and another Ellastone is a memorable village, though to me its greatest attraction is way out northward, over the Weaver Hills, the Binton Hills of *Adam Bede*, of which George Eliot writes: 'High up against the horizon were the huge conical masses of hills, like giant mounds intended to fortify this region of corn and grass against the keen and hungry winds of the north.' The description is overdone. The Weavers are bland hills with clean but not overpowering skylines. Here is turf as green and crisp as you could wish – the first mile or so of England's mountain spine, the Pennine Chain.

The first village on the Churnet as one follows it north-westward from the Dove Valley is Denstone, famous for its college and for awards as the best-kept village in Staffordshire. It offers contrasting views of the bare limestone of the Weavers, and the sylvan valley up which we shall follow the Churnet, but its mid-nineteenth century church, by G. E. Street, is fussy, with an atmosphere of Roman Catholicism, and the nave is very gloomy.

My son returned from his first visit to the Churnet Valley after a June ramble in 1973, not certain what he had seen but full of enthusiasm for the area.

'There's one building, a castle around Alton, exactly like Colditz in the television series', he said – and I envied him the physical comparison, though the enchanted fairy atmosphere of this nineteenth century convent on the site of a Norman castle is far removed from the grim aura of Colditz. From its lofty eminence the occupants can peep across the River Churnet and over the outer tree fringe into Charles Talbot's extravaganza at Alton Towers.

Despite the crowds and the coachloads of visitors to Alton Towers the village of Alton is as sequestered a spot as I know, where a car can be casually abandoned a yard out in the road without it seeming a social crime fit to qualify the perpetrator for incarceration in the village lock-up. This is a circular structure of dark stone with a heavily-studded door curving into its circumference and crowned by a cupola. By way of the 'Bull's Head' and the 'White Hart' the visitor to Alton comes to the massive gates of St Peter's overgrown churchyard where the deceased lose their identities behind the tall summer grasses to regain them when winter reveals their headstones. In contrast to Denstone Church, Alton chancel is gloomy and its nave light and pleasant, with a slim rounded south arcade and a heavier, more Norman one to the north aisle, which seems sacred to the Bill family of Farley, including a Robert and a Lydia who had 13 children, and another Lieutenant Robert who died at Gibraltar during the siege. A Colonel Charles Bill was the founder-chairman of the Leek and Manifold Light Railway, and an ancestress of his, another Lydia, married John Gilbert who, as agent to the Duke of Bridgwater, introduced to him that illiterate genius, James Brindley who became engineer of the Duke of Bridgwater's Canal.

The earliest vicar of Alton in 1166 was one Adam. Next came a nameless incumbent appointed by the Abbot of Crokysden – Croxden, two miles southward, a Cistercian house founded by the builder of the original Alton Castle, Bertram de Verdun, a Crusader, who would probably not be happy to think that the 'heart of the worst king England ever had' – to quote Mee's *Staffordshire* – may lie in Croxden's picturesque ruins. King John, whom I persist in regarding as an infinitely better king than his swashbuckling absentee brother, Richard I, was attended on his death bed at Newark by monks who came either from Croxden or from Croxton in Leicestershire, and who bore away his heart, leaving his body to be taken for burial in the cathedral he loved at Worcester.

Passing the Wild Duck Inn on the one-in-ten drop from Alton village, one finds a Talbot Inn near the bridge, its heraldic sign blazoning the arms of the Earls of Shrewsbury with talbot hounds as supporters. Across the Churnet bridge with vestiges of the canal and the railway beneath its farther end, Charles Talbot, 15th Earl of Shrewsbury, early last century played Kubla Khan to a wooded tract of his territory and gave us Alton Towers. It was Sir John Talbot who in 1406 acquired Alton Castle when he married Maud Nevill, Baroness Furnivall – the Furnivalls having also come by it through marriage with a Verdun heiress. John Talbot was Henry V's great captain in the French wars, being created Earl of Shrewsbury, Shakespeare's 'valiant Talbot' of *King Henry VI*, and dying of wounds at Chastillon aged 62 after proving victorious in some 40 battles and major skirmishes. In 1694 Charles, 12th Earl of Shrewsbury, was created Duke of Shrewsbury and Marquis of Alton, but these titles died with him, the earldom reverting to a cousin.

It was Charles Talbot, the 15th Earl, who perpetrated Alton Towers in the 1820s, and his successor, his nephew John, who added to his uncle's gross conceit by enlarging the house itself, aided by Pugin. Alton Towers passed from the Talbots in 1924 and the great house is now given over to the largest known electric model railway and refreshment rooms for those who come to wonder at the Chinese temple, the pagoda on an island from which a fountain is thrown so high that it can be seen from afar, the five-storeyed flag tower 90 feet tall, the conservatory with seven domes above seven terraces running down to the river, the magnificent trees, walks, and parterres – and that inevitable concomitant to modern mass enjoyment, a pool of sea lions.

Alton Towers' next door neighbour comes as something of a surprise. If, as we hope, you have come unawares on Moor Court and stopped to read the lengthy notice at the entrance gateway you will see that this begins with a recital of the penalties for aiding and abetting a prisoner to escape. Moor Court is a prison – in exquisite surroundings, if that is any consolation to its inmates.

Cradled in encircling tree-clad hills, Oakamoor's situation, if not the village itself, should inspire a poet, as Wordsworth was inspired by the sylvan Forest of Dean at Tintern Abbey. Somewhere through that protective green wall the River Churnet enters; somewhere departs; but from the bridge at Oakamoor the breaches are not apparent. Yet, cut off from the world, it was the workpeople of Oakamoor who were largely responsible for voices crossing the vast Atlantic in 1858 between Newfoundland and Valencia, Co. Kerry. Today, from the bridge where the Churnet runs down a four-stepped weir, a grass-grown area with outcrops of broken concrete is described as 'Dangerous' on warning notices. Here was once the copper works of Thomas Bolton – now operating at Froghall three miles upstream – and in them was made the 20,000 miles of copper wire forming the core of the first Atlantic cable.

Across the river from Bolton's was a limestone works, the old kilns still visible. Something of an incongruity is the name and sign of the Cricketers Arms, with a top-hatted batsman at the stumps, which left me wondering where in Oakamoor a field could be found flat enough to play cricket.

Towering above the riverside, Oakamoor Church bears evidence to the slope out of the village. From its west front it juts into space so that a crypt, used as the church hall, had to be built beneath to support it, and below the ecclesiastical east window of the church is the secular and plainly useful window of the lower room. Is any other church built on its church hall? The war memorial records that a Bolton, whether of the copper family or no, was killed in each of the world wars, while Clement Wragge died of wounds received at Lone Pine, Gallipoli. At Oakamoor I found an epitaph which I have seen only twice before, in each case in Staffordshire, at Croxton, near Eccleshall, and at Walsall Wood. On headstones of young children, it reads:

> *When the Archangel's trump shall sound,*
> *And souls with bodies join;*
> *Thousands will wish their stay on earth*
> *Had been as short as mine.*

A mile up the Cheadle road from Oakamoor the Masefield Gates stand beside a striking tall house incongruously named Hawksmoor Cottage and bearing the initials W. E. B. This was the late W. E. Bowers of Caverswall Castle, nearer the Potteries, who also owned Hawksmoor to which the gates afford entrance. Bought by public subscription and presented to the National Trust, Hawksmoor Nature Reserve and Bird Sanctuary was opened by Lord Grey of Falloden on 7 May 1927. The founder of the reserve was John Richard Beech Masefield, and on 21 October 1933 the gates were dedicated to him by his cousin the late Poet Laureate, John Masefield. A plaque says of the founder : 'He was a great naturalist with an unrivalled knowledge of the flora and fauna of his native county. For 49 years he was a member and four times president of the North Staffordshire Field Club, and was ever ready to help and encourage others in the study of natural history.'

Poetry ran in the Masefield family. J. R. B. was the father of Charles John Beech Masefield, who was making a name as a poet when he was killed in action at Lens in June 1917. He had written a novel *Gilbert Hermer*, set in and around Cheadle, which he called 'Cradleby', and a *Little Guide to Staffordshire*, but to me two poignant lines from a poem written in the month before his death are sufficient memorial :

> *Grief though it be to die, 'tis grief yet more*
> *To live and count the dear dead comrades o'er.*

I have my own reservations as a walker about the nature reserves and trails which have come to proliferate over Britain of recent years. They take the visitor too firmly by the hand and, in part, destroy the thrill of exploring. Having said which, I am full of praise for Hawksmoor's 250 acres, and especially for its splendid explanatory pamphlet from which I crib gratefully.

Carboniferous rock around 300 million years old underlies Hawksmoor; one of these coal seams, the Crabtree, outcropping near the Churnet. Above this bedrock on a landscape of deep glens and steep ridges with occasional breathtaking distant views, the sandstone of the Bunter pebble beds supports scrub, bracken, bilberry, dwarf oaks, and birch, with Forestry Commission plantings of beech, sycamore, pines, fir, larch, cypress, and hemlock. Birds abound in great variety as do mammals, with the occasional grass snake. One section is moorland enough to be designated 'curlew country'; elsewhere once stood a pheasantry, and in Gibridding Wood there is a memorial stone to a man who fell dead in 1892 during a pheasant shoot.

East Wall Farm is incorporated in the reserve – its name is distinguishable in twelfth-century documents as Heystiswell – while one of the Churnet Valley's most recent industries comes into full view with the works and quarry of British Industrial Sand, where over 100 are employed. Here the most modern sand purification and processing plant in Europe provide flint glass sand used in the manufacture of such items as milk bottles, pottery paint, and glazes, asbestos sheeting and abrasive cleanser. The sand is supplied particularly to the Lancashire glass industry around St Helens, and the quarry is estimated to hold 40 years' supply.

Not the least interesting feature of Hawksmoor Reserve is the industrial archaeology. A hut in Lightoaks Wood was the home of 'Charcoal Jack', one of several charcoal-burners employed up to the end of last century by Bolton's copper works. An earth embankment marks the line of a tramway which carried coal from the Cheadle collieries to a wharf, traces of which exist, on the Froghall–Uttoxeter Canal, while the remains of a winding drum can still be seen in Gibridding Wood. Following the towpath you find Morris's or California Lock with the masonry almost intact. Iron slag unearthed in East Wall farmyard is evidence of a smelting furnace there when the Churnet Valley had an important ironstone mining industry. Bars of iron from Consall Forge were transported on mules to Oakamoor tin mill where they were made into tin plate.

The reserve is open free of charge to the public and the three sections of nature trail are 2½, 1½, and 1½ miles long. For his work in developing the reserve as an educational and field study centre the secretary and warden, Mr Peter Wilson, was presented with one of the 'Countryside in 1970' awards.

Cheadle is an undistinguished chocolate-coloured town with a smattering of Tudor black-and-white standing between the two streams which join to southward to form the River Tean. Even its one great feature, the splendidly proportioned, crocketed spire, 200 feet tall, of Pugin's Roman Catholic church, completed in 1846, attracts only to repel. The two enormous gold rampant lions on the red west door are a warning of the over-ornate bad taste of the interior. The parish church provides little of interest – a small tablet to 85-year-old Charlotte Plant who died in 1869, 'the faithful and devoted nurse of the Earl of Belfast and his sister, Lady Harriet Ashley', but the churchyard has a memorial to Joseph Atkinson of Melfield, Co. Dublin, with a poem by Thomas Moore of five verses, the first being:

> *If ever lot was prosperously cast,*
> *If ever life was like the lengthened flow*
> *Of some sweet music, sweetness to the last,*
> *'Twas his who, mourned by many, sleeps below.*

Moore had earlier written a fulsome poem to Atkinson from Bermuda, where the poet had gone on being appointed Registrar in the Admiralty Court of that Atlantic island. Finding Bermuda little to his liking Moore appointed a deputy and returned to Britain, eventually to marry Bessy Dyke, with whom, and their daughters Barbara and Olivia, he retired in 1813 to Mayfield on the Staffordshire side of the River Dove from Ashbourne. Moore had been given an advance of 3,000 guineas by Longman's to write an epic poem, and for four years, until 1817, he worked on his oriental masterpiece 'Lalla Rookh'. Surely no one grapples with its turgid length today, though many still take pleasure in a trifle of Moore's Mayfield days, 'Those Evening Bells', inspired by the chimes of Ashbourne wafting across the border from Derbyshire.

'I could not possibly have a more rural or secluded corner to court the Muses in' wrote Moore of Mayfield, though it brought him the loss of little Olivia who was buried in Mayfield churchyard in the year of Waterloo.

Moore's old home is now Stancliffe Farm, and I remember in May 1961 squelching there through waterlogged meadows to the grey cottage where the occupant gave me shelter from the rain, showed me Moore's study heaped with dandelion heads for brewing dandelion beer, and paid her tribute to the poet by quoting 'Those Evening Bells' in full.

Cheadle, too, had its poets. Captain Masefield has been mentioned, but another, Thomas Bakewell, produced 'The Moorland Bard' or 'Poetical Recollections of a Weaver in the Moorlands of Staffordshire'. In earlier life he was foreman of a tape mill – Cheadle still has a Tape Street – but he moved to Trentham where he set up a private asylum for the insane, and, dying aged 74 he was buried at Stone where his tomb is one of few to have survived a drastic clearance of the church-yard.

The traditional textile manufacture of the area still affords employment in Cheadle, but a newcomer is the firm making power boats.

A couple of miles north of Cheadle the Blacksmiths Arms at Kingsley Holt flaunts a quotation from Dr Samuel Johnson above its entrance door – 'There is nothing which has yet been contrived by man by which so much happiness is provided as by a good tavern or inn.' Of all the verbose doctor's pontifications this commends itself to me the least. Normally friendly and talkative, I become morose and taciturn under the dead hand of artificial bonhomie, eye-searing tobacco smoke, and unwanted liquor on the unhappy occasions when I enter a pub.

Now a churchyard – as readers will have noted – fills me with eager interest and questing vitality, and they have a beauty at St Werburgh's, Kingsley.

'What a populous churchyard for so small a village', I once re-marked to a woman cleaning the church.

'Yes', she replied, not quite comprehending me, 'and they nearly all come to the services' – a macabre vision.

Here at Kingsley, as in other churchyards, are the 'short and simple annals' of generations of villagers. If one story bores you, you move on in a way you could not readily do in a pub. So, browsing among the engraved social history of Kingsley, we meet John Lomax –

> *His widow after paying his just debts*
> *To his lamented name this stone erects.*

Here lies Thomas Alcock, 'borne to his grave by six of his sons' in 1816 – the same stalwart sextet acting as bearers two years later to their sister Elizabeth. Prolific characters, these Alcocks. I almost entitled this chapter 'The Alcock Country'. Their name appears everywhere around the Churnet, above shops, on vans, and, at last, on tombstones. The Carnwells, too, have left their mark at Kingsley on memorial stools near the organ, while up among the red, white, and blue sallies on the ringing platform is a frame recording chimes on 18 October 1944, to celebrate Henry Carnwell's 55 years as a change ringer. Returning from a war when England's bells held themselves silent to sound a warning of invasion, a Kingsley ringer wrote a verse which hangs in the ringing chamber :

> *And thou, grey, friendly, sturdy tower*
> *That changelessly looks down on night and day;*
> *Art thou rejoiced to have thy sons once more,*
> *And feel them shake thy stones in noisy play?*

What oldest inhabitant, drooling into a pint on my expense account in the 'Swan' could have told me so succinctly and authoritatively as does his memorial tablet in Kingsley Church of the death of Lieut. Rowland Auriol James Beech of the 16th (Queen's) Lancers? In 1914 he had the distinction of being among the first list of officers mentioned in despatches. But, before his oak leaves could burgeon in their first spring, came the fatal 21 February 1915, when, near Ypres, 'The enemy having blown up a mine under the trenches of a squadron of his regiment on his left at dawn, he at once took the men near him to their assistance, and to repel the inrushing enemy he placed his men in a trench, but remaining crouched outside himself to observe their fire, he was killed instantly.'

Well might Froghall call its pub the 'Railway' and display an ancient engine on the sign – though in green livery not crimson lake – for it is associated with the ancestry of the 'Knotty'. In 1776 the Trent and Mersey Canal proprietors were empowered to construct a plateway or railway between the limestone quarries at Caldon Low and a proposed canal basin at Froghall, the line being opened in 1777 with a drop of 649 feet in four miles.

Today Froghall is little more than a large factory – Bolton's – with rows of parked employees' cars, the Railway Inn, and the river bridge at the bottom of a steep road switchback from Kingsley Holt to Ipstones.

Topping the 1,000-feet contour, Ipstones Edge forms the northern wall of the Churnet Valley on the river's middle course, and the road that winds the two uphill miles from Froghall to the village of Ipstones introduces the traveller to the grimy gritstone walls which bespeak the moorlands. Considerable new building and a wide smooth road are, however, uncharacteristic of the moors, and it is not until one turns past the pub – nameless, but with a fine pictorial sign which, I was assured, features the Marquis of Granby wearing the wig he lost leading a charge at the Battle of Minden – and seeks the church, that the upland nature of Ipstones becomes apparent. On the western fringe of the village St Leonard's Church commands a wide view westward past the trig point, where a typical stone-wall track skirts Noonsun Common. A spacious blue-washed church, St Leonard's includes among others in its east window its name saint, with the fetters which proclaim him the patron saint of prisoners, and remote though Ipstones may be its sons have gone out to die in two wars in Flanders, Salonica, and such far-off places as Imphal, Kohima in Burma, and Longstop Hill, Tunisia.

A large genealogical tree on the north wall conducts nine generations of the Clowes family from Robert, married in Ipstones Church in 1649, a farmer who was paying Hearth Tax in Charles II's reign, to Harold, born in 1903, who became Lord Mayor of Stoke-on-Trent. Harold's father, Samuel Clowes (1864–1928) was also an alderman of Stoke, M.P. for Hanley, and general secretary of the National Society of Pottery Workers. But despite these illustrious men I was most intrigued by one William Clowes (1789–1866) described as a 'farmer and breeder of funeral horses at Holeshouse Farm, Bucknall.'

Urn memorials in a window recess commemorate the Sneyd family, one of them a vicar, one the planter of many trees which still thrive hereabouts, while a third, 18-year-old Edmund Lionel Sneyd, died on board the *Emma Watts* in 1853 on his voyage home from New Orleans.

Ipstones people drop down those two winding miles to work at Thomas Bolton's in Froghall. One retired native, learning that I came from Birmingham, told me that he used to travel from Froghall to Birmingham daily on a Bolton's lorry, making a dozen calls in the city delivering copper sheet and coil.

Three miles south of Leek the Churnet flows beneath the A.520, the fast modern successor to the Sandon-Leek Turnpike. Beside the river is its close companion over five miles to Froghall, the Caldon Canal – and sandwiched between the two at Cheddleton is the flint mill. Industrial archaeology is all the vogue today and the Churnet Flint Mill Preservation Society rescued a gem from decay and opened it to the public in 1969.

Here, in that earthy fragrance of turbulent water the Churnet foams down a weir, leaving a mill race to turn the two large under-shot wheels alongside the red brick buildings. Natural flints, it is explained, came by canal boat from Gravesend and were loaded into two kilns, which can be seen, in three-inch layers separated by coal slack. After three or four days burning in the kiln the calcinated flints were easier to grind, and after grinding the flint powder was loaded, at the canal whence it had come, for transport to the Potteries. Here it was added to the clay to give strength to the pottery products. Other items displayed include a two-wheel cart used by the millers and potters, made by Wood Brothers of Wetley Rocks, and a centre feed mill once used for grinding pepper, but brought to an Etruria firm for grinding fine china clay.

The 17½ miles of the Caldon Canal from Etruria to Froghall is being cleared by Staffordshire County Council, the British Waterways Board, and Stoke Corporation, and in 1973 a boat hire firm was confidently advertising that one of its narrow boats would ply from Cheddleton in 1974. In fact the County Council seems to be backing the Churnet Valley as Staffordshire's foremost tourist area, with a 'walkway' known as the Churnet Way from Denstone to Oakamoor, picnic areas at Wall Grange, Froghall, and Oakamoor, and a nature study centre at Hayles Wood.

In Cheddleton Church a series of windows featuring unusual potentates such as Constantine, Charlemagne, Ludovic, Ethelbert, and Peada of Mercia, commemorates members of the Powys family of Westwood Manor, as does the Powys Arms at nearby Wetley Rocks. Cheddleton's east window is a memorial to Thomas Powys, a veteran of Waterloo who was largely responsible for quelling the Pottery Riots in 1842 during the Chartist agitation.

To reach Cheddleton the Churnet has half encircled Leek from the west, coming down from its source in the moors north of that town through Tittesworth Reservoir where, in its infancy, it is pressed into service as a water supply by the North Staffordshire Water Board.

CHAPTER ELEVEN

The Potteries

Thirteen might have seemed an unlucky number to Josiah Wedgwood, the great potter, for at the age of eleven this last, and thirteenth, child of Thomas and Mary Wedgwood, born in 1730 at Burslem, was crippled in the right knee by a smallpox complication. Such, however, was his genius and application – of which more later – that he died in 1795 at Etruria Hall leaving a thriving world-famous business, and half a million pounds to be divided between his children, of whom he and his wife, Sarah Wedgwood, a third cousin, had seven. His namesake among them, Josiah Wedgwood II, was able to live in some state at Maer Hall. Beckoned by the alluring Maer Hills, when the verdure of spring was beginning to cover the winter's dead bracken, I came one day in May 1973 to the village of Maer where the church rises above the hall.

An amiable priest-in-charge was in the church of which he talked with obvious love before taking me into the vestry and producing the current marriage register. In so small a community this is not much in demand, and the date of only the second entry was as long ago as 29 January 1839, when a marriage was solemnized between Emma Wedgwood, daughter of Josiah II, and her cousin, Charles Robert Darwin, so that I found myself gazing at a signature in the same hand that had written the epoch-making *Origin of Species* and *A Naturalist's Voyage in the Beagle*. Nearly eight years before the marriage Darwin had visited Maer Hall and asked his uncle's advice on the offer made to him of a place on the scientific world voyage of the *Beagle* – rather belatedly, for because his father felt acceptance would interfere with his son's plans to become a clergyman, Darwin had already written declining the offer. His uncle was apparently so persuasive that on 31 August 1831 Darwin wrote again reversing his decision of only 24 hours earlier.

Place-names on old gravestones in Maer's steep churchyard – Mare Moss and Mareway Lane – were clues to a corruption in the name of the village of 'Mere'. Other evidence was the sight of the beautiful lake or mere behind the hall, with green slopes rising beyond, through a gap in which the infant River Tern sets out on its course to join the Severn downstream of Shrewsbury. This part of Staffordshire, on the Cheshire border, shares with its neighbour an abundance of small pools or 'flashes' which dot the ordnance map like the tiny blue eyes of speedwell among meadow grass. These pools are caused by subsidence from the pumping of brine out of the red marl at the Cheshire salt towns.

The Maer Hills are privately owned by two landowners. Maer has an interesting inn, the 'Swan with Two Necks', though the casual visitor would not realise it. There is no sign, the licensee is not allowed to advertise its function, and it has only a six-day licence – all in conformity with the wishes of a late owner of the Maer Estate.

Eastward of Maer, across Swynnerton Old Park and the Hanchurch Hills, the M.6 Motorway slices through Trentham Park and continues north-westward to give a glimpse of the sylvan environs which harbour that reddest of red-brick universities, Keele. Trentham Church occupies the site of St Werburgh's nunnery, and Trentham Hall, home of the Leveson-Gower family who became Dukes of Sutherland, was originally a Tudor house. In 1840 the second duke commissioned Sir Charles Barry to build instead an Italian palace, but 65 years later the very feature that had attracted the Leveson-Gowers to the area – the tree-fringed Trent – had become so polluted in its course through the Potteries that the fourth duke and his family moved from Trentham in 1905. The stately home was demolished but for the ballroom and one large hall, though Trentham Gardens remain as the playground for Staffordshire people, and a statue of the first Duke of Sutherland looks down from a hill on their enjoyment of his old estate – which was the Brentham of Disraeli's novel *Lothair*. A great attraction of Trentham Gardens in 1973 is its all-in entry fee of 40p

29   *Leek Church stands comparison in interest with any parish church in England*

adults, 25p children and pensioners, or £1 for a family, which gives the freedom of boating on the mile-long lake, of the mini-train, the swimming pool, and the fun fair.

Keele Park, seen under snow, was described by the Grand Duke Michael of Russia, who lived there with his family from 1901 to 1910, as 'the Switzerland of England'. The hall in which the Grand Duke lived was built around 1860 for Mr Ralph Sneyd, many generations of whose family had lived in the previous hall which was demolished, their memorials still gracing the church.

Whitmore, to southward, was the birthplace of Samuel Stone who wrote the famous hymn 'The Church's one foundation'. Madeley, too, has its literary associations, in the dedication by Izaak Walton of *The Compleat Angler* to his friend Sir John Offley of the manor house which preceded the modern buildings. A timbered hall has survived in Madeley, and its walls bear an inscription more consistent with a sundial – 'Walk knave. What lookest at?' Audley on the Roman Ryknield Street, has an alabaster figure on a sunken tomb in the chancel of Richard Delves who fought at Poitiers, one of four squires who carried their wounded knight, Sir James Audley, from the field. He had occupied the position of honour in front of the army, and, as he was borne back to his tent the Black Prince stopped his squires and confirmed that as 'the bravest knight in the battle' he had nobly justified his place of honour.

We have come now right against the Cheshire border to Betley, where the village grocer once told me of an ancient feud between the two great houses, the seventeenth-century hall and the nine-teenth-century court which stand on either side of the road not quite opposite each other.

'You'll see a clock tower on the stables of the court', he said, 'and you'll notice it has a clock face on three sides only. The blank side is visible down the drive from the hall, and the family at the court wasn't going to have its rivals telling the time by their clock.'

Many people have come to Kidsgrove from southward under-ground by one of the two Harecastle tunnels which carry the Trent and Mersey Canal from Cheshire into the Potteries, often with cargoes of Cornish clay. James Brindley constructed the first of the tunnels in 1777, incidentally finding a prolific seam of coal which gave the

30 (above)   *Milldale on the River Dove – haunt of the trout fisherman*
31   *A lake that gave its name to a poet, Rudyard Lake, near Leek, where Rudyard Kipling's parents first met at a picnic*

major impetus to the working of the modern North Staffordshire coal-field. Thomas Telford, the other great canal engineer, built the second tunnel 50 years later. Kidsgrove is an industrial extension of the Potteries, but it has a charming sylvan backwater called Acres Nook, with a lake which, during the magnificent summer of 1947 I watched steadily dry up while bur marigold followed the receding water down its bed.

North-eastward of Kidsgrove the land rises to Biddulph Moor, with the grim village of Mow Cop perched above its western escarpment. Up there one morning, walking out of Cheshire along Congleton Edge into Staffordshire, I was stopped by a police inspector and invited, quite courteously, to explain my presence there in walking kit. Satisfied – I hope, impressed – by my story that I was walking the entire boundary of Staffordshire, he told me that they were seeking 'some other hiker.' At this I bridled. You can suspect me of sleeping in a barn and making off with a pilfered pullet in my pack. You can call me walker, rambler, or any other kind of fool, but 'hiker' is a term I detest. So, delivering a slightly pompous lecture on philology, I went my way.

Mow Cop's higgledy-piggledy village is dominated by the mock ruin of Mow Cop Castle, built to enhance the view from Rode Hall, three miles distant on the Cheshire plain. A lesser protuberance is the Old Man of Mow, a pillar of rock left behind in a quarry and vividly reminiscent to one who knows Orkney of the Old Man of Hoy. On the Cheshire boundary up here there is a 360-degree view which includes the radio telescope at Jodrell Bank, nine miles distant in Cheshire, sometimes a full moon, at others a crescent.

One Sunday in May 1807 Mow Cop gave birth to Primitive Methodism when Hugh Bourne, a Stoke-on-Trent wheelwright, and William Clowes, a champion dancer from Burslem, called a camp meeting which lasted 14 hours. When Mow Cop Castle was given to the National Trust in 1937, 10,000 Methodists marked the occasion with a meeting on the hill. Maybe it was memories of this which led to two startling replies I got when I asked villagers if there was any local memorial to the birth of Primitive Methodism.

'No', said one, 'but they have a centenary now and then.' The other had an equal Rip Van Winkle disregard for the passage of time

– 'I don't think there's a memorial, but they hold a centenary occasionally.'

Just eastward of Mow Cop the Victoria pit is the northernmost of the eight North Staffordshire collieries which between them, in the year ending 31 March 1973, employed 7,800 men and produced 4,182,219 tons of coal, Hem Heath, the southernmost, just topping the million tons with 1,680 workers, though Silverdale, at 76 cwts, had the greatest output per man-shift.

The 'Five Towns' of Arnold Bennett had become six in 1910, taking in Fenton when they amalgamated to form Stoke-on-Trent, the coat-of-arms of which reveals much of the history of these towns. '*Vis unita fortior*', the joint motto, translates as 'Strength is the stronger for unity'. The crest, of an ancient Egyptian potter at his wheel, sums up the trade which has brought fame to the area as The Potteries, and the Portland vase in the first quarter comes from the old Tunstall arms and commemorates Wedgwood's jasper reproduction of an antique – a glass cameo vase – the Portland or Barberini Vase. In the second quarter a camel comes from the crest of John Ridgway, first Mayor of Hanley. An eagle represents Longton, and in the fourth quarter the scythe or snead pops up yet again in this book as the emblem of the Sneyd family of Keele, and appeared in the original arms of Tunstall and Burslem. The cross gules, fretted with gold, is a Fenton device, but is also a play on the arms of the Audley family in Burslem's old arms, while the boar's head, from the earlier Stoke and Longton arms, comes from the Sandford family. Finally, two Stafford knots recall one in the Tunstall arms, and a reminder, too, that the North Stafford Railway – the 'Knotty' – wound a small octopus of lines around the Potteries, had a works at Stoke, and ran a famous service to Newcastle-under-Lyme from which miners travelling to the old Leycett Colliery would jump before the station and rush to the lamp house.

The Wedgwoods were a very prolific family, the most famous of them, Josiah, born in 1730, being the thirteenth and youngest child of Thomas and Mary Wedgwood. So, despite the family being comfortable property owners, the younger sons had to work at the industry indigenous to their neighbourhood. Thus Josiah's father was a potter and his death, when Josiah was only nine, necessitated the boy leaving school and starting an apprenticeship in the Burslem pottery of his eldest brother, Thomas. Two years later, smallpox having permanently weakened Josiah's knee, he had to abandon the 'throwing' at which he had become so proficient.

He took up other skills within the industry and developed a progressive artistic conception which commended itself neither to his brother nor another firm, but met with the approval of Thomas Whieldon, a Fenton master-potter with whom Josiah worked until setting up his own business in 1759 at Ivy House Works, Burslem. Here Wedgwood was indefatigable as creative artist, potter and administrator, and within five years he was making donations towards schools and roads, and helping develop the canal system. In 1762 he was appointed Queen's Potter when he produced a 'Queen's Ware' tea service for Queen Charlotte, and in the same year he took additional premises at Brick House and Works, still in Burslem, where he remained until 1773 when he finally moved to Etruria which he had established on a site between Burslem and Stoke, building a garden village for his workers, Etruria Hall as his own residence, and a factory opened in 1769. His products went from strength to strength, both utilitarian and decorative, and his cream, black basalt, variegated marble, and ultimately blue jasper ware became world famous. As inventor of the pyrometer for measuring extreme heat Josiah was elected a Fellow of the Royal Society, and another side of the man is perpetuated in his medallions inscribed 'Am I not a man and a brother?', produced to raise money for slave emancipation.

In 1764 Josiah married his third cousin, Sarah Wedgwood, by whom he had seven children, and four years later he rid himself by amputation of the encumbrance of his diseased right leg. His activity thus enhanced, he continued his canal efforts and the Trent and Mersey Canal, opened in 1777 with Josiah as its first treasurer, passed through the Etruria Works to their great benefit. Among Wedgwood's great productions, two dinner services for Catherine ii, Empress of Russia, embodied 952 pieces of decorated cream-coloured ware. It has been written of Josiah Wedgwood that 'no other potter of modern times so successfully welded into one harmonious whole the prose and poetry of the ceramic art.' He died, aged 64, at Etruria on 3 January 1795 and lies buried in the churchyard of St Peter ad

Vincula at Stoke, where a Flaxman monument in the chancel records
that he 'converted a rude and inconsiderable manufactory into an
elegant art and an important part of national commerce.' Today his
works have moved to a country site at Barlaston, six miles from
Stoke, and there over 2,200 are employed, while the Wedgwood
Group, one of the world's largest pottery concerns, employs 8,000.

Two other eighteenth-century North Staffordshire potters of vastly
different upbringing were Josiah Spode, who at the age of six in
1739 saw his father buried in a pauper's grave, and Thomas Minton,
born in 1765 and educated at Shrewsbury School. Each founded a
firm and produced work much prized by collectors – the Spode Works,
still on their original site in the centre of Stoke, now being in the
hands of W. T. Copeland and Sons Ltd; while Mintons, though a
member of the Royal Doulton Group, still operate from the site
of the original china works though in a new factory with a charming
garden frontage.

In 1887 Henry Doulton extended to Burslem a pottery business
pioneered by his father, John Doulton, at Lambeth, London, in 1815,
and though the name Doulton is still associated with modern sanita-
tion Royal Doulton is a synonym for fine china ware, figurines and
toby-jugs so precious to collectors. Henry Doulton was the first
potter to receive a knighthood, in 1887.

A plaque on the building at the corner of Hope Street and Hanover
Street, Hanley, records the birth on 27 May 1867, in a previous house
and shop on the site, of Arnold Bennett, whose novels *The Old
Wives' Tale*, *Clayhanger*, *The Card*, and *Anna of the Five Towns*,
were set in the Potteries. By 1880 he was living at 205, Waterloo
Road, Burslem, now maintained by Stoke as the Arnold Bennett
Museum, but, leaving for London, aged 21, Bennett never again lived
in the area with which he is associated. The Bennett 'country' is a
restricted area around the centre of Burslem, his 'Bursley', where he
transforms Moorland Road into Moorthorne Road, Swan Bank into
Duck Bank, Nile Street into Aboukir Street, and Waterloo Road into
Trafalgar Road. St John's Church becomes St Luke's, but Burslem's
old Town Hall with its golden angel was used in several novels, particularly in *The Card*, where a ball is held in the assembly room.
In 1960 the City Council and Civic Trust redeveloped 'The

Shambles' as a garden with a pedestal on which is a portrait plaque to the author fashioned by Wedgwood's. Bennett died on 27 March 1931 and his ashes were interred in Burslem Cemetery.

In Broad Street, Hanley, the Mitchell Memorial Youth Centre commemorates Reginald Mitchell, designer of the Spitfire aircraft, who was born at 115, Congleton Road, Butt Lane, Talke. An inn with an aircraft sign, the 'Tiger Moth' stands on the A.520 at Meir, near the airport, and other Potteries pubs span the years from the 'Lump of Coal' at Brown Edge to the 'Man in Space 'at Trentham.

Stoke's two traditional industries, coal-mining and pottery making with the consequent extraction of clay marl, left the area a problem of derelict 'heaps and holes'. For two reasons this should make Stoke a focus for town-planners. The first is that its actual acreage of derelict area at 1648, and its percentage of derelict area at 7.2, raised it on 1969 figures far above any other local authority in England. Second is the splendid way in which Stoke is coping with its problem, transforming these areas into attractive amenity sites and linking them with 'walkways' along disused passenger and mineral railways. Today, for instance, Central Forest Park is growing out of the spoil of Hanley Deep Pit. This consisted mainly of three slag heaps known as the Three Ugly Sisters. One is now gone, while the others have been landscaped and incorporate a golf course, ski slopes, a nature reserve, camp site, adventure playground, picnic area and a flower garden. Schoolchildren planted trees and were thus involved in the scheme. Overlooking all this, just as it towered above the previous desolation, the pithead gear of Hanley Deep is preserved as an industrial monument and an elevated lookout point.

In the north-west of the conurbation Westport Water Park has been hewn out of a grim waterlogged area between the Trent and Mersey Canal and the London to Manchester railway line, and is already immensely popular for water sports. At Clanway, Tunstall, a partly-filled marl hole has become a sports stadium. Berry Hill was lucky in having a colliery spoil mound almost above a marl hole of similar proportions, so the one was conveniently pushed into the other to reclaim 70 acres for housing and industry. The enormous mountain of the Sneyd Colliery spoil has been re-shaped and seeded, and the Vesuvius-like tip of Mossfield Colliery is now seen from a section of the Greenway which pursues a serpentine course among the reclaimed land. Constructed along much of the loop line that once served the Potteries towns, it is hoped that eventually the Greenway will provide a traffic-free walk along the entire 13-mile north-south axis of the Stoke-on-Trent federation.

Stoke has a high loss of population to outlying areas – 21,000 over 1955–64 – with all that this has meant of new housing in green and pleasant land. Most cities have had similar problems, but Stoke has certainly more imagination than other authorities in restoring grass and trees in its depopulated urban areas to replace the surrounding countryside swallowed up by the outward migration of its population. Not only Stoke Corporation, but national and private bodies have undertaken the task of reclamation. The National Coal Board is filling in a marl hole adjacent to the defunct Stafford Colliery with spoil from Hem Heath Colliery still in operation, and the Shelton Iron and Steeel Works have tidied up some of the 80 acres within their province. Another project is that mounted by Brownhills School in clearing the Scotia Valley between Longport and Tunstall, an area including a tip from a tile works. Planting over 1,000 trees and shrubs given by the city the school authorities hope to include a nature trail among the new amenities they are creating.

Strenuous efforts are being made to clean up the River Trent in Stoke. In 1970 a national survey listed the Upper Trent as the most polluted river in England, but a £10 million scheme is expected to bring back fish to the city by 1975, followed soon after by allowing swimming in the river.

Staffordshire's neighbour, Derbyshire, is noted for half-a-dozen villages which celebrate 'well-dressing' on different occasions throughout the year. The custom spills over into one Staffordshire village north-east of the Potteries – Endon, where the well is decorated with flowers and a Well-Dressing Queen is crowned on the Spring Bank Holiday Saturday. Wily Will Willett, buried in Endon churchyard, made his bid for fame by dancing for 12 days and nights in the mid-eighteenth century. He used those 'missing eleven days' referred to in Chapter One when we altered the calendar, dancing from late on September 2, 1752 to the morning of September 14 – actually the next day.

CHAPTER TWELVE

Leek and the Moors

From the moors in the north of Staffordshire, frosted over with myriad heads of bog cotton, I anxiously watched the mists gathering beneath the setting sun. Not that I had any fear of being benighted up among that loneliness of heather, the lapwing and curlew my only companions – my anxiety arose from the mists, for I had a date with the sunset that night, 22 June 1972, in Leek churchyard five miles distant. I could make it in time, but would the sun be prematurely swallowed in those vapours? Alas, it was as I hurried past that remote hostelry, the 'Mermaid', loftily perched on the Morridge, and isolated until the Staffordshire Gliding Club came to keep it company.

Once again I was baulked in an attempt to see Leek's phenomenon of a 'double sunset', visible if conditions permit on the midsummer nights of 20, 21, and 22 June. On those nights if the sky is clear people gather in the north-east corner of Leek churchyard – the 'Doctors' Corner' because eight doctors are buried there – to watch the double sunset behind Bosley Cloud which touches the thousand foot contour on the Staffordshire–Cheshire border seven miles north-westward beyond Rudyard Lake. To be more exact Bosley Cloud's northern escarpment falls to the Cheshire Plain from the moorland plateau north of Biddulph, into which, at the summer solstice the sun sets, to reappear a few minutes later round the escarpment before its second and final setting.

Leek is known as the 'Capital of the Moorlands', an attractive town with over 20,000 population largely employed as textile and dyeing workers in several huge mills of many storeys. It has some interesting pub names, and if the 'Cock' in the cobbled Market Square is only ordinary it does display a plaque explaining that the first meeting of the founders of the Amalgamated Society of Textile Workers and Kindred Trades was held there on 21 April 1871. The 'Union' celebrates the marriage of Henry Tudor of Lancaster – Henry VII – and Elizabeth of York which ended the Wars of the Roses. The 'Quiet Woman', which occurs again eight miles away at Earl Sterndale, Derbyshire, is something of a gibe at female chatter, for the Leek sign shows a woman minus her head. A 'Quiet Woman' inn sign at Halstock, Dorset, where the lady has her head tucked underneath her arm, refers to a local St Judith or Judwardine, decapitated for her Christian faith in the sixth century. Leek has also a 'Wilkes Head' recalling John Wilkes, M.P. for Aylesbury and Middlesex in the mid-eighteenth century, a considerable rabble rouser in the Commons versus King agitation, though I can find no particular association of his with Leek.

In 1297 a fire destroyed the church at Leek and it was rebuilt some 20 years later, undergoing a restoration in 1856. Then in 1867 G. E. Street rebuilt the chancel, but architecturally the showpiece probably remains in the splendid timber roof of the nave, where, it is boasted, each cross-beam was hewn from a separate oak tree. Certainly the church is a focal point in any view of this pleasant town. 'Indeed', writes the vicar, the Rev. P. D. S. Blake, in the guidebook, 'as one drops down over Ladderedge and sees below one the sight of Leek on its hill in its valley, one is reminded of coming over the Mount of Olives and seeing Jerusalem standing on Mount Zion.'

Until 1215 Leek had rectors, the title being changed to vicar when the Lord of the Manor, Ranulf de Blundeville, 6th Earl of Chester, founded the Abbey of Dieulacres just across the Churnet, now a ruin. Rectors worked their glebe lands; vicars were paid by tithes as the representatives of those owning the rectorial dues, in Leek's case with the establishment of Dieulacres, the Abbot, who thereafter appointed a senior monk as vicar of Leek. The parish has one unique legal appointment, that of Warden of Leek instead of the normal vicar's warden and people's warden. Any ratepayer may be nominated, irrespective of religion, at the annual vestry meeting, which all ratepayers of Leek are entitled to attend. If more than three are nominated a town election is necessary, and this has happened recently; otherwise the vicar makes the choice and announces it on Easter Sunday.

On 6 February 1800 Hannah Rogers died aged 75 at Hob-house, Leek, followed on 12 February by her 79-year-old husband, George. They lie together in Leek churchyard with this epitaph :

> *From nuptial years, till creeping to fourscore,*
> *The various turns of Wedlock's bonds we bore,*
> *When my dear Mate did all her cares compose,*
> *On me devolved a double weight of Woes.*
> *Six days I labour'd hard with grief opprest*
> *Which Christ beheld with mercy-teeming breast,*
> *And sent a Sabbath of eternal rest.*

Am I wrong in thinking this of greater general interest than the various Saxon preaching crosses in the churchyard, though these are intriguing as ancient crosses go, with Leek near the boundary of the kingdoms of Mercia and Northumbria ? The tall cylindrical cross is said to have been raised by St Wilfred, Bishop of Ripon, whose Roman-style Christianity triumphed over the northern Celtic tradition at the Synod of Whitby in 664. Leek Church is dedicated to St Edward the Confessor, the quisling king so largely responsible for the Norman Conquest, who nevertheless redeemed himself as the builder of Westminster Abbey. The town and church have another association with the Conquest in the proudest production of the Leek School of Embroidery, an exact copy of the Bayeux Tapestry, now in Reading Museum, while the church has other examples of the school's work, notably four exquisite altar frontals. It was Mrs Thomas Wardle – later Dame Elizabeth – wife of the silk manufacturer, who founded the School of Embroidery in the 1870s to encourage the use of silk as a yarn for embroidering clothes. A rose window commemorates her.

A memorial tablet in the church to Thomas Osborn, who died in 1749, starts on a familiar graveyard theme, but concludes with a line of 'you can't take it with you' philosophy :

> *As I was, so be ye,*
> *As I am, ye shall be,*

That I gave, that I have;
What I spent, that I had,
Thus I end, all my cost,
What I left, that I lost.

The Ashenhurst brass beside the pulpit was so popular with brass-rubbers that a prohibition has been clamped on their activities to prevent further wear and tear. John Ashenhurst, who died in 1597, came of a well-known Leek family which moved to Park Hall, near Stafford. He was well blessed in life with four wives who gave him four sons and six daughters, and the entire rugger team is depicted on the brass, piously kneeling with hands clasped in prayer.

There is some divergence of opinion whether the Leek silk industry came with French Huguenot refugees or from Spitalfields by way of Derby. A memorial in the north wall recalls one of the Huguenot families, the Van Tuyls, wealthy refugees from Roman Catholic oppression who arrived in England in the guise of fruit peddlars carrying their sons in fruit panniers. These young men emigrated to America in 1700, John Peter Van Tuyl becoming a founder of the city of New York. It was a Peter Bogart Van Tuyl who married Olive Bullock of Leek, and the memorial commemorates both families.

Leek Grammar School was founded in 1723 by a native of the town, Thomas Parker, who became Lord Chancellor and the 1st Earl of Macclesfield, but was impeached for corruption and fined £30,000. He emerged from the privacy into which he retired only to become pall bearer to Sir Isaac Newton. Another prominent Leek native, Sir Arthur Nicholson, who raised the dominant clock tower in Ashbourne Road as a First World War memorial to his own son and other local men who fell in action, still has his family name perpetuated in the firm of Brough, Nicholson and Hall, textile manufacturers at Leek and Cheadle.

On 13 February 1947 a Halifax aircraft crashed on Grindon Moor, five miles east of Leek. That crash, more than anything else, emphasises the surprising remoteness of a large area of this heavily-populated, highly-developed county with its intricate communication network. A memorial in Grindon Church records that the six R.A.F. men who died in the crash were 'bringing relief to the stricken villages during the great blizzard of 1947'. Dying with them, as they dropped food by parachute. were two press photographers. During the phenomenal weather of that 1947 winter the villages of Grindon, Onecote, Wetton, and Butterton were competely cut off from road transport. In less severe winters it is unusual if at least once the Mermaid Inn upon the Morridge fails to make the news columns when it provides a night's shelter for schoolchildren and other travellers marooned by a snowstorm.

The isolation of these moorlands is underlined too by an ethnological phenomenon with which I made acquaintance when, during a walk in 1968, I joined a council gang for their dinner break in the portable shelter that defied a bitter June wind high among the gritstone uplands. The foreman took a swig of tea.

'I suppose', he said, 'it's because there were no facilities for travel that you have these predominant surnames around here.'

'Chaps had to court girls in their own villages and often married their cousins,' added another. 'Here in Butterton it's the Salts, in Grindon the Mycocks, and in Alstonfield the Beresfords.'

I had met my first Salt of Butterton at 8 a.m. – 'Curly' Jim Salt, an energetic 81, receiving his weekly churn of water specially brought from Ashbourne on the milk lorry. Water was not on tap at his home, Ivy Cottage, in the Holloway which climbs steeply to Butterton's tall spire from the Hoo Brook ford.

'My grandfather worked in the copper mine at Ecton – James Salt,' Curly told me, and seeing my interest in his clogs added: 'I've always worn clogs. Used to work on t'roads and found them comfortable. Still get 'em in Leek. No, I've never been to London, but I used to travel up Cheshire way. Aye, there's a lot of mixed-up Salts in this village.'

Mix-ups there were, like Raymond John Salt's daughter Ruby, from 'Bottom o' Town', who married Joe Salt of Brook House; mix-ups like Jim Salt at the Stores who, further to confuse the postmistress, came from nearby Waterhouses to marry a Butterton Salt, Doreen.

'She's my sister,' said Reuben Salt of Lane House Farm. 'She and Jim weren't related.'

Of Reuben's four sisters, one more, Frances, married another Salt – her cousin Harold of Grindon, which pokes up a neighbourly spire barely a mile distant from Butterton and has its spillover of seven Salts on the electoral roll.

'We are strong church people', Reuben, organist and secretary of Butterton Church Council, told me. 'I had a great-uncle, the Rev. Enoch Salt, lived at Crofts Heads and I think he once kept the Black Lion Inn. My father, Richard Salt, married Ella Salt of this village. He was a farmer and milk carrier from Elkstone to the dairy factory at Ecton, which closed when the Manifold Valley Railway did.'

The vicar, the Rev. Michael Bromfield, told me that the earliest local Salt to his knowledge was a Rev. Ralph Salt, curate in 1586 at Onecote near by.

'As a new vicar feeling my way about Butterton, if I said "Hello Mr Salt" or "Good morning, Mrs Salt" I was fairly certain to be right', he added, 'but to be more specific there's Colin Salt of Nook House, Geoffrey of Elkstone, Annie of Greenlow Head, Fred at Heathy Roods Farm, Charlie at Steps Cottage, Joe at Brooke House, Bill at Wardle Cottage; the Salts of Bollands Hall, at Town End; and Reuben had four brothers – Bill of Causeway House, Edgar at Tatton Mill, Bernard at Waterfall, and John at Grindon.'

There was, too, Leslie Salt of Mount Pleasant – I bumped into his wife in the village.

'Leslie's father was Hezekiah Salt', she told me, 'a brother of Raymond at Bottom o' Town.'

This was where I had come in. I had gone full circle with the Salts, with stories of problems in the school register where so many of the children are Salts, and of the football match when a Butterton XI incorporating ten Salts lost heavily to Leek. 'Butterton Salts peppered by Leek' was the headline in the local paper.

Yet the Salts make only a modest show in Butterton churchyard. Other village families, the Stubbs, the Cantrells, and the Hambletons are there in as great force. When in 1775 Mrs Ruth Stubbs gave £5 and 'the profits of one half a beast grass in the Clews to the poor of Butterton for ever' the name of John Cantrell appeared as church-warden on the charity board in the church. Rowland Cantrell and William Hambleton, with Joseph Wood, are commended on a tablet for sacrificing their lives in an 'unsuccessful but heroic attempt to rescue from death a youth, Joseph Shenton, who had descended an unused shaft on August 30, 1842.'

A stone pillar stands near Grindon Church gate, whither I walked after leaving the council workers. It bears one readable inscription: 'The Lord of the Manor of Grindon established his right to this rindle at the Stafford Assizes, March 17, 1862'. A rindle is a brook, and I could see its course passing the stone, though it was dry and over-grown with grass. Maybe, like the winterbournes of chalk country, it flows only in wet weather.

On Grindon Church memorial to the First World War are two Mycocks killed in action and two who returned. A plaque on the organ records that John Mycock, one of the casualties, had been organist for 20 years. Such scant reference inside the church did not prepare me for the congregation of Mycocks gathered in the church-yard. Never have I seen such a forest of headstones bearing the same name – Mycocks of Saucefields, Porch Farm, Ladyside, Willcroft Hill, Lilac Cottage, Summerhill, Hillsdale, Martin's Lowe, Berkham-sytch. The most recent burial seemed to be Ernest Higton Mycock of Greenhouse Farm, who died in 1964; the longest ago John Mycock, interred in 1832. As with the Salts, there has been intermarriage among the Mycocks.

'But', said Charles William Mycock of Ladyside, 'one Miss Maggie Mycock moved outside the clan. She married a John Alcock of Elk-stone. Her father was William Mycock of Ossams Hall Farm. We called him "Lloyd George" because he broke with the Conservative tradition of the Mycocks by being a staunch Liberal.'

The Grindon Mycocks seem to have originated in two brothers who came from Derbyshire over 300 years ago. One was a stone-mason, the other a shoemaker, so that the present-day Mycocks are either stonemasons or cobblers according to their descent, though a sub-division of butchers probably stems from a James Thomas Mycock, whose mother nicknamed him 'Butcher'. in 1968 Mrs Mary Mycock, aged 89, was the matriarch of the clan. She had five daughters and four sons who grew to maturity, and they belong to the 'stonemason' line. Her daughter, Edith, told me:

'I'm a Crown Farm Mycock and I married my second cousin Arthur Mycock of Deepdale. Arthur's grandfather was always known as

"Mylord" Mycock. Mylord had a brother who was a well-known bandleader, and another who kept the Royal Hotel at Blackpool. He was the most successful Mycock and left £72,000. Another Mycock hotelier was Thomas, son of Mylord, who kept the Albion Hotel, Blackpool.'

The Staffordshire Mycocks are not restricted to Grindon. There are, in 1973, no fewer than eight of the 'stonemason' Mycocks on the Waterhouses telephone exchange. The Mycocks appear to have been quiet, law-abiding people. All my efforts to discover any exciting stories about them in Grindon foundered on the rocks not of a Mycock, but of a Smith about whom they insisted on telling me. He was the vicar some 50 years ago, who shot and killed his maid and himself.

To walkers from the Black Country and Birmingham the most accessible of the limestone dales – so often thought all to belong to Derbyshire – is that of the River Hamps, its entire length in Staffordshire, and a good day afoot might well start in the southernmost hills of the Pennines, the Weaver Hills, as it did for Stanley Whitehead and me one June day in 1971. Abandoning my car at Wootton we took a track west of the village and gained the grassy slopes which led us up the Weavers to the trig point at 1,217 feet. From this breezy spot the nearer verdant hillsides were criss-crossed with white limestone walls, quarries spoiled the view in the middle distance, but south and eastward was a vast if featureless expanse including Cannock Chase, Charnwood Forest, and the Needwood Forest across the Dove Valley. Our way lay northward, downhill towards the track to Wardlow. Descending beside busy quarries we turned momentarily left on the main Stoke road, right again to Caldon Grange, and so by fields and Stoneyrock Farm to the gap in the hills where the River Hamps runs northward to join the Manifold. This tract is dominated by a cement works which must deter the little people whom Mary Howitt, a local poetess, once saw on Caldon Low:

> *A hundred fairies danced last night,*
> *And the harpers they were nine.*

But she laughed at their antics and broke the spell:

And then on the top of Caldon Low
There was no one left but me.

The Hamps is unusual among rivers because it disappears from time to time down 'swallet holes' and runs underground, leaving a dry surface bed of cream-coloured smooth limestone rocks. Such was the river's state when we struck it at Waterhouses, and dry it remained for the four miles to Beeston Tor, with butterbur, that virile plant of the limestone valleys, prolific among the rocks. As if it were not enough to follow a river without any water, we actually walked on a railway without any rails. This was the track of the Leek and Manifold Valley Light Railway, closed in 1934, the eight miles of which, from Hulme End to Waterhouses are now a macadamised walkers' path.

The railway was constructed on a 2 foot 6 inch gauge as a result of the Light Railways Act of 1896 which aimed to give less populous districts the benefit of cheaper rail communication. In addition to anticipating freight in coal, milk, cattle feed, limestone, and building stone, the promoters hoped for the revival of Ecton Copper and Lead Mines on the route, though this did not materialise. Tourist traffic was expected, and interesting estimates were made of prospective local passenger traffic. According to 'Manifold' in his 1965 book on the railway, of a total population in 1891 of 3,366 for Alstonfield, Butterton, Fawfieldhead, Grindon, Longnor, Sheen, Warslow, Wetton, and Throwley it was expected that 7% would travel once weekly to Leek Market, and that 3% would use the railway on the other six days of the week, making 35,000 single journeys in a year.

The opening ceremony was on 27 June 1904, the inn at Hulme End modernising its name for the occasion from the 'Wagon and Horses' to the Light Railway Hotel. Unhappily the railway was a constant failure, and the last public train ran on 10 March 1934. It was Sir Josiah Stamp, chairman of the L.M.S. Railway, who, on 23 July 1937, declared the footpath open.

Redstarts seem to favour the dales, and several times we saw their fiery tails flitting among the bushes. When a young bull, grazing beside the track, began following us with no good intent we were glad to take evasive action by nipping into the dry river bed, to be told by an onlooker that we could not have sought such salvation three weeks earlier when the river was a roaring torrent. Shortly after midday we found our valley barred by the great limestone outcrop of Beeston Tor where, in St Bertram's Cave, Saxon jewels and coins have been found. The Manifold, another 'disappearing' river, joins the Hamps beneath Beeston Tor, and a mile upstream Thor's Cave gapes from the hillside above. Here, too, treasure was found by those great explorers of these uplands, Thomas Bateman, and the Wetton schoolmaster, Samuel Carrington, on whose grave in Wetton churchyard are carved the shells and fossils he so often unearthed from this limestone.

The confluence of the Hamps and Manifold beneath the tor was quite dry, and we had no need of the stepping stones to reach the steep grassy path up the tor to the road above. From this road we could appreciate Soles Hill and Oldpark Hill, which reared their pointed heads 1,100 feet above the dale we had just walked. In this Staffordshire and Derbyshire limestone it is the dales, scored deep by their rivers, which constitute the features. The hills, lovely and green as they are, bare of untidy hedgerows and trees, are habitable by man and beast, while walls of white limestone chequer the emerald grass to their summits. Whenever I walk this glorious area I laugh at all the enthusiasm for that other stone-wall countryside, the Cotswolds. Stanley and I agreed that the Cotswolds cannot hold a candle to the dales and their hills.

Our upland way now took us by field paths and open country with ancient mine shafts, passing through several local slit stiles – narrow gaps in the stone walls tapering downwards which deter plump walkers. On the two miles down to Ilam the road verges beneath the stone walls were laced with the flowers of sweet cicely, smelling pungently of aniseed, one of the prolific plants of Staffordshire limestone.

Among the lusher beauties of a spot called Paradise the Manifold emerges from its underground course to flow through the Swiss-like village of Ilam which owes its 'model' charms to Jesse Watts Russell, who also raised the 'Eleanor' cross to his wife's memory. St Bertram or Bertelin is buried in Ilam Church, which has also some of those sad relics known as maiden garlands – the white gloves and artificial flowers from the coffin of an unmarried girl. Ilam Hall, given in 1935 by Robert McDougall of Manchester, is one of the largest youth hostels in Britain, and it has introduced many thousands of youngsters to the glorious walking country of the dales.

Blore Church was our next landmark, and the last three of our 18 miles, by Lady Low, Swinscoe, Brown Edge, and Blake Low brought us from the austere white beauty of the hedgeless limestone back through hedgerow country on to the less attractive gritstone where the stone walls look grimier.

Another splendid walk of a dozen miles or so starts from the car park at the southern end of Dovedale, where a field path behind the Izaak Walton Hotel debouches on the road at Ilam. Here we enter Paradise, an Elysian stretch of magnificently-wooded country which so impressed Dr Samuel Johnson that he moved the entire area to Abyssinia in the novel *Rasselas* which he wrote to pay for his mother's funeral. A number of its great trees still lie aslant or recumbent where they fell on the terrific night of 16 February 1962 when a hurricane did so much damage in Sheffield.

Enclosed by a wooden fence in Paradise Walk is the Battle Stone, the shaft of an ancient cross which was unearthed from the foundations of a cottage during the rebuilding of Ilam in 1840. Although traditionally associated with a battle between the Saxons and the Danes, the stone has carvings similar to those on crosses at Ilam and Checkley, and my map describes it as the Cross Stone. A bridge carries the public footpath across to the west of the Manifold after half a mile of Paradise Walk. To the east in another half-mile a lodge cottage displays a notice ordering the payment of a toll for having used the private path. The lodge where this toll was collected bears the inscription 'The first stone of River Lodge was laid on May 6, 1840, by Jemima, Countess of Monteglas.'

An uphill track climbing into the stone-wall country past the solid grey bulk of Castern Hall and through a farmyard leads to upper slopes yellow and purple with ragwort and thistles, and the walker can look down entranced into a lost valley – a remote stretch of greensward backed by Cheshire Wood and bounded otherwise by the dry bed of the Manifold and the grey crags of Beeston Tor. It always reminds me of R. D. Blackmore's description of the Doone Valley on

Exmoor: 'It looked as if no frost could enter, neither wind go ruffling; only spring, and hope, and comfort breathe to one another. . . .'

Hereabouts the track ends at some old lead-mine workings, leaving an uncharted way towards Wetton involving several crossings of stone walls. The careful walker tries not to dislodge stones from these walls or, if he does, he replaces them, noticing in them perhaps some brachipods or fossilised sea-lilies. In his poem 'Sussex' Rudyard Kipling writes:

> *We have no waters to delight*
> *Our broad and brookless vales –*
> *Only the dewpond on the height,*
> *Unfed, which never fails.*

These Staffordshire hills, where Kipling's parents first met, have water all right, but the limestone is so porous that it seeps through, so artificial dewponds are made to water the cattle, several being passed on the way to Wetton.

In 1905 Caroline Joseph Adams of Newton, Massachusetts, gave Wetton church clock in memory of her grandfather, Ralph Adams, and ten years later, 43 men who regulated their youthful comings and goings by that clock were fighting in the First World War. Six of them died, three being Gilmans. Wetton churchyard has no outstanding epitaph, but I like the simplicity of the verse to Francis Singleton,

> *A friend so true there were but few*
> *And difficult to find;*
> *A man more just and true to trust*
> *There is not left behind.*

A path across a mile of crisp pasture with slit stiles at the walls brings the walker from Wetton to Alstonfield by way of its football pitch. 'As I'm an honest man, a very pretty church', said the 'Compleat Angler', Izaak Walton, when first he came to the village with his friend Charles Cotton. A track across the front of the church continues as a delightful lane to the picturesque village of Milldale, where the Dove is spanned by a successor to the Viator's Bridge of Walton's famous book.

From Milldale the four best-known miles of Dovedale run southward with the river through a limestone canyon to the stepping stones below Thorpe Cloud. The path through Dovedale is actually in Derbyshire, following, as it does, the left bank of the Dove, which is here the county boundary. I frankly prefer the moorlands to the dales, and Dovedale can often be dank and sloppy to the walker, with the humidity so frequently engendered by the blanket of trees on the almost vertical limestone which encloses the dale. Up among those leaves and branches are such features as Reynard's Cave, reached by those with a head for heights up a breakneck boulder slope spanned by a natural arch. The Derbyshire limestone rises to Pickering Tor and Tissington Spires, while on the Staffordshire side Jacob's Ladder, falling from Ilam Tops, offers a steep access to or exit from the dale, with the Twelve Apostles keeping watch and ward to southward. Sufficient sunlight penetrates the trees to impart a sparkle to the Dove as, helped by a number of small weirs, it pursues its downhill course, with many trout to be seen cruising in the stiller reaches.

To emerge from Dovedale when the sun is behind Thorpe Cloud is to see the dark shadow of this Matterhorn in miniature thrown across the river from Derbyshire on to the bulk of Bunster Hill in Staffordshire, where Castle Cave is a magnet to the venturesome.

Back to Milldale – and half a mile eastward of the village, after running parallel with the road, the Dove comes down beneath Shining Tor from Wolfscote Dale and Beresford Dale, country I much prefer to Dovedale. Here the limestone is free from trees, so that the eye travels from the scintillating stream up green slopes with dazzling white outcrops. The wise man walks upstream here. The rise is not sufficient to be tiring, and, with the sun at one's back, the many little weirs give life to the river. The ravine known as Narrowdale provides another solar phenomenon, the same today as when Dr Plot wrote nearly 300 years ago – 'the inhabitants, for that quarter of the year when the sun is nearest the Tropic of Capricorn, never see it at all; and at length when it does begin to appear again they never see it till about one by the clock, which they call thereabouts the

Narrowdale noon'. Were there inhabitants in Narrowdale in the seventeenth century? There is none today.

Where the austere beauty of Wolfscote Dale merges with the more sylvan charms of Beresford Dale and meadows border the river we are in the heart of the fishing country shared by Izaak Walton and his friend Charles Cotton of Beresford Hall, 40 years younger, who entwined their initials in the little fishing house he built beside the Dove. Beresford Hall is gone, but the fishing house is still there, embowered by trees and difficult of access. Here, too, is Pike Pool – 'But what have we got here? A rock springing up in the middle of the river. This is one of the oddest sights I ever saw.' These were Viator's words on first seeing the limestone pinnacle or pike in the Dove as recorded by Cotton in the second part of *The Compleat Angler*, which he wrote in ten days.

Cotton's own canopied pew can still be seen in Alstonfield Church, competing in its decoration with the two-decker pulpit, an ornate feature, though less lavish in the text carved upon it, which presupposes an acquaintance with Revelation, Chapter 2 – 'Be faithful, etc.; and I will give thee a crowne, etc.'

A mile west of the Dove I was once walking towards Hulme End when, in the angle of the stone walls where a road struck north towards Sheen, I noticed a small enclosure beneath a yew with taller trees rising above. A slight mound suggested a burial, probably a pet's grave. An enquiry at a cottage across the road revealed that it was the grave of a John Bonsall who, some 200 years ago, wanted to be buried on his own land, though I could not gather if the plot was ever consecrated. My informant was herself a Mrs Bonsall and she added that the builder's initials, R.B. 1725, on her cottage were those of one Richard Bonsall, an ancestor of her husband.

South of Hulme End, Ecton Hill raises its noble bulk to form an impressive backcloth to Warslow, a pleasant village with lime trees around its church. Here a box pew was used by the Harpur-Crewe family from Calke Abbey, Derbyshire, when they stayed at Warslow Hall for the grouse shooting, and an east window commemorates Sir Thomas Wardle, the Leek silk magnate, who built the chancel. Sir Thomas had an estate at Swainley in the Manifold valley nearby. A director and leading spirit in the Manifold Valley Railway, he never-theless did not intend it to spoil his view, so it was tunneled – motor-way construction units please copy. It was thought by the promoters of the railway that tourists would not relish the dry river beds of the Hamps and Manifold, so Sir Thomas, who was a geologist, tried to close with cement the swallet holes down which the rivers disappear, but the pressure of water blew out the concrete and left us with the phenomenon.

Situated between the Dove and the Manifold where these rivers are not a mile apart, and where the high bare moors to westward have dropped into more verdant country, Longnor is a village of considerable character. Its buildings certainly reflect the seeming grime of gritstone, and its church, with plain warehouse-like windows, has been called the ugliest in Staffordshire. But there are fascinating narrow flagged passages such as Chapel Street and Queen Street abut-ting on a wide space where the Harpur-Crewe coats-of-arms on the Market Hall and the Crewe and Harpur Arms face one another across the heart of the village, while the 'Cheshire Cheese' round the corner has a cheese on its sign complete with cutting wires. The church interior is plain, neat, and chapel-like, but with a reredos from which an arch of delicate plaster work reminiscent of Adam encloses the east window.

Rising from the cobbles, the façade of the Market Hall still records the tolls exacted by Sir Vauncy Harpur Crewe in 1903. The seller of every pen of sheep or other livestock, for instance, paid fourpence; of a basket of eggs one penny.

Longnor churchyard is prolific in epitaphs which record much social history and link the area with the national scene. That of William Billinge describes him as 'born in a cornfield at Fawfieldhead 1679. At the age of 23 he enlisted into H.M. Service under Sir George Rooke and was at the taking of the fortress of Gibraltar, 1704, served under Marlborough at Ramillies and wounded by a musket shot in the thigh. He afterwards returned to his native country and with manly courage defended his Sovereign's rights at the rebellions in 1715 and 1745. He died within the space of 150 yards of where he was born and was interred here 30 January 1791 aged 112 years.' William's original headstone crumbled, but the people of Longnor, with a laudable sense of history, subscribed for a new stone in 1903, adding this couplet:

> *Billeted by death, I quartered here remain;*
> *When the trumpet sounds I'll rise and march again.*

The 1745 rebellion came perilously near William's cornfield, for not only did Bonnie Prince Charlie stay a night in Leek vicarage during his invasion which reached as far south as Derby, he also stayed at the Royal Cottage Inn on the Buxton road where, in the absence of any other explanation, I take Bareleg Hill beside the inn to refer to the Young Pretender's kilted bravoes.

Barely accessible against Longnor church wall and hidden by an elder tree is the headstone of Samuel Bagshaw, carpenter, part of whose verse I deciphered as:

> *For seventy-one revolving years*
> *He sowed no seeds of strife,*
> *With wood and saw, line, rule, and square*
> *Employed his useful life.*

He lived at Hardings Booth, still a farm near Longnor, as did Isaac Bagshaw, whose epitaph is the customary verse of his blacksmith's trade, seen also at Aston, Birmingham and Bilton, Rugby:

> *My sledge and hammer lie reclined,*
> *My bellows, too, have lost their wind, etc.*

One decayed headstone Longnor did not restore, but the vicar had kept a copy and I am glad to give it permanence here. It read: 'Dedicated to the memory of Jane Simms who unintentionally effected an ignominious exit of her inglorious career on the 21st day of April, 1830, aged 22 years –

> *I place this here kind friends to let you know,*
> *A subtile lover prov'd my overthrow;*
> *Perfidious suitors all I did beware,*

For Doomsday shall their secret deeds declare,
And though I'm vanished far from human view,
Yet at God's bar I surely shall meet you;
Where female wrongs shall amply be redrest,
And fraud and guile for ever be supprest.

In the burial register there is written in the margin of this entry:
'In consequence of poison.'

In January 1972 Longnor flashed into international significance
when a television company, seeking an isolated village for a programme on tobacco smoking habits, settled on Longnor. The basis
of the programme was for smoking villagers to give up for one
week during which pubs and shops stopped selling tobacco and
cigarettes.

'What the pubs lost on tobacco they made up in beer sales', the
vicar told me, 'as all the national papers descended on us, as did
Dutch and French television, while we had enquiries from U.S.A.'

A village meeting was held at which prominent anti-smoking
doctors spoke, and a follow-up television programme six months
later revealed, happily, that some 20 erstwhile smokers had continued
to abstain.

Let us now cross to westward of the Leek-Buxton road at Upper
Hulme into climbers' Staffordshire of the Ramshaw Rocks and the
Five Clouds of the Roaches with Hen Cloud isolated from them
by Windygates gap. But even as we turn our backs on the eastern
moorlands we have perforce to cast one rearward glance at the
Mermaid Inn, stranded lonely on the Morridge like the Ark on Ararat.
Its saucy sign seems inappropriate to these inland hills, yet it derives
from a good legend. Northward of the inn, where Merryton Low rises
to 1,603 feet, is Black Mere or Mermaid Pool, where, it is said, a
beautiful young woman was once drowned as a witch. Shortly
afterwards her chief tormenter, Joshua Linnet, was himself found
drowned in the pool with talon scratches on his face. Local gossips
declare that no bird will fly over Mermaid Pool, yet one summer
evening as I sat lonely beside it watching the sun set over Cheshire,
half fearing, half hoping that a shapely arm would rise and beckon
me into the depths, I saw curlew, lapwings, and snipe cross the

fatal mere. Mercifully, in a changing world, a certain pristine change-lessness broods up in this Staffordshire 'White Country' blanketed with bog cotton. In April 1952 the 'Mermaid' reverted to a seven-day license, and the first pint drawn on the Sunday was drunk by John Mellor who had downed the last pint on a Sunday before the six-day license came into force 40 years earlier.

The stupendous outcropping of the Roaches and the Ramshaw Rocks, where tall pillars lean drunkenly like the battlements of a fortress overwhelmed in some titanic struggle of giants. From the Buxton road a phenomenon known as the 'Winking Eye' caused by the alternate background of rock and sky to a gap in the hillside, gives a blinking effect as though one of the dying titans is taking a last look at the battlefield. In fact, warfare is not unassociated with the Roaches which, it is said, were christened Les Roches – the Rocks – by French prisoners from the Napoleonic wars.

From Upper Hulme a sporting road enables a five-mile circuit of the Roaches and their outliers, but this is walking country, and a half-mile across moorland from the village brings you to the foot of Hen Cloud, a scrambling ascent and a meandering walk on the crest beset with many crags. For the climber there is the Central Route, the Great Chimney, and the Arete.

The Roaches, which raise their two-mile spiky spine half a mile north-west of Hen Cloud, are private property and strictly a small fee for disporting oneself on them should be paid at the gamekeeper's cottage tucked in at the western foot of the outcrops. The lower western slopes are tree-clad, and the cottage seems almost part of the Lower Tier of gritstone. To the left a climb to the Promenade brings you to grips with the Upper Tier. Here a walk to your left among the trees, with some forbidding overhangs on your right ultimately discloses a break in the cliff wall with a gully surmountable by the walker, who attains a lofty ridge which can be followed north-westward giving splendid panoramic views past Skyline Buttress with its pool and trig point at 1,656 feet, to a safe descent of 300 feet by a path to the road at Roaches End.

The climber meanwhile will be pitting his skills against Saul's Crack and the Sloth, where the Great Slab and the Pedestal lead to the crux of the Overhang which involves a hair-raising free swing.

Joe Brown, the doyen of British rock climbers, does not scorn these climbs and has found them an excellent training ground for his pupils.

North of the Roaches across Goldsitch Moss the village pub at Flash, the New Inn, proclaims on its sign 'Highest Village in England, 1,158 feet above sea level.' Next door a notice read 'Flash Village Store, Quarnford Post Office', a duality occasioned by Quarnford being a civil parish without any community of that name, and Flash the centre of population, such as it is. It nestles, one short street, with plane trees around the church, on the southern slope of Oliver Hill, the highest point of Staffordshire at 1,684 feet. An occasional bungalow or detached farm raises the population of Flash by a score or so. The name is said variously to derive from counterfeit or 'flash' coins once struck at Pastures Farm under the legitimate guise of a button press, and from cheap or 'flash' trinkets sold at a moorland market nearby, the haunt of shady or 'flash' characters who could quickly cross the Derby or Cheshire border to evade the Staffordshire police.

A grim place in winter snows, on a sunny June day Flash distils a pastoral peace melodious with lark-song, the cows and ponies belly-deep among buttercups and ox-eye daisies in fields surrounded by gritstone walls. Across the Buxton road the bland expansive and featureless moors are so different from the view southward where the hills rear up like a succession of advancing wave crests. Among the bird-foot trefoil at the roadside near Flash can be found patches of rarish dyer's greenweed, a paler yellow and more upright than the trefoil, and to stray from the road is to bring down the wrath of lapwings whose nests are in the heather and pasture.

An anemometer spins in the upland breezes at the home of Mrs Margaret Kidd, who succeeded her mother-in-law, Florence Kidd, as an auxiliary weather observer. She is phoned by the Meteorological Office at Ringway Airport, Manchester, every hour from 6.50 a.m. to 5.50 p.m. for a report on wind direction and speed, and the amount and height of cloud. Mrs Kidd senior was still operating as observer into her nineties.

Flash Church is distinguished by the coat-of-arms of the ubiquitous Harpur-Crewes in a window, a charming little mouse half hidden beneath one of the carved apples around the pulpit, and no fewer than eleven Mellors who served in the First World War. Of Ellen Day her epitaph in the churchyard says 'Plain was her form, yet rich her mind.'

A favourite day's walk of Midland ramblers, with coach support, starts from Flash and provides a lovely and varied 14 miles to Rudyard village, near Leek. Beside the Wesleyan Chapel at Flash a narrow hill track between stone walls to Wolf Edge, the western slope of Oliver Hill, where the tremulous notes of the curlew greet the walker in a trackless wilderness of bog, bilberry, and tufted heather. Aiming downhill for the track to Knotbury, we cross a peaty stream bridged by a great uncut slab of gritstone. A mile of narrow walled track now brings us to a last farm above the ravine cut by a tributary as it hurries to meet the River Dane at Three Shires Head where, in the scenery of a Highland glen, Staffordshire, Cheshire, and Derbyshire meet, and the Dane takes over the job of Staffordshire's boundary abandoned by the Dove at its source a mile eastward. Between the two rivers the northernmost salient of Staffordshire thrusts on to Axe Edge Moor with the Congleton-Buxton road far above.

Three Shires Head is an idyllic place with only foot tracks converging there – a seductive spot liable to make a walker linger as I have often done in peaceful sunshine, with the rushing of water beneath the bridge and down the tiny falls where dippers dive and pied wagtails and white-rumped wheatears bob and curtsey. Here the quiet of the hills enfolds the footslogger and he is apt to stretch out with his head on his pack.

Instead, with seven miles still to go, let us sort out the Stoke One Inch Ordnance Survey Sheet – we need it in another mile. A sandy path on the Cheshire side of the Dane climbs Cut Thorn Hill before dropping across fields to Knar Farm, with a grand view ahead of the serrated ridge of the Roaches. This land belonged to the Earls of Derby, and the farmer at Knar once told me that, while he had never been to the Roaches he once went to London to the wedding feast of an Earl of Derby at the Savoy Hotel.

Reaching the road west of the Dane bridge, our route crosses into Staffordshire again, and turns back downstream beside the river along a footpath. On this walk do watch the map religiously hereabouts. The paths around Gradbach, which take you past the Peter

Wilson Memorial Camp of Buxton Scouts, are not easy to interpret. I well remember my first venture on to Gradbach Hill, when I did a Blondin-like stepping stone crossing of Black Brook, only to find a footbridge just downstream, from which a path veers right and climbs unremittingly beneath arching branches for half a mile with delightful glimpses of the Dane farther below at every gap in the trees. High up here beside the grouse moor of Back Forest is one of the secret wonders of Staffordshire – Lud's Church. Near the top of the ascent the bastion of Castle Cliff Rocks rises on the right of the path. Nearly opposite a path runs back, and 150 yards along it on the right is the narrow cleft which leads to Lud's Church, a place of macabre compulsion. It is a natural 'church' formed by some seismic convulsion, with a 'nave' 200 yards long between 60 foot high walls rising sheer only eight feet apart. Ferns and other vegetation cling to the walls and a dank air enshrouds the place. At the extremity of the 'nave', if you continue beyond the steps up to the moor, there is a considerable cave. Beyond the 'chancel' at the other end lies a second cave.

Lud's Church gets its name from Walter de Lud-Auk, one of Wycliff's Lollards who worshipped here in secret during the fourteeenth century when the sect was persecuted. When soldiers discovered and attacked Lud's Church, Lud-Auk's 18-year-old grand-daughter, Alice, was killed in a struggle, and an oak at the opening of the chasm is said to mark her grave, while her effigy in wood once stood on a rock ledge in the 'church'. Lud's Church has one of the 'leap' legends so popular in England, witness Douglas's Leap on Haughmond Hill, where the Black Douglas was captured after the Battle of Shrewsbury; the Major's Leap on Wenlock Edge, Shropshire, and Winter's Leap on the lower Wye, these last two Cavalier escapes from pursuing Roundheads. At Lud's Church it is Trafford's Leap, where a squire of Swythamley leapt the chasm while hunting.

I wonder if Lud's Church could provide Staffordshire's greatest surprise; an all-the-year-round snowfield. On 7 July some 300 years ago a man emptied a sack of snow in Leek Market Square, which he had got from Lud's Church. I have seen packed snow there in May. Might it be that some year, of heavy and late snowfall, when the summer was unusually cold and dry, that the last snow lingered to the first snow of another winter?

From Lud's Church the track continues across grouse moors 1,250 feet up on Back Forest. There are two great eye-catchers hereabouts – Shutlingsloe, an alluring conical hill rising three miles north in Cheshire like a miniature Schiehallion; and the Hangingstone, seemingly defying gravity on the slope above Swythamley Park. This massive rock has a couple of memorials, one to 'Burke', a mastiff, the other, dated 1949, to Lieut. Col. Conley Brocklehurst of the Royal Hussars. Sir Philip Brocklehurst introduced wallabies into Swythamley deer park, but a number escaped in 1938 and for some years were reported to be breeding and running wild on the moors. Another animal – the badger – appears in the Brocklehurst coat-of-arms, a heraldic rebus or pun on 'Brock', an old country name for the badger.

Earlier squires of Swythamley, the Traffords, have left us not only Trafford's Leap but the stone in Leek Church inscribed to 'William Trafford of Swythamley Esqr. died December 10th 1967, aged 93'. William is depicted on the stone wearing a country workman's smock and holding a flail with a wheatsheaf at his feet, but with the Trafford motto 'Now Thus' beside him. He raised a troop for the king during the Civil War, but returned home on the king's capture. Followed by Cromwellian soldiers, he disguised himself in the smock and continued safely threshing corn in a barn while a search was mounted for him.

A gated road skirts Swythamley Park and drops down a 1 in $5\frac{1}{2}$ gradient at Bearda Hill, a name smacking of Manx. The Dane is close on the right, still the county boundary, and we follow one of its tributary brooks to a riverside path and eventually a lane into Rushton Spencer. Crossing the Leek-Macclesfield road, a stream, and a railway, an uphill track leads to Rushton Spencer Church, the 'chapel in the wilderness'. A wooden building, though encased in stone, with a timber belfry and dormers, it is dedicated to St Laurence, and I have never found it open. This rendered a notice I once saw in the porch superfluous – 'No money is ever left in this church and it contains nothing of value to thieves. Keep my hands from picking and stealing – Church Catechism.' Thus does Christian charity descend to the level of what it deplores.

In 1781 Thomas Meaykin came to his second burial in Rushton Spencer churchyard, where his stone is inscribed 'As a man falleth before wicked men: so fell I.' They say that he was in love above his station with his employer's daughter and that her father had him drugged and taken to Stone where he was buried alive. Friends who exhumed him found him thrown face down in a coffin, which was brought back to his boyhood home at Rushton Spencer.

A mile south of the church, pleasantly accessible by lanes and field paths, is Rudyard Lake, artificial but beautiful, and reminding me of a smaller Bassenthwaite. Two miles long, and on average a quarter of a mile wide, it was constructed in 1831 as a feeder for the Macclesfield Canal, and our walk from Flash and the austere moors ends in a sylvan mile or so to Rudyard village beneath the trees at the water's edge on the western shore of the lake. Rudyard Kipling got his forename from the lake, beside which his parents met on a picnic in the spring of 1863. They married, travelled to India, and their son was born at Bombay in 1865.

Rudyard village is a miniature lake resort. Nearby Horton is the resting place of George Heath who, as a builder's apprentice, worked on the fabric of the church and, as a poet of 25, his songs still unsung, was buried in the churchyard. His runic cross says of him, in his own words,

> His life is a fragment – a broken clue,
> His harp had a musical string or two;
> The tension was great and they sprang and flew. . . .

I stayed a night in June 1973 at a farm above Rudyard Lake on the Leek-Macclesfield road. As dusk fell the lake became a sheet of glass and one becalmed yacht lay 'idle as a painted ship upon a painted ocean'. Yet the road was an inferno, and all night I was kept awake by lorries tearing along, many carrying the stone which was once Derbyshire to be put to nefarious road-building projects. Derbyshire is becoming one vast hole, and Staffordshire suffers much of the transport of the rock quarried from its neighbour.

Staffordshire, too, has its environmental problems. The county holds nothing more beautiful than Rudyard Lake, so the County

Structure Plan, published in 1973, embodies a blueprint for its destruction. This reads: 'The County Council intend to develop fully the potential of this area in conjunction with the Waterways Board. The first phase will be the development of a 35-acre picnic site on the eastern side of the lake. This will be followed by the creation of a Country Park exploiting the sandy beaches on the north-west shores of the lake, together with car parks and ancillary uses. The lake has further potential for sailing, fishing, and canoeing and in addition rowing and pleasure boating will be encouraged.'

I hope that your journey with me round this often maligned county will have revealed unsuspected pleasures, and that further acquaintance will bring you, like me, to think of it as Staffordshire the surprising.

INDEX

Abbots Bromley, 104–6, 109; Horn Dance, 107–8; St Mary and St Anne's School, 108
Acton Hill Farm, 81
Acton Trussell, 81
Adam Bede, 25, 167–9
Adbaston, 155–6
Addison, Joseph, 20
Admaston, 105
Ainger, Rev. A., 37
Alcock family, 176
Aldersley Junction, 143
Allsopp collection, 32
Alrewas, 13, 36–7
Alsopp, Samuel, 100
Alstonfield, 196, 200, 203, 205
Alton – and Towers 88, 164, 168, 170–1
Amalgamated Society of Textile Workers, 192
Anker, River 29
Ansculf, 46
Anson family, 116–17
Anuk and Ali, 46, 123
Aqualate, 152–5
Arderne, Sir Thomas, 35–6
Argyll, Amelia Duchess of, 88
Argyll, Louise Duchess of, 25
Arkwright, Richard, 33
Armitage, 110
Asbury, Francis, 63
Ashbourne, 23, 168, 175, 196
Ashley, 159–61
Ashmole, Elias, 16
Ashton, Colonel, 151
Astley family, 71–2
Aston Hall, nr Stone, 24, 141
Aston, Lord, 137
Astronauts, 33
Athelstan, 30, 32
Atlantic Cable, 172
Audley, 185
Audley, Sir James and family, 185, 187
Audley, Lord, 159
Austen, Jane, 33
Autherley Junction, 143–4, 149

Back Brook, 151
Back Forest, 212–13
Baggeridge Pool, 48
Bagnall, W. G. Ltd., 128, 133
Bagot family, 35, 104–8
Bagot Park, 104–5
Bakewell, Thomas, 176

Balfour, Sir Graham, 117
Bamford, Dr., 119
Bamford, Joseph C., 167
Bareleg Hill, 207
Barnett's Breach, 49
Barnfield, Richard, 141
Barlaston, 189
Barr Beacon, 43, 120
Barry, Sir Charles, 182
Barton-under-Needwood, 85–6
Bass, M. T. (Lord Burton), and William. Brewery, 98–9, 101
Baswich, 81
Batchacre Hall, 155
Bayley, James, 161
Bayly, Henry Wm. (1st Marquis of Anglesey), 115
Bayly, Sir Nicholas, 116
Beaudesert, 114–15, 121
Beeston Tor, 200–2
Bennett, Arnold, 187, 189–90
Bentley Canal, 38
Bentley Hall, Willenhall, 55, 60, 83
Beresfords of Alstonfield, 196
Beresford, Admiral Lord Charles, 28
Beresford Dale and Hall, 139, 204–5
Berridge, Leslie and family, 143–5
Betley, 153, 185
Biddulph, and Moor, 13, 186, 192
Bill family, 170
Bilston, 41, 56
Birch, Marie Cecil, 36
Birchills Power Station, 60
Birmingham, 13, 15, 24, 29, 35, 41–3, 50, 59, 81, 140, 144, 199
Birmingham Canal, 143
Bishop's Wood, 156, 160
Black Brook, 33
Black Country, 38, 44, 64, 82, 123, 143, 153, 199
   Museum, 45–6
   Society, 46
Black Lake Colliery, 63
Blake, Rev. P. D. S., 193
Blithbury, 109
Blithe, River, 85, 103–4, 109, 138
Blithfield Hall, 104–7
Blithfield Reservoir, 104
Blore, 202
Blore Heath, Battle of, 159
Blymhill, 151
Blythebridge, 104
Bloxwich, 124
Bodley, George, 87

Index

Boleyn, Anne, 109
Bolton, Thomas – Copper Works, 172, 174, 177, 179
Booker, Rev. Luke, 48
Borrow, George, 38, 131
Borrowcop Hill, 14
Boscobel, House and Oak, 24, 77, 78, 83, 152
Bostock family, 81, 131
Bosley Cloud, 192
Boughey family, 153–4
Boulton, Matthew, 19
Bourne, Hugh, 186
Bowker, Thomas, 156
Bowyer, Sir William, 139
Bradley, 151
Brereton, Sir William, 47
Brewood, 55, 77–8, 144
Bridgeman family (Earls of Bradford) 88, 151–2
Brierley Hill, 42
Brindley, James, 82, 170, 185
British Industrial Sand, 174
British Plaster Board Industries Ltd., 96
British Waterways Board, 44, 179
Brocklehursts of Swythamley, 213
Brocton, 131
Bromfield, Rev. M., 197
Bromley family, 160
Bromshall, 138
Brooke, Lord, 15
Brooke, Sir Basil, 23
Broughton, Church and Hall, 156–8
Brown, 'Capability', 74
Brownhills, 122
Bughole Bridge, 51
Bunbury, Sir Charles, 126
Burndhurst Mill, 104
Burne-Jones, Sir Edward, 68, 70, 104
Burntwood, 122
Burritt, Elihu, 41, 64
Burslem, 181, 186–90
Burston Church, 141
Burton-on-Trent, 13, 15, 36, 89, 96, 98-101
Burton-on-Trent, Battle of, 90
Burton Chronicle, 95
Burton, Richard and family, 81
Byron, Lord, 34

Calf Heath Marina, 82
Canal Cruising Co. Ltd., 140
Canaway, W. H., 109
Cannock, 41–2, 60, 73, 80, 82, 114, 117, 122–3, 125, 127
Cannock Chase, 59, 113–17, 120, 131, 144–6, 199
Cannock Collieries, 122
Carless, Colonel William, 78
Carter, Archbishop, 62
Cary, Henry, 122

Castle Ring, 120
Caverswall, 103, 173
Cawarden family, 109–10
Cellarhead, 103
Chadwick family, 109–10
Chamberlain, Joseph, 61
Chambers, Catherine, 24
Champagne, Jane, 115–16
Chantrey, 25, 142, 160
Chapel Ash, 56
Chapel Wood, 157
Charlemont Hall, 63
Charnes Hall, 156–8
Chartley, 32, 77, 91, 133, 136–8
Chasewater Reservoir, 44, 122
Cheadle, 173–4, 176, 195
Cheadle and Kingsley Moor Coalfield, 164
Cheadle Copper and Brass Works, 164
Checkley, 202
Cheddleton, 179–80
Cheslyn Hay, 123–4
Chesterfield, Lord, 23
Chetwynd family, 131
Church Eaton, 150
Church Eaton Brook, 79
Church Leigh, 104
Churnet Flint Mill Presn Society, 179
Churnet, River, 88, 164, 169-74, 177–80, 193
Churnet Way, 179
Churton, Bishop, 62
Clay, Bob, 121
Clifford, Hon Thomas and B., 132
Clifton Campville, 34
Cloke, Geoffrey, 37
Clowes family, Ipstones and Stoke, 178
Clowes, William, 186
Coates family, 37
Codsall, 73
Collingwood, Father, 24
Colton, 92, 120
Colwich, 116–17
Compton family, Earls of Northampton, 32, 133
Conan-Doyle, Sir Arthur, 125
Congleton Edge, 186
Congreve, 78–9
Congreve family, 79, 138
Consall Forge, 174
Cook, John Parsons, 118–19
Cooke, Mrs. H. R., 27–8
Copeland, W. T. and Sons Ltd., 189
Corfield family, 15–16
Corrugated Iron Company, 54
Coseley, 41
Cotton, Charles, 139, 204–5
Coven, 73
Coventry Canal, 29, 37, 140
Cradley, 42, 50

Index

Cradley Heath, 42, 49
Cradock, Matthew, 103
Cromwell, Oliver, 23–4, 110
Croxall Hall, 34
Croxden Abbey, 170–1
Croxton, 156, 172
Cuba Pit, 48
Cullis, Stanley, 54

Dane, River, 211–12
Darby, Abraham, 47
Darlaston, 41, 50–2
Dartmouth, 4th Earl. Collieries, 62
Darwin, Charles, 16, 181–2
Darwin, Erasmus, 16, 19
Day, Thomas, 19, 20
Delves, Richard, 185
Denbigh, Earl of, 60
Denstone, and College, 163–4, 169–70, 179
Devereux family, Earls of Essex, 137–8
Devil's Dressing Room, 33
Devil's Finger and Ring, 159
De Wint, Peter, 142
Dieulacres Abbey, 193
Digby family, 135
Dixon's Green, 48
Doulton, Henry and John 189
Dove, River, 85, 89, 90, 95, 96, 103, 163–4, 168–9, 175, 199, 204–6
Dovedale, 139, 168, 202, 204
Draycott-in-the-Clay, 92
Drayton Bassett, and Manor, 29, 121
Dudley, 41–2, 45–8, 50, 65–7
Dudley, Prebendary A., 24
Dudley 'Dud', 47
Dudley Canal, 44–5, 50
Dudley, Lord Guildford and family, 46–8, 66–7
Dudley and Ward, 2nd Viscount, 45
Dugdale, Stephen, 137
Dumble Derry, 44
Dunston, 81, 117
Dyott family, 15, 23

Eaton, Captain James, 63
Eaton's Cross, Joan, 150
Eccleshall, 149, 157, 161–2, 172
Ecton, 197, 200, 205
Edalji family, 124–5
Edgeworth, Maria and R.L., 19, 20
Editha, 30, 32
Edith of Polesworth, 30–1
Ednam, Viscount and Viscountess, 47, 66–7
Edwards, Canon James, 61
Egerton, Sir John, 97
Elbow Street, Old Hill, 52–3
Elde family, 139
Elford, 34–6

Eliot, George (Mary Ann Evans), 25, 167, 169
Elkstone, 197–8
Ellastone, 168–9
Ellesmere Port, 54
Endon, 191
English Electric Co., 128
Enville, 64–5
Erdeswick family, 135
Essington, 126–7
Evans, George, 25, 168
Ethelfleda, Lady of the Mercians, 30
Etruria, 28, 179
Etruria Hall, 181, 188
Eve Hill, 48

Farewell, 121
Farley, 170
Farmer, Edward, 32
Fauld, 85, 92, 96–7
Fawfieldhead, 200, 206
Fazeley, 29
Fazeley Canal, 29
Fenton, 187–8
Ferrers family, 31–2, 90, 137–8
Fisher, Rev., George, 51–2
Fitzherbert family – Lords of Stafford, 24, 137, 141
Fitzherbert, Mrs, 80
Five Clouds, 208
Five Towns, 187
Flash, 210–11, 214
Fleetwood, Sir R., 167
Fletcher, Sir Thomas, 153
Floyd, Julia, 122
Ford, Sergeant J. B., 36
Ford, Peter and mine, 92, 96
Forester, Lady, 142
Forestry Commission, 120
Forton, 151, 153–5
Fowell family, 189
Fowke, Dr Phineas, 125
Fowler–Butler family, 73
Fox, Charles James, 80
Fradley Heath, 14
Fradley Junction, 29, 37
'Fram', 34–5
Freeford, 15, 27
Freville de, family, 31
Froghall, 172, 177–8, 179
Froghall–Uttoxeter Canal, 164, 174
Furnivall family, 171

Gailey and Cruisers, 82
'Gansey', The, 43
Garrick, David, 18, 20, 55
Gaunt, John of, 85, 91
Gentleshaw, 120
Gerard family, 160–1
Gerrards Bromley, 160

Index

Gibbons, Grinling, 136
Giffard family of Chillington Hall, 73–4, 77–8, 144.
Gnosall, 149
Goddard and Gibbs, 106
Gornal, 46, 48–9
Gradbach, 211–12
Graham, Mary N., 101
Grand Union Canal, 29, 140
Great Bridge, 43
Gratwick, 104
Great Haywood, 82, 117
Great Northern Railway, 133
Great Wyrley, 123–5
Green, John Henry, 125
Greene, Mrs John Wollaston, 153–4
Grindley, 133, 138
Grindon, 195–200
Gurney, Rachel, Countess of Dudley, 66
Guy, Thomas, 33
Gwinnett, Button, 56

Hacket, John, Bishop of Lichfield, 23
Halesowen, 41
Halfpenny Green, 65
Halfhead Cottage, 139
Halifax, 2nd Viscount, 87
Hallam, Henry, 63
Hallam Hospital, 63
Hallchurch, Diana, 80
Hanbury, 97
Hamps, River, 199–201, 206
Hanbury, Sir John, 97
Hanchurch Hills, 182
Handsacre family and hall, 110
Hangingstone, 213
Hanley, 27–8, 87, 189–90
Harecastle Tunnels, 185
Harper family, 46
Harpur family, 60
Harpur–Crewe family, 205–6, 210
Haselour Hall, 34
Hattons, The, 73
Haunton, 33
Hawcroft Grange, 120
Hawksmoor Nature Reserve, 173–4
Hedda, Bishop, 24
Hednesford, and hills, 104, 121–3
Hemp Mill Brook, 159
Hen Cloud, 208–9
Highgate Common, 64
High Hades, 80
High Offley, 149
High Onn, 150
Hilton, Jack of, 126
Hilton Park, 51, 125–6
Himley Hall, 47, 65–7
Hints, 33
Hoar Cross Church and Hall, 86–8, 160
Hodshead, Henry, 24

Holland family, 86
Holland, Josh, 37
Hollinshead, Reg., 121
Hopton Heath, 133
Hopwas, 33
Horninglow, 101
Horton, 214
Horton, William, 131
Hough, Bishop John, 122
Howard family, 35–6
Hulme End, 200–205
Huntington, 122
Hurd, Richard, 55
Huskisson, William, 78

Ilam, 201–2, 204
India Pale Ale, 98
Ingestre, 133, 136
'In Memoriam', Tennyson, 63
Inns: Anglesey, Hednesford, 121
   Bell, Barton-under-Needwood, 86
   Blithe Spirit, Blythebridge, 104
   Bull and Spectacles, Blithbury, 109
   Cat, Enville, 54–5
   Chadwick Arms, Hill Ridware, 109
   Chetwynd Arms, Brocton, 131
   Colliers Arms, Cheslyn Hay, 124
   Dog and Doublet, Sandon, 134
   Dog and Partridge, Tutbury, 97
   Four Counties, 33
   George and Fox, Penkridge, 80
   Glynne Arms, Crooked House, 48
   Haberdashers Arms, 155
   Hartley Arms, Wheaton Aston, 145
   Lane Arms, Bentley, 53
   Marquis of Lorne, Burton, 99
   Mermaid, near Leek, 192, 196, 208–9
   Prince Alfred, Burton, 100
   Quiet Woman, Leek, 193
   Shrewsbury Arms, Rugeley, 118
   Spread Eagle, Rolleston, 101
   Stewponey and Foley Arms, 64
   Swan with Two Necks, Longdon, 121
   Three Loggerheads, 158
   Turk's Head, Wednesbury, 50
   Walsall Inns, 59
   Wheatsheaf, Great Wyrley, 124
   White Hart, Penkridge, 80
Ipstones, 178

Jackson, Georgina, 149
Jefferson, F. T., 61
Jellyman stories, 123
Jerome, Jerome K., 59, 127
Jervis, Admiral Sir John (Earl St Vincent), 142
Johnson, Alice 52–3
Johnson, Dr Samuel, 15–16, 20, 24, 55, 82, 121, 163, 176, 202
Jones, John, 54

Index

Jones, Peter, 54
Joules Brewery and family, 140

Keele University and Park, 154, 160, 182–3
Kempe, C. E., 68–70
Ken, Bishop, 106, 139
Kenrick, Archibald and family, 61–2
Kenrick and Jefferson Ltd, 61
Kent, George, Duke of, 67
Kidsgrove, 185–6
King Alfred the Great, 13, 30
 Charles I, 16, 32, 66, 92, 131, 155, 162
 Charles II, 24–5, 55, 70–1, 77–8, 83–4, 105, 151, 157
 Edward I, 89, 162
 Edward II, 89, 90, 162
 Edward IV, 71, 153
 Edward VI, 26
 Edward VI Grammar School, Lichfield, 20
 Edward VII, 78
 George II, 15
 George III, 52
 George IV, 80
 George V, 70
 Henry II, 90
 Henry III, 46, 89, 90, 141
 Henry IV, 85, 91, 110
 Henry VI, 159
 Henry VII, 36, 72, 85
 Henry VIII, 31, 72, 74, 86, 107, 115
 James I, 32, 92
 James II, 70–1, 122
 John 79, 100, 160, 170
 Richard II, 28
 Richard III, 36, 137
 William III, 71, 121–2
King, Edward, Bishop of Lincoln 87
King's Bromley, 109
Kingshill S.M. School, Lichfield, 20
Kingsley, 176–7
Kingsley Holt, 176–8
Kinnersley, Thomas of Clough Hall, 160
Kingswinford, 65
Kinver, 64
Kipling, Rudyard, 203, 214
Knighton, 149
Knox-Little, Canon, 88

'Ladies of the Vale', 13
Lady Bridge, 30
Lane, Jane, 55, 83
Lane, Colonel John, 55, 60, 83–4
Lancaster, Earls Edmund and Thomas, 90
Langton, Bishop Walter, 162
Lapley, 145, 149, 151
Lascelles, Henry, 83
Lavengro, 38
Leacroft Hall, 122

Lee, Jenny (Baroness Asheridge), 118
Leek, 103, 164, 179, 180, 192–5, 197, 200, 205, 207, 211–13
Leek and Manifold Light Railway, 170, 197, 200, 206
Legge family, Earls of Dartmouth, 70–1
Leigh, Sir Edward and Dame, 60
Leomonsley, 27
Leper House Farm, 73
Leveson, John, 24
Leveson–Gower family, Dukes of Sutherland, 55, 142, 182
Leyland Steam Boiler Co., 96
Lichfield, 13–16, 19, 20, 23–8, 30, 32–3, 35, 55, 61, 78, 87–8, 106, 110, 114–15, 120–2, 160–2
Lichfield, Lord, 127
Little Blithe, 109
Little Bloxwich, 44
Little Onn, 150
Littleton family, 79–80
Little Wyrley, 125
Liverpool and Manchester Railway, 162
Lonco Brook, 156
London, Midland and Scottish Railway, 164
London and North Eastern Railway, 135
London and North Western Railway, 133
Longdon, 120–1
Longnor, 200, 206–8
Longport, 191
Longton, 187
Lothair, 182
Lower Gornal, 49
Lower Green, 73
Loxton, Second-Lieut Charles, 122
Lucretia, 19
Lud's Church, 212–13
Lunar Society, 16
Lymsey, Bishop Robert de, 25

Macclesfield Canal, 214
Madeley, 185
Maer, 181–2
Maer Hills, 181–2
Madeley, 185
Manifold, River, 199, 201–2, 205–6
Marina, Princess, 67
Marmion, Robert de, 30–1
Marston, John, 54
Masefield, Charles J. B., 173
Masefield, John R. B., 173
Matthews, Lady Diana, 70
Mavesyn family, 109–10
Mayfield, 175
Meaford Halls, 140, 142
Mease, River, 33–4
Meece Brook, 138–9
Meir, 190

Index

Mercia, 13, 23, 29, 132, 140, 149, 153
'Merrie England', 123
Merryton Low, 208
Mesurier Le, P. and Misses, 68
Meynell Hunt, 89
Meynell–Ingram family, 86–9
Meynell Trustees, 161
Michael, Grand Duke of Russia, 185
Midland Railway, 98, 133
Milford, 117
Milford Common, 114
Millar, Gertie, Countess of Dudley, 66
Milldale, 203–4
Milnes, Esther, 20
Mitchell, Reginald, 190
Mohun, Lord Charles, 134
Monckton family, 78
Monckton, Lionel, 66
Monmouth, James Duke of, 70–2
Montague, Lady Mary Wortley, 20
Moreton, Rev. William, 51–2
Moore, Thomas, 34, 175
Morridge, 192, 196, 208
Morris, William, 32, 68–70
Moseley Old Hall, 83
Mosley family, 101–2
Mountrath, Countess of 152
Mow Cop, 137, 186–7
Mucklestone, 159
Mullett family, 45
Mumpers Dingle, 38
Murray, David C., 62
Mycocks of Grindon, 196, 198

Narrowdale, 204–5
National Coal Board, 65, 67, 123
National Pig Breeders' Association, 37
National Trust, 14, 68, 117, 186
Neaum, Rev. D., 104
Needwood Forest, 85–6, 89, 91, 97, 107, 159, 199
Needwood Plaster and Cement Co., 92
Nestlé's, Tutbury, 96
Netherton Tunnel, 50
Neville, Lady Isabella, 35–6
Newbolt, Sir Henry, 56
Newborough, 89
Newport Canal, 149
Newport, Lady Anne, 152
Newton Junction, 43
Newton, William, 92
Nicholson, Sir Arthur, 195
No Man's Heath, 33
Nonconformist Chapels, 53
Noonsun Common, 178
Norbury, Derbyshire, 168
Norbury, Staffs, 149, 153–4
North Staffordshire Coalfield, 186–7
    Field Club, 173
    Railway, 92, 95–6, 133, 164, 177, 187

Water Board, 180
Norton, Mrs Ellen, 83
Noyes, Alfred, 27, 56, 123

Oakamoor, 164, 172–4, 179
'Oakly', 34
Oates, Titus, 137
Ocker Bank, 43
Offa, King, 13, 29, 30, 35
Oldbury, 42, 44, 143–4
Old Hill, 42, 52
Old Side Forge, 45
Oliver Hill, 210–11
Oliver's School, Dame, 16
Onecote, 196–7
Orme family (Fauld), 92
Orme, Captain Thomas, 121
Overton, Bishop William, 161

Paganel family, 46
Paget family, 28, 101, 114–16, 121
Paget, Rev. Francis, 36
Paget, Lord, of Longdon, 27
Palmer, Dr William, 119–20
Paradise, 201–2
Parker, 'Buff Coat', 103
Parker, Admiral Sir William, 33
Parkhead, 44–5
Parton, Mrs, 79
Patshull, 70–2
Paulet, Lady Elizabeth, 101
Paulet, Sir Amyas, 91, 101
Peel, Sir Robert, father, 31
Peel, Sir Robert, son, Premier, 29, 31, 121
Pelsall Hall Colliery, 63
Pendeford, 73
Penderell family, 77
Penk, River, 73, 78–9, 81, 144
Penkridge, 73, 79, 80, 114
Penn Common, 64
Petrie, Mr and Mrs, 83
Phillips, Charles, 55
Pigot family, 72
Pillaton Hall, 80
Plant, Charlie, 44
Plot, Dr, *History of Staffordshire*, 85, 136, 160–1
Plumb, Bishop C. E., 62
Plum Pudding Tunnel, 110
Plunket, Richard, 104
Polesworth Abbey, 30–1
Popple, James, 140
Porter, John, 120
Porter, Lucy, 24
Potteries, 27, 97, 153, 167, 182, 185–7, 189, 190–1
Pottery Riots, 180
Powys family, 179
Price, Claude, 61
Price, Sir Frank, 44

221

Index

Primitive Methodism, 186
Pugin, A. W., 164, 171, 175
Pusey, Dr Edward, 87

Quarnford, 210
Quarry Bank, 42
Queen Caroline of Brunswick, 80
  Elizabeth I, 77, 80, 91, 101, 137, 139
  Margaret, 159
  Mary of Scots, 77, 91–2, 101, 136–7
  Mary Tudor, 26, 47, 56, 59
Queen Mary's Grammar School, Walsall, 56,59
'Quondam', Lord, 46

Ramshaw Rocks, 208–9
Rattle Chain and Stour Valley Brickworks, 49
'Red Stockings', 156–7
Rennie, James, 164
Ridware villages, 109
Roaches, The, 208–11
Robinson, Canon William, 25
Rocester, 95–6, 164, 167
Rolleston, 96, 101–2
Romany Rye, The, 131
Rowley Regis, 42
Royal Doulton Group, 189
Rubery-Owen Works, 41, 46
Rudyard Lake, 192, 214
Rudyard village, 211, 214
Ruffin's Well, 29, 141
Rugeley, 92, 114, 117–20, 122, 124
Rugeley street names, 118
Ruiton, 46
Rushall, and hall, 44, 59, 60–1, 83
Rushall Canal, 43
Rushton Spencer, 213–14
Russell Hall, 24
Russell, Jesse Watts, 201
Ryder family (Earls of Harrowby), 134–5
Ryknield Street, 185

Sabrina, 19–20
'Saddlers', The, 59, 82
Sadler, Sir Ralph, 91
Saint Aidan, 23, 25
  Ambrose, 120
  Bertram, 201
  Boniface, 150
  Chad, 23–5, 29, 87, 141
  Crispin, 131
  Gertrude, 33
  Giles, 51–2
  Hubert, 122
  Modwena, 100
  Nicholas, 121
  Remigius, 150
  Werburgh, 97
Salt, 133–5

Salt family, Stafford, 128
Salt Library, 14, 128
Salts of Butterton, 196–7
Sandon, 134–5
Sandwell Hall, 71
Saredon Brook, 73
Scholastica, Mother, 34
Scott, Captain R. F. and Lady, 27–8
Scott, Sir Walter, 31
Scropton Sidings, 96
Sedgley, 24
Sedgley Park, 47
Seighford, 138–9
Selwyn, Bishop, 26, 37, 87, 161
Selwyn, Clara and John, 37
Selwyn College, Cambridge, 26, 37
Seven Sisters Cave, 45
Seward Anna, The Swan of Lichfield, 16
Shakespeare, 69, 101, 141
Shallowford, 139
Shareshill, 83, 121
Sheen, 200, 205
Shenstone, 33
Sherbrook Valley, 114
Sheridan, Richard Brinsley, 80, 131
Shirleys of Chartley, 32
Shirley, Sir Robert, 138
Shobnall Mills, 92
Shrewsbury Foundling Hospital, 19
Shropshire Union Canal, 143, 149, 151, 155
Shrubbery Ironworks, 53
Shugborough Hall, 117, 128
Shutlingsloe, 213
Sihtric, King of Northumbria, 30
Simon de Montfort, 46
Sister Dora, 124
Skelhorn, Mary, 159
Skrymsher, Thomas, 153–4
'Sleeping Children', The, 25
Small, Dr William, 19
Smethwick, 41, 121
Smith, Bob (The Favourite), 50–1
Smith, Commander E. J., 27–8
Smith, Francis, 74
Smyth, Sir William, 35
Sneyd, Anne, Lady Skrymsher, 154
Sneyd, Elizabeth Honora, 19
Sneyd family of Keele, 185, 187
Sneyd, Rev. John, 36
Sneyd, Captain Richard, 132
Soane, Sir John, 74
Soho House, Handsworth, 19
Somerford Park, 73, 78–9
Somerville, Sir Robert, 90
Somery de, family, 46, 153
South Staffordshire Coalfield, 82
South Staffordshire Waterworks Co., 104
Sow, River, 73, 78, 117, 128, 131, 138
Speedwell Castle, 78

Index

Spode, Josiah, 189
Spurrier, Henry, 96
Stafford, 14, 71, 73, 80–3, 124–5, 128, 131–3, 140, 145, 156, 162, 195
  Committee, 60
  Gaol, 119, 132
  Railway Building Society, 128
Stafford de, family, 106, 131
Staffordshire County Council, 179
Staffordshire County Museum, 117
Staffordshire Gliding Club, 192
Staffordshire and Uttoxeter Railway (Clog and Knocker), 133, 135–6, 138
Staffordshire and Worcestershire Canal, 45, 80–2, 143
Stamford, Earl of, 64
Stanley family, 34–6
Statfold, 33
Staton, J. Clarke Company, 92, 96
Staunton, Anne, 35
Stevens, 'Caggy', 42–4
Stoke-on-Trent, 164, 186–91, 199
Stoke Corporation, 179
Stone, 24, 131, 140–2, 176
Stone, Samuel, 185
Stourbridge, 41–2
Stour Valley Ironworks, 54
Stowe (Lichfield), 23, 24, 29
Stowe (near Stafford), 133, 137
Stowe House, Lichfield, 19
Stratford, Troop Sgt-Major, 55
Street, G. E., 169, 193
Stretton, near Burton, 96
Stretton Hall, 78
Stretton Mill, 79
Stronginthearme, Thomas, 109
Stuart, 'Athenian', 117
Sudbury, 89–90
Summit Foundry, 61
Sunbeamland, 54
Survey of Staffordshire, 135
Swainley, 205
Swan Village, 38
Swarbourn Brook, 86
Swynnerton family of Hilton Hall, 126
Swynnerton Hall, 24
Swynnerton Park, Stone, 137
Swynnerton Old Park, 182
Swythamley, 212–3

Talbot family, Earls of Shrewsbury, 170–1
Talke, 190
Tame, River, 29, 30, 35–6, 43, 59
Tamworth, 13, 29, 30–3, 60
Tamworth pigs, 37
Taylor family, 86
Tean, River, 174
Teddesley Park and Hall, 80–1
Telford, Thomas, 62, 144, 186
Tern, River 182

Thomas, Earl of Lancaster, 90
Thomas, Ernest, 82
Thompson, Robert of Kilburn, 33
Thorneycroft family, 53–4
Thorp Cloud, 204
Thorpe Constantine, 33
Thor's Cave, 201
Three Shires Head, 211
Throckmorton, Barbara, 74
Throwley, 200
'Tilly of Bloomsbury', 49
Tipton, 41, 44–5, 49, 53
'Titanic', 27
Tittesworth Reservoir, 180
Tividale Junction, 42
Tixall, 136–7
Tomlinson, Elizabeth, 47
Tortoishell family, 136
Townsend family, 32
Townson, Rev. Thomas, 105
Trafford, Agnes de, 34
Trafford's Leap, 212
Trent and Mersey Canal, 29, 37, 82, 85, 92, 98, 110, 140, 144, 177, 185, 188, 190
Trentham, 97, 176, 182, 190
Trent, River, 13, 37, 86, 89, 98, 103, 109, 110, 116–17, 120, 134, 136, 191
Trubshaw, Thomas, 116
Tunstall, 187, 190–1
Tutbury, 85, 89–92, 95–8
'Tutbury Jennie', 96
Tutbury Mill Company, 95

Ullathorne, Bishop, 141
Upper Hulme, 208–9
Upper Longdon, 120–1
Uttoxeter, 106, 163–4, 168

Vacuum Salt Works, 81
Valley Training Centre, 123
Van Tuyl family, 195
Venables, August Caesar, 161
Vernon, Admiral 'Grog', 126
Vernons of Hilton Park, 51, 125–6
Viator's Bridge, 204
Villiers, Barbara, 105
Villiers, Lady Caroline, 115

Wakeley, William, 155
Walks in the Black Country and Its Green Borderland, 41, 64
Wall (Letocetum), 13
Wallace, Mrs Frank, 125
Walsall, 41, 44, 56, 59, 60–1, 82–3, 124–5, 152
Walsall Canal, 51
Walsall Wood, 44, 61, 172
Walsall Wood Colliery, 44
Walsingham, Sir Francis, 77, 101
Walter, Lucy, 70

Walton, Izaak, 132, 138–40, 157, 185, 203–5
    Hotel, 202
Ward, Humble, 47
Wardle, Dame Elizabeth, 193
Wardle, Sir Thomas, 69, 205–6
Wardlow, 199
Warley, 67
Warley Senior Schools Band, 44
Warwickshire Coalfield, 29
Waterfall, 197
Waterhouses, 196, 199, 200
Watford Gap, 13
Watling Street, 13, 29, 82, 123, 127, 144, 151
Watton family, 46
Weaver Hills, 169, 199
Webb Stone, 151
Wedgwood, Josiah and family, 181, 187, 188, 189, 190
Wednesbury, 41, 50
Weeford, 33
Weeping Cross, 128
Wellesley, Lady Charlotte, 115
Wesley, John, 53
West Bromwich, 42, 44, 61–3, 71, 136
Westminster Abbey, 56, 59
Weston, John, 120
Weston Jones Mill, 156
Weston Park, 151–2
Weston-on-Trent, 133, 136
Weston-under-Lizard, 151
Wetley Rocks, 179
Wetton, 196, 200–1, 203
Wheaton Aston, 144–5
Wheeler, Jack, 45
Whieldon, Thomas, 188
Whiffen, Marcus, *Stuart and Georgian Churches*, 136
Whimsey Bridge, 42
Whiston Brook, 151
White, William, *History of Staffordshire*, 92

Whitehead, Stanley, 34–5, 199, 201
Whiteley family, 116
Whitmore, 185
Whitmore, Mark, 154
Whittington, 14–15, 36
Whitworth, Admiral Richard, 155–6
Wightwick Manor, 67–70
Wilkes, Dr, 55
Willenhall, 38, 41, 51, 52, 55, 83
William of Gloucester, Prince, 65
Williams, Henry, 25
Willoughbridge, 161
Wilmot-Horton, Lady Anne, 34
Wilmot, Lord, 83
Wilson, Peter, 174
Windsor, Duke of, 65, 67
Wolf Edge, 211
Wolfscote Dale, 139, 204–5
Wolseley, Field-Marshal Viscount, 116–17
Wolseley Park and Plain, 116–17
Wolseley, Sir William, 117
Wolverhampton, 15, 38, 41–2, 53–6, 67–9, 73–4, 78, 84, 143, 145
Wolverhampton Canal, 82
Wombourn, 65
Woodsetton, 24
Wootton Lodge, 167
Worthington, William 98
Wren, Christopher, 136
Wren's Nest, 41, 45
Wright, Bishop, 162
Wulfhade, 29, 141–2
Wulhere, King, 25, 29, 140–1
Wyatt, James (inventor), 33
Wyatt, James and Samuel (architects), 117
Wyggeston, William, 101
Wyrley and Essington Canal, 27, 44
Wyrley Gang, 124–5

Yevele, Henry, 163
Yonge family, 157–8
Yoxall, 85–6